The American Lie

The American Lie

GOVERNMENT BY THE PEOPLE
AND OTHER POLITICAL FABLES

Benjamin Ginsberg

Paradigm Publishers
Boulder • London

Copyright © 2007 Paradigm Publishers

Published in the United States by Paradigm Publishers, 3360 Mitchell Lane Suite E, Boulder, CO 80301 USA

Paradigm Publishers is the trade name of Birkenkamp & Company, LLC, Dean Birkenkamp, President and Publisher.

Library of Congress Cataloging-in-Publication Data

Ginsberg, Benjamin.
The American lie : government by the people and other political fables / Benjamin Ginsberg.
    p.   cm.
Includes bibliographical references and index.
ISBN 978-1-59451-412-8 (hc)—ISBN 978-1-59451-413-5 (pbk)
1. Political ethics—United States.   2. Power (Social sciences)—United States.
3. United States—Politics and government.   4. Political corruption—United States.   5. Elections—United States.   6. Representative government and representation—United States.   7. Voting—United States.   I. Title.

JK468.E7G56   2007
320.973—dc22

                                                                 2007014795

Printed and bound in the United States of America on acid-free paper that meets the standards of the American National Standard for Permanence of Paper for Printed Library Materials.

Designed and Typeset by Straight Creek Bookmakers.

11 10 09 08 07   1 2 3 4 5

For Ted Lowi

Contents

Preface

Americans are constantly urged to involve themselves in political life, to pay attention to the issues, to vote for the best candidates, and above all to avoid succumbing to political apathy and cynicism. The unpleasant truth, though, is that for most individuals, most of the time, politics is a rather unrewarding enterprise. Prussian military strategist Carl von Clausewitz was correct to equate war and politics. Both are nasty, sometimes brutish activities from which ordinary participants secure few benefits. And yet, like war, politics is sometimes forced upon us, and we must defend ourselves.

Self-defense requires some understanding of the realities of political struggle. To begin with, much of what we see and hear in the political world consists of lies and deceptions. The issues addressed by competing cliques of politicians are typically developed for tactical purposes and cannot be taken at face value. Politicians are generally, albeit not always, a currish lot, driven by a desire to acquire power or status or wealth rather than commitment to the public interest. Indeed, because politicians, political parties, and other political actors habitually lie, citizens who heed the frequent injunction to abjure cynicism are likely to be duped into contributing their tax dollars and even their lives for dubious purposes such as building democracy in Iraq. Those who actually work in the political arena—politicians, journalists, consultants, lobbyists, and other political practitioners—are a notoriously cynical bunch. Although they encourage ordinary citizens to trust the government and the political class, members of the political class are not so foolish as to trust one another.

Five hundred years ago, Niccolo Machiavelli dedicated his masterpiece of political realism, *The Prince,* to Florentine ruler Lorenzo de' Medici, whose favor Machiavelli hoped to win. In truth, Lorenzo did not need Machiavelli's advice; he already practiced what Machiavelli preached. Whether in the sixteenth century or the twenty-first, it is credulous citizens, not calculating and rapacious princes, who need a firmer understanding of political realities. Ordinary citizens usually do what is asked of them, steadfastly offering their support and trust only to be victimized by the Machiavellian tactics of their rulers. Thus, contra Machiavelli, this book is not dedicated to the education of would-be princes. Instead, it is designed to arm their subjects against them.

A number of individuals helped me to formulate the ideas and arguments presented in this book. I am especially grateful to Matthew A. Crenson, Howard Egeth, Alexander B. Ginsberg, Roby Harrington, John Irwin, Robert Kargon, Martin Shefter, Robert Worley, and Robert Weissberg. I also want to thank my editor at Paradigm, Jennifer Knerr. I'm glad we finally had a chance to do a book together. This book is dedicated to my favorite teacher and longtime colleague, Theodore J. Lowi, who constantly claims that I am too cynical. I say that when it comes to understanding politics, one cannot be too cynical.

I

Interests and Principles
in Political Life

For more than 200 years, the tale of George Washington and the cherry tree
has symbolized the virtue of America's first president and, by his example,
the importance of integrity as an attribute of political leadership. Unfortunately, the cherry-tree story is a myth, concocted in 1806 by an enterprising
preacher, Mason L. Weems, who hoped to bolster the flagging sales of his
rather shallow biography of Washington.[1]

Although it may seem ironic that an anecdote designed to highlight the
importance of truth-telling is itself a fabrication, this irony is precisely the
significance of the story. Parson Weems's fable helps to illustrate the duplicity and hypocrisy so often at the heart of the political process. Politics is a
realm in which bold assertions about the importance of the truth are often
lies, and charges about the duplicity of others are typically hypocritical efforts to divert attention from the speaker's own misdeeds.

Take the contemporary debate between Democrats and Republicans
on the question of ethics. Could anything be more obviously hypocritical
and dishonest than the tiresome daily spectacle of party functionaries accusing one another of ethics violations? In 2006, Republican lobbying and
fund-raising improprieties helped Democrats trounce the Grand Old Party
(GOP) at the polls, as similar scandals had helped Republicans turn out the
Democrats in 1994. Not surprisingly, once they regained power, Democrats
again had trouble finding their own ethical footing. Within a week of the
election and in clear violation of congressional rules, Rep. William Jefferson
(D-LA) sent out a franked letter on official stationery to solicit contributions

1

to retire his campaign debt.[2] Of course, by Rep. Jefferson's standards, this was a minor ethical lapse. As he mailed out solicitation letters at taxpayers' expense, the congressman was also busy explaining to federal investigators how he came to have $90,000 in cash hidden in a freezer in his Capitol Hill home. By the beginning of 2007, members of both parties had learned how to circumvent the new ethics rules and resume their normal activities. Washington was again open for business.[3] Rather than being known by their current donkey and elephant symbols, the two parties should be identified as the pots and the kettles. This terminology would give voters a better understanding of the meaning of the steady barrage of partisan charges and countercharges to which they are subjected.

Perhaps political figures should be forgiven for their hypocrisy. Like other human beings, politicians are usually driven by personal desires and private ambitions. Yet individuals in public life are compelled to provide publicly acceptable justifications for their actions. Accordingly, they explain what often is self-interested conduct in terms of high-minded goals, civic needs, and national interests. Honesty would so frequently be politically damaging that virtually all politicians and public officials become practiced liars.

Critics who insist on pointing out the regular discrepancies between politicians' claims and their true purposes are inevitably accused of fostering public cynicism. The news media, in particular, are regularly charged with promoting cynicism through their negative coverage of politicians and government officials. This charge is made so often that even many journalists have come to believe it. Nearly 40 percent of the journalists responding to a recent survey agreed that journalists are too cynical.[4] Some analysts assert that public doubts about the government and politicians diminish popular participation and undermine political institutions. Harvard political scientist Joseph Nye has said that cynicism about the political process tends to reduce the "quality" of American democracy.[5] Several scholars have recently proposed that the government and private institutions should work to develop educational programs and other initiatives to promote popular political trust.[6] A number of states, indeed, have already launched civic education campaigns designed to combat political cynicism among young people.[7] And, even as they regularly present rather unflattering accounts of governmental and political processes, members of the national news media frequently urge Americans to eschew cynicism. "Cynicism can destroy our nation as readily as enemy bombs," wrote one columnist who apparently loves hyperbole as much as he abhors cynicism.[8]

These condemnations of cynicism, though, seem rather misguided. Perhaps members of the nation's political class have reason to be concerned about cynicism. After all, cynical citizens hardly make enthusiastic subjects or reliable followers. Yet popular cynicism is hardly an aberration or a malady to be cured through the dissemination of more effective propaganda materials. Instead, cynicism should be understood as a reasonable, if mainly intuitive, popular response to the realities of politics. Millions of Americans see over and over again that politicians and government officials routinely deceive, mislead, and misinform them, offering pretexts while masking their true plans and purposes.[9]

"I have previously stated and I repeat now that the United States plans no military intervention in Cuba," said President John F. Kennedy in 1961 as he planned military action in Cuba. "As president, it is my duty to the American people to report that renewed hostile actions against United States ships on the high seas in the Gulf of Tonkin have today required me to order the military forces of the United States to take action in reply," said President Lyndon Johnson in 1964 as he fabricated an incident to justify expansion of American involvement in Vietnam. "We did not, I repeat, did not trade weapons or anything else [to Iran] for hostages, nor will we," said President Ronald Reagan in November 1986, four months before admitting that U.S. arms had been traded to Iran in exchange for Americans being held hostage there. "Simply stated, there is no doubt that Saddam Hussein now has weapons of mass destruction," said Vice President Dick Cheney in 2002. When it turned out that these weapons did not exist, Assistant Defense Secretary Paul Wolfowitz explained, "For bureaucratic reasons, we settled on one issue, weapons of mass destruction [as justification for invading Iraq] because it was the one reason everyone could agree on."[10]

Because politicians and public officials are hypocrites, it is quite appropriate for ordinary citizens to be cynics. Ambrose Bierce defined a cynic as a "blackguard whose faulty vision sees things as they are, not as they ought to be."[11] If anything, too many Americans lack a requisite sense of cynicism. About half of those responding to University of Michigan surveys say the government *can be trusted* most of the time, and nearly two-thirds *disagree* with the proposition that public officials don't really care what people think. These recent percentages actually represent an increase in public trust after some decline between the 1960s and 1990s.[12] But shouldn't every American be just a bit distrustful of a class of individuals whose most prominent members, contrary to all logic and evidence, claim never to have inhaled, aver that they hardly even knew that pesky Ms. Lewinsky, or suggest that they reluctantly agreed to forgo the opportunity to serve in Vietnam in order to undertake the more onerous task of defending the airspace over Texas? For that matter, can anyone truly believe the legions of lesser politicians who portentously declare that they are driven by an overwhelming urge to "fight" for the right of every last geezer to receive a pension check? Far from being a pathological condition, cynicism is a useful defense against such duplicity.

Yet cynicism alone is hardly an adequate guide to the reality of politics. Political cynics often see through the lies of politicians only to fall prey to even more bizarre fantasies. Millions of Americans, for example, who don't trust the government also believe that federal officials are hiding evidence of extraterrestrial visitors at a secret base in New Mexico.[13] These individuals are ready to spurn official claims but, in their place, accept science fiction tales as reality. An understanding of politics requires not only a willingness to reject falsehoods but also the ability to assess objective evidence and arrive at the truth. The Chinese call this marriage of cynicism and objectivity "cynical realism," connoting an effort to substitute a true and accurate picture of political life for the lies told by the authorities.[14]

THE PRINCIPLES OF CYNICAL REALISM

Cynics are sometimes accused of being without principles. Cynical realism, however, is based upon three core principles of political analysis. The first is that politics mainly revolves around self-interest. In particular, actors generally compete in the political arena to increase their resources and stature. Individuals strive to enhance their own wealth, their own power, and their own status rather than for more altruistic or public-spirited purposes. Second, even if political actors actually have less-selfish aims, they must almost always, nevertheless, work to acquire wealth, power, or status to achieve these other goals. As Machiavelli observed, prophets generally must arm themselves if they hope to succeed.[15] Unfortunately, though, the effort to maximize these interests often becomes an end in and of itself, even if it was not a political actor's primary initial goal. The quest for power can be as corrupting as its exercise. Third, the issues and ideas publicly espoused by political actors are more often the weapons of political struggle than its actual goals. What politicians say cannot be taken at face value but is important, nonetheless.

The idea that political action is governed by selfish motives is hardly novel. Indeed, for centuries, political and social theorists have conceived self-interested conduct to be a fundamental reflection of human nature, "For it may be said of men in general," said Machiavelli, "that they are ungrateful, voluble, dissemblers, anxious to avoid danger, and covetous of gain."[16] This rather bleak view of human nature has a substantial scientific basis. Evolutionary psychologists argue that power, status, and possession of material resources have been associated with reproductive success throughout the evolution of the human species. Hence, the desire to acquire these assets is a potent driving force. Psychologist Steven Pinker wrote that although humans have not evolved the rigid pecking orders characteristic of some animal species, in all human societies "high-ranking men are deferred to, have a greater voice in group decisions ... and always have more wives, more lovers, and more affairs with other men's wives."[17] Of course, individuals vary enormously in the extent to which they are driven by greed or the lust for power and status. Yet those drawn to political life are, by virtue of self-selection, more likely than others to desire the substance, trappings, and privileges of rank.[18]

Though politics is driven by the self-interest of individuals, typically, individuals do not work alone to achieve their political goals. They band together in various forms of associations and alliances—cabals, cliques, factions, interest groups, political parties—that they believe will enhance their ability to acquire wealth, status, or power. These groups may change the appearance but not the fundamental character of politics. Associations seldom arise spontaneously. They are most often created by particularly energetic and ambitious individuals who undertake the task of recruiting followers to help them accomplish their purposes. Today's Democratic Party, for example, owes its existence to the organizational efforts of Martin Van Buren and other supporters of Andrew Jackson in the 1820s. In a similar vein, the cornerstone of the Republican Party was laid in the 1850s by Salmon Chase and other Northern politicians who sought to mobilize supporters behind the idea of opposition to the expansion of slavery to America's Western territories. Subsequent generations of party leaders built upon these foundations to create the organizations that play important roles in American politics today.

If they succeed, political alliances seldom provide equal rewards for all who participate in them. Leaders almost always take a larger portion of the spoils of victory, sharing as little as possible with followers in exchange for their support. Take the contemporary Republican Party, for example. Since the 1980s, Republican leaders have courted the support of religious conservatives while actually doing very little to outlaw abortion, to restore school prayer, or to give religion a more prominent place in public life. Many prominent Republicans believe that an all-out effort to realize their religious followers' aspirations would countermine the agenda of tax and regulatory reform sought by the GOP's business leadership. Religious voters, for their part, have been unhappy but have continued to support the GOP as the best available alternative.

The members of political associations can often develop durable loyalties to the group. Millions of Americans, for example, feel a strong bond to either the Democratic or Republican Party and considerable antipathy for the opposition.[19] Such loyalties sometimes survive the original purposes of the relationship. Indeed, some Americans identify with a political party on the basis of affiliations first established by their parents or grandparents. In a similar vein, some of today's ethnic and religious attachments probably have their roots in tribal loyalties formed centuries or even millennia in the past.

Of course, these irredentist sentiments are often encouraged by politicians who see in religion and ethnicity powerful tools for mobilizing and maintaining popular followings even if their own piety or communal commitments may be questionable. In recent years, many Republicans have publicly courted the support of religious conservatives while privately calling them "goofy" or "the nuts."[20] So often in politics, expressed principles mainly function as vehicles for interests. And so often in political life, leaders view associations instrumentally while followers develop strong emotional attachments to them. Leaders tend to be more cunning and calculating and are typically in a better position to know their options and act upon them. A telling example from antiquity is that of the Athenian general Alcibiades, a man who, according to Plutarch, had an inordinate love of distinction and fame.[21] After losing a political struggle in Athens, Alcibiades took advantage of his family's ties to members of the Spartan elite and sought to make himself a leader in Sparta, Athens's mortal enemy. After his political foes came to power in Sparta, Alcibiades sought to make himself a leader among the Persians. And after losing favor with the Persians, Alcibiades was able to take command of an Athenian army. In every instance, Alcibiades appealed to the patriotic sentiments of his followers, calling upon them to fight and die for their country while he was, himself, prepared to change countries whenever it suited his interests.

Perhaps Alcibiades' modern-day equivalent is the General Motors Corporation. General Motors (GM) is well-known for advertising campaigns based upon nationalistic slogans such as "Keep America Rolling," and "Our Country—Our Trucks." GM also is justifiably proud of its contribution to America's defense effort, especially in World War II, when its aircraft engines powered many of the nation's bombers and fighters. GM, however, seldom mentions the fact that during that same war, the company also made a major contribution to Germany's military efforts. While GM built equipment for the U.S. Army, its German subsidiary, Adam Opel, built trucks, aircraft engines, and torpedoes for the Germans.[22] As corporate officials exhorted American workers to make an all-out effort to defeat the Germans, their colleagues in Germany urged German workers to do the same to defeat the Americans. The company profited from military contracts in both countries. Indeed, in the United States, the company took a huge tax deduction for allegedly abandoning its German plants—which it reclaimed after the war—and then collected reparations from the U.S. government for bombing its German plants during the war. Alcibiades would have been proud. Let us consider, in turn, each of the driving forces of politics, beginning with money and material resources.

Money

James Madison wrote in *Federalist* 10, "The latent causes of faction are thus sown in the nature of man ... a zeal for different opinions concerning religion, concerning government and many other points have divided mankind.... But the most common and durable source of faction has been the various and unequal distribution of property. Those who hold and those who are without property ... those who are creditors and those who are debtors, a landed interest, a manufacturing interest, a mercantile interest, a moneyed interest." These, according to Madison, "have ever formed distinct interests in society."[23] As Madison suggested, private pecuniary interests play a ubiquitous role in political affairs. In the United States today, local politics is often dominated by property developers and state politics by manufacturers. Even national security decisions are affected by the financial considerations of those involved in decision-making. At the beginning of World War II, for example, Secretary of War Henry Stimson advised President Franklin Roosevelt to "hire" industrialists by providing them with lucrative military contracts. "If you are going to try to go to war, or to prepare for war, in a capitalist country, you have got to let business make money out of the process or business won't work," Stimson said.[24]

Often competition among different groups and forces over money engages armies of lawyers and lobbyists and focuses on seemingly minor changes in statutes or administrative regulations. For example, in 2005, the multibillion-dollar life insurance industry prepared for an all-out battle to prevent President Bush from bringing about the enactment of a change in the tax code that promised to lower the tax rate on individual savings accounts. In particular, Bush had proposed the creation of tax-free Lifetime

Savings Accounts that would permit individuals to save up to $5,000 a year without ever being required to pay taxes on the earnings.

Why would the life insurance industry be concerned about this seemingly innocuous measure? Since 1916, life insurance proceeds have been exempt from taxation to protect surviving dependents when a family's breadwinner died. Over the years, the industry managed, through assiduous lobbying, to persuade Congress to extend various forms of tax-exempt or tax-deferred status to virtually all insurance products, including annuities and other investment vehicles, which today account for hundreds of billions of dollars in income for the industry. The president's proposal threatened to create a simpler and more efficient vehicle through which individuals could obtain tax-exempt status for their savings. This, in turn, would probably divert at least some of the billions flowing into the coffers of the insurers. In response, a coalition of corporations that own insurance companies, including General Electric and Massachusetts Mutual Life Insurance Company as well as trade associations for independent life insurance salespeople, mobilized their forces. Leading the fight for the insurers was former Oklahoma governor and self-proclaimed "populist" Frank Keating, president of the American Council of Life Insurers, a trade association representing the industry. As a practiced politician, Keating knew better than to explain that he was fighting for the pecuniary interests of a congeries of huge and enormously profitable firms. Instead, he explained that the industry's only concerns were to make certain that Americans saved for retirement and to prevent investors from receiving unfair tax advantages at the expense of workers.[25] Surely cynicism is the only appropriate response to this rank hypocrisy.

This fight over insurance is just one example of the thousands of battles over money that are such prominent features of political life. Approximately 25,000 associations employing several hundred thousand representatives and lobbyists are active in Washington today. More than three-fourths of these organizations represent business or professional interests, with nearly half representing business corporations. Public interest, civil rights, social welfare, and other ideologically motivated groups make up only about 20 percent of the total.[26] These representatives of business and professional groups lobby members of Congress and work to influence top government officials, including the president and vice president. Lobbyists also work tirelessly to influence the bureaucratic rule-making process. And, in a similar vein, hundreds of corporate law firms use the courts to fight for their sponsors' interests and against laws, rules, or the actions of regulatory agencies that might prove inimical to their clients' economic interests.

One major Washington law firm, for instance, advertises that it can help clients facing government agency investigation win disputes against other firms and thwart any government enforcement proceedings directed against them. This firm, like many others, boasts that it employs attorneys who previously worked for the Department of Justice or the major regulatory agencies and, hence, will have an insider's familiarity with the tactics these agencies might employ. The cost of this expertise is astronomical. Corporate law firms bill hundreds of dollars per attorney per hour, and a major case can cost a client tens of millions of dollars. That corporations are willing to pay such staggering amounts is an indication of the financial stakes of the battle. Speaking of money, corporate and professional groups also contribute hundreds of millions of dollars to political campaigns at the national, state, and local levels to help elect sympathetic politicians or, at least, to win the sympathies of those who are elected. A prominent former member of Congress once said that money was the "mother's milk" of politics. Who could argue?

Power

A second goal of the participants in political struggle is power. Thomas Hobbes said, "A restless desire for power is in all men ... a perpetual and restless desire of power after power, that ceaseth only in death."[27] To be sure, individuals vary in the extent to which they are affected by Hobbes's "restless desire." Some seem content to lead quiet lives in which they command nothing more challenging than their television tuners. Others, however, appear to perpetually strive for important offices and positions that place them in charge of people, resources, and significant policy decisions. Power, of course, has many meanings. In the international arena, power usually connotes possession of personnel, weapons, and economic resources capable of intimidating or defeating potential foes. In the realm of domestic politics, though, the quest for power typically entails an effort to gain command over positions and turf. That is, individuals compete with one another to control important governmental offices, while those who control such posts vie to expand the sphere of authority or "turf" of their office vis-à-vis their rivals. Of course, some politicians seek power in order to make money. One former member of Congress, North Carolina Republican Charles Taylor, used his position in Congress to fund federal projects that aided companies he controlled.[28] Taylor was defeated for reelection in 2006.

The most visible aspect of the struggle for power in the United States is the electoral process. Every year, thousands of individuals compete for local, state, and national political office. Some seem driven to constantly strive for higher and higher office, seemingly equating the desirability of the position with the power its occupant commands. Every year, local politicians seek opportunities to run for state office. State-level politicians constantly eye national offices. And national politicians often harbor presidential ambitions. A number of well-known American politicians invested years, or even decades, in seeking election to the presidency. Men such as Henry Clay, Stephen A. Douglas, and Albert Gore Jr. devoted large fractions of their lives to unsuccessful presidential quests. Others, such as Richard Nixon and Bill Clinton, struggled for years and finally succeeded. But what drives such individuals to commit themselves to a life of meetings, official dinners, and deals, a life of fund-raising and negotiation, a life of media scrutiny? According to presidential scholar Richard Shenkman, these aspirants for high office are "frighteningly overambitious, willing to sacrifice their health, family, loyalty and values as they sought to overcome the obstacles to power."[29] The modern presidential selection system, which virtually requires aspirants to devote years to a single-minded quest for office, probably selects for an extraordinary level of ambition and, perhaps, ruthlessness among the major contenders for office.[30]

Electoral politics, of course, is only one route to political power in the United States. Many prominent and ambitious individuals compete vigorously for positions on the federal bench or in the bureaucracy. Competition for appointive office in the United States can be every bit as intense and engaging as electoral politics. Take, for example, President George W. Bush's former secretary of defense Donald Rumsfeld. After a brief stint in Congress during the 1960s, Rumsfeld resigned in 1969 to join President Richard Nixon's cabinet as director of the Office of Economic Opportunity. Since that time, Rumsfeld has sought and won a succession of ever more important and powerful appointive posts in Republican administrations. A skilled and ferocious bureaucratic infighter, Rumsfeld was able to defeat or circumvent other powerful figures, including such luminaries as Henry Kissinger and Colin Powell. During his career, Rumsfeld served as ambassador to NATO, President Gerald Ford's chief of staff, and, of course, twice as defense secretary, a position whose occupant exercises enormous power, not only in the United States but in the world at large. In 2006, of course, the failures of U.S. efforts in Iraq led to Rumsfeld's ouster. During the course of American history, many of the nation's most important public officials, including such towering figures as secretaries of state Dean Acheson and George C. Marshall, rose to power and prominence through the appointment process rather than electoral politics.

Both elected and appointed officials, of course, hold formal office. Some individuals choose to strive for power through informal channels. Rather than seek office, these individuals attempt to influence the behavior of those in office from behind the scenes. The "wire puller," or power behind the throne, is a staple of political history, literature, and film, perhaps epitomized by Cardinal Mazarin, presented as the power behind Louis XIV's throne in Alexandre Dumas's swashbuckling novel *The Three Musketeers.* There are two types of wire pullers: agents and independent actors. Some wire pullers seek power by attaching themselves to and becoming the agents of prominent and powerful politicians. These agents can be very important figures so long as they retain their sponsor's confidence. Many presidents have elevated trusted staffers to positions of authority. Such Washington relationships have included Abraham Lincoln and Thurlow Weed; Franklin D. Roosevelt and Harry Hopkins; and, of course, George W. Bush and Karl Rove. Other wire pullers operate more independently, making use of their own resources and connections to help their associates and dependents rise to positions of power. One of the classic examples of the independent actor is the late Joseph P. Kennedy, father of President John Kennedy and senators Robert and Edward Kennedy. Joseph Kennedy made a fortune in a variety of businesses, including the illicit sale of alcohol, between the two world wars. He used his wife's family connections to become a major behind-the-scenes power broker in Massachusetts politics and his money to help finance Franklin D. Roosevelt's presidential campaign in 1932. After the election, FDR rewarded Kennedy with an appointment as head of the newly created Securities and Exchange Commission (SEC). Roosevelt reportedly explained the appointment of this rather shady character to a law enforcement post by saying that it takes a thief to catch a thief. As his influence in national politics grew, Kennedy groomed his sons for high political office, using his influence and money to launch each on a political career. Kennedy never held office after brief stints as SEC chairman and ambassador to Great Britain. He preferred to exercise influence behind the scenes and to pave the way for his sons' political success.

Closely related to political power is the notion of "turf." When individuals are able to secure positions of power, they often perceive an interest in expanding the power of the position they hold. In effect, the position becomes an extension of the individual whose "restless desire for power" is expressed by enhancing the prominence of the institution at his or her command. This effort can lead to competition among rival institutions. Battles between the federal government and the states, between Congress and the White House, among bureaucratic agencies, and between the judiciary and

Capitol Hill are common in the United States. Indeed, the framers of the Constitution expected such struggles when they devised America's twin systems of separation of powers and federalism. They saw such struggles as an antidote to tyranny. "Ambition must be made to counteract ambition," said Madison in *Federalist* 51.[31]

Bureaucratic turf wars are waged on an almost constant basis in Washington as rival agencies battle over jurisdiction, budgets, programs, and prestige. These struggles can last for years, and sometimes decades. For example, since the creation of the Department of Defense (DoD) and the Central Intelligence Agency (CIA) in 1947, the secretary of defense and the director of central intelligence have been locked in battle over the collection and evaluation of intelligence materials. Successive secretaries of defense have sought to marginalize the CIA and to give the intelligence agencies within the DoD a monopoly in the intelligence field. This battle has been marked by skirmishes in which the CIA and DoD have refused to share information or to cooperate on intelligence matters, fights in which the two agencies have sought to pin the blame for intelligence failures on one another, and pitched battles in which each agency has sought to seize offices and functions from the other. Lack of cooperation between these rival agencies was one of the factors cited by the National 9/11 Commission to explain why a small group of Islamic terrorists was able to wreak so much havoc in the United States in September 2001.[32] Struggles over turf had seemingly become more important than the purposes for which all of the various intelligence agencies had nominally been created. Interestingly, in 2004, when Congress created a new cabinet-level intelligence position to oversee all U.S. intelligence efforts, the CIA and DoD temporarily joined forces against this interloper, who represented a threat to both bureaucratic empires.

The most important turf fight in Washington over the past century has been a result of the ongoing effort of successive presidents to expand the power of the White House at the expense of Congress. Over the past several decades, presidents have gained effective control over the power to make war and over federal spending, the two most important powers granted to Congress under the Constitution.[33] Presidents in recent years have also moved to circumvent Congress by relying, whenever possible, upon executive orders rather than legislation and upon executive agreements rather than treaties requiring Senate approval. Presidents have also taken more and more direct control over the administrative rule-making process through a practice known as regulatory review. This practice involves presidential directives to administrative agencies outlining the rules and regulations the president expects them to promulgate.[34] In these and a host of other ways, presidents have sought to satisfy their restless desire for power by expanding their turf.

Of course, international competition is the ultimate species of turf war. For millennia, the leaders of rival nations have struggled to enhance the power, position, and territorial sweep of the nation-states they controlled.[35] This struggle has involved diplomacy, economic competition, and war. In recent centuries, the leaders of rival states have often devised complex ideologies, heroic historical narratives, creative interpretations of God's will, and stirring anthems to help them rally popular support for their battles.

Status

Status is a third major goal for which individuals will often struggle in the political arena. Competition over status, or precedence in the human pecking order, is of course a common theme in the literature of politics. Indeed, one of the oldest literary accounts of a political assassination involved a rivalry over status. "And the Lord had respect unto Abel and to his offering; but unto Cain and to his offering He had not respect. And Cain was very wroth.... And it came to pass, when they were in the field, that Cain rose up against Abel his brother, and slew him."[36] Shakespeare also saw competition over status as an important force in politics. In *Julius Caesar,* Cassius seeks to turn Brutus against Caesar, telling him, "Brutus and Caesar: What should be in that Caesar? Why should that name be sounded more? ... Upon what meat doth this our Caesar feed, That he has grown so great?"[37] Brutus, of course, is swayed by Cassius's appeal to his pride and joins the conspiracy to murder Caesar. Some evolutionary psychologists have argued that the desire for status or dominance over others is among the most powerful human drives. Steven Pinker, for example, wrote, "People everywhere strive for a ghostly substance called authority, cachet, dignity, dominance, eminence, esteem, face, position, preeminence, prestige, rank, regard, repute, respect, standing, stature or status. People go hungry, risk their lives, and exhaust their wealth in pursuit of bits of ribbon and metal."[38]

Status, of course, takes many different forms. Wealth and power can give individuals status in their communities. However, wealth and power are not identical to status. Indeed, some individuals systematically reduce their wealth in order to increase their status. This practice is known as philanthropy. Similarly, some individuals endeavor to increase their status by relinquishing power. The Roman general Lucius Quinctius Cincinnatus, who gave up power to return to his farm, is a model of this sort of conduct.

Prestigious awards and occupations can confer status. Graduation from an elite university can confer status. Membership in a famous family such as the Kennedys or the Rockefellers can provide a person with considerable status. Four of the most important forms of status that individuals can acquire through political activity are fame, rank, respect, and standing.

Fame is public renown and widespread recognition of an individual's superior endowments and accomplishments. John Adams said, "The desire for the esteem of others is as real a want of nature as hunger."[39] For many individuals in public life, the desire for fame seems, indeed, to be a potent driving force. One notable example is America's first president, George Washington. Unlike most men of his era, Washington did not fully believe in the concept of an afterlife. As a result, he was determined to become famous in this life and to live in the memory of succeeding generations.[40] Washington even saw his postrevolutionary retirement as contributing to his subsequent fame. He viewed himself as a latter-day Cincinnatus, trading current power for subsequent fame.[41] John Adams was another prominent member of America's founding generation who eagerly sought fame. Adams was jealous of the renown won by men he regarded as his inferiors, particularly George Washington and Benjamin Franklin. In one letter to his friend Benjamin Rush, Adams wrote, "The History of our Revolution will be one continued lye from one end to the other. The essence of the whole will be that Dr. Franklin's electric rod smote the earth and out sprang General Washington."[42]

Rank refers to the rung on the ladder or place in the pecking order that an individual occupies. Individuals seek political rank for its own sake as well as for the status such rank can confer in the larger society. Of course, societies vary in the extent to which even the most ambitious and talented persons are able to enhance their social and political rank. In societies, however, where mobility is a possibility, talented individuals who began life near the lower rungs of the social ladder are sometimes intensely driven to improve their rank in society through political effort. For example, as a young man, George Washington aspired, without much success, to be accepted into the elite social circles inhabited by his half-brother, Lawrence. Throughout his life, Washington seemed determined, through military success, marriage, and prodigious political effort, to achieve the rank he desperately desired. Joseph Ellis wrote of Washington, "Because he lacked both the presumptive superiority of a British aristocrat and the economic resources of a Tidewater grandee, Washington could only rely on the hard core of his own merit."[43] Another famous American politician whose original lack of social standing led him to strive for rank was Alexander Hamilton. Hamilton's illegitimate birth in the West Indies was often, as he wrote, "the subject of the most humiliating criticism."[44] Hamilton hoped, however, that his facility with words "would someday free him from his humble birth and place him on a par with the most powerful men of his age."[45] More recent American politicians driven to prodigious efforts to overcome humble beginnings include Richard Nixon and Bill Clinton. And, of course, Lyndon Johnson strove for rank after the failure of his father's business interests and political career left him feeling deeply humiliated.[46]

Respect refers to the way in which an individual is viewed and treated by colleagues, coworkers, and others with whom he or she is likely to come into contact. Individuals who possess fame and rank may, as a result, be respected, but often enough, famous and important individuals are not held in very high esteem by their colleagues and intimates. For example, John Kennedy possessed about as much fame and rank as any person could hope for. In Washington, however, most members of Congress who had served with Kennedy dismissed him as a "lightweight" and paid little attention to his views on policy issues.[47] Indeed, many proposals that had languished in the Senate during Kennedy's tenure were enacted after Lyndon Johnson took office. Senate barons who had been disdainful of Kennedy were ready to follow the lead of Johnson—a colleague whom they respected. In contemporary national politics, reporters often appear to assiduously demand respect. Early in the Clinton years, for example, the national press presented several unflattering stories about the president after staffers limited media access to the White House and refused to make the president available for press conferences. Correspondents felt that they had not been treated with proper respect. The president was forced to mend fences with the reporters. Respect was very much on the mind of the late Phil Graham, publisher of one of America's premier newspapers, the *Washington Post*. When Graham took over the *Post* from his wife's father, it was an unimportant paper that relied upon the wire services even for local political coverage. Graham was determined to transform the *Post* into a periodical that would be widely respected in the Washington political community. He hired talented political writers, increased the paper's investigative coverage, launched the career of the political cartoonist Herblock, involved the paper in national politics through relentless attacks on Senator Joseph P. McCarthy, and allied the paper with important national politicians such as Lyndon Johnson. Graham confided that his goal was to make his *Post* a "miniature *New York Times*," referring to what was then the nation's most prestigious newspaper.[48] Today, of course, the *Post* and Graham's legacy are widely respected in Washington, where the newspaper is seen as even more important than its New York rival.

Standing refers to a place in the community. For many individuals, a goal of political involvement is simply to be involved, to have a recognized place in political affairs, to be an "insider" with standing. Many individuals volunteer for partisan political activity or take part in community service efforts as much because such involvement gives them standing in political and community life as because of their commitment to the nominal cause. Many activists in the not-for-profit and public interest sectors seem motivated by a desire for standing. One prominent public interest activist told me that he constantly sought to develop and promote new political issues because these were the vehicles through which he was able to play an active part in politics. This individual relished the role of participant and insider and vigorously sought to avoid having to sit on the political sidelines.

Altruism and Interests

The desire for wealth, power, and status is an extremely powerful force in political life. Yet politics does not consist solely of self-interested conduct. Human beings are certainly capable of altruistic behavior. Take, for example, the international health care and advocacy group Doctors Without Borders (Médecins sans Frontières, or MSF), established in France in 1971 and now operating from offices in nineteen countries, including the United States. Each year, MSF sends about 2,500 volunteer doctors, nurses, and other medical professionals to provide medical aid in more than eighty poor nations. MSF volunteers often work under extremely hazardous conditions, sometimes combating deadly plagues such as the 2005 outbreak of Marburg virus in Angola and working in the middle of revolutions and civil wars when no other health care is available. And MSF has been willing to publicize human-rights violations even when its own personnel faced threats of retribution from the perpetrators of abuses. The organization's staff members are almost all volunteers, and barely 5 percent of its annual expenditures are used to pay administrative costs. On every score, MSF is a model of altruistic conduct, surely worthy of the Nobel Peace Prize it received in 1999.

The level of altruism exhibited by MSF's organizers and volunteers is, however, extraordinary in public life. For every individual or organization like MSF that eschews wealth, power, and status, there is probably another seeking all three. One need only think of other nominally charitable organizations—the International Red Cross is an example—for which much of the charity ends as well as begins at home. But certainly, altruistic conduct does occur. Even usually cynical evolutionary psychologists concede that "reciprocal altruism"—performance of acts beneficial to others with the expectation or hope of recompense—is also part of humanity's evolutionary endowment and is necessary for any creature that engages in cooperative social behavior.[49] Perhaps this notion of reciprocal altruism helps to explain why some fundamentally self-interested individuals make a point of being ethical, particularly when their behavior is likely to be scrutinized by others. Such individuals endeavor to pursue their interests in ways that also serve, or at least do no harm to, others. Their goal is to establish mutually beneficial relationships or to profit later from their virtuous conduct. Examples of reciprocal altruism can be seen every day on committees, in business relationships, and even within families. Students who undertake unpaid public service jobs to burnish their résumés are engaging in acts of reciprocal altruism. In a sense, they are seeking to do well by doing good. Of course, many religions have long distinguished between truly altruistic conduct and beneficence undertaken in the hope of reward or recognition. For example, the Jewish Talmud asserts that true charity must be given in secret so that neither the recipient nor anyone else will know its source.[50] One who gives charity in secret is "greater than Moses," according to the Talmud.[51]

Politicians certainly engage in reciprocally altruistic conduct and occasionally, perhaps, in truly altruistic conduct. Without a doubt, some individuals enter public life because they hope to do good, to "make a difference" to the welfare of the community. The problem, however, is that before an individual in public life can do good, with or without the expectation of later reward, they must acquire resources. In essence, and with very few exceptions, they must seek wealth, power, and status before they can achieve any other goals they might wish to pursue. And this is the problem. The effort to acquire these resources, even if undertaken for the best of reasons, can become all consuming.

The corrupting impact of seeking power is a recurrent theme in literary treatments of politics. One of many examples is a popular 1972 film titled *The Candidate*. In this film, an idealistic, handsome, and articulate liberal California lawyer, Bill McKay (portrayed by Robert Redford), is recruited by a cynical political consultant to run for the U.S. Senate in an apparently hopeless race against an entrenched incumbent. McKay agrees to run, but only on the understanding that he will be free to express his political views regardless of their popularity. Initially, McKay says exactly what he thinks about every major topic, using the campaign to increase public awareness of the issues he deems important. The candidate's refreshing candor impresses the public, and McKay's standing in the polls improves, turning the once hopeless contest into a tight race. As he continues to campaign, McKay wants more and more to win. He begins to accept his manager's advice and to take positions on the basis of political calculations rather than his own beliefs. Indeed, as the campaign progresses, McKay completely loses sight of his initial goals and ideals. Winning the senatorial race gradually becomes the only goal in his life. Finally, when the votes are tallied and McKay finds that he has won, he turns to his manager and asks, "What do we do now?"

Another, even more famous work of fiction that explores the corrosive impact of the quest to acquire and maintain political power is Robert Penn Warren's 1947 Pulitzer Prize–winning novel, *All the King's Men*. The central character of the novel is Willie Stark, a poor, honest, and idealistic rural Louisiana lawyer who pursues a political career in order to help his impoverished fellow citizens. After suffering a defeat in his first gubernatorial campaign, Willie feels a sense of anger and humiliation and vows never to lose again. He begins to surrender his ideals and puts victory ahead of all other goals. Willie eventually wins elections by making a series of deals with the very same corrupt interests against which he previously campaigned. He avers, however, that his compromises were necessary means to achieve a higher end. He says he will "make a deal with the devil" if it achieves his purposes. In the end, Willie has lost his original honesty and idealism, and there is little to distinguish him from the vicious and corrupt politicians he initially set out to vanquish.

Warren's fictional Willie Stark was loosely based upon the character of Louisiana Governor Huey Long, the notorious "Kingfish" who ruled the state during the Great Depression. The real Huey Long appears to have been driven mainly by intense personal ambition from the outset. At the age of twenty-four, he told his future wife that he planned to begin with a secondary state office, then become governor, and in due course win election to the presidency of the United States.[52] Other noteworthy politicians, though, seem to have become more and more ambitious as their careers progressed. Take President Harry S. Truman, for example. Truman was rather dismayed by his initial exposure to political reality, which came when he was elected to a minor Missouri judicial post in 1928. "While it looks good from the sidelines to have control and get your name in both papers every day and pictures every other day, it's not a pleasant position," he said. "Politics should make a thief, a roué and a pessimist of anyone."[53] Yet, by 1948, Truman discovered that he "liked being in charge."[54] "The greatest ambition Harry Truman had," according to his aide, Clark Clifford, "was to get elected in his own right."[55] Truman often said he wanted to take on the Republicans "in an all-out, full-scale, championship fight."[56]

Examples of the steady growth of political ambition among politicians are numerous. Take, for instance, one of America's great nineteenth-century statesmen, Henry Clay. Though he never lacked political ambition, early in his career, Clay appeared to put the national interest ahead of private goals. For example, in 1820, at substantial personal and political cost to himself, Clay was one of the principal brokers of the Missouri Compromise, which preserved the Union for another three decades. As his biographer Robert Remini observed, "Both sides of the question slowly acknowledged that Clay, the slaveholder, was not politicking but intent solely on preserving the Union."[57] Within a few years, however, Clay began competing furiously for the presidency. Clay's defeat in 1824, which Remini described as a "stinging blow to his pride," seems to have left Clay with a single-minded obsession for the White House.[58] And when he was defeated again in 1828, Clay's megalomania had grown to the point that he saw his own loss as a national tragedy. "The dark cloud which has so long been suspended over our devoted country," he wrote, "has become more dense, more menacing, more alarming. Whether we shall ever see light, and law and liberty again, is very questionable."[59]

To take a more recent example, 2004 Democratic presidential candidate John Kerry seems, like Henry Clay, to have been deeply affected by his electoral defeat. Early in his career, Kerry championed a number of liberal issues and causes and was, in particular, prominently identified with the anti–Vietnam War movement. As he prepared to run for the presidency, however, Kerry appeared to shift his positions. Kerry voted in favor of a congressional resolution supporting President Bush's plan to attack Iraq, though he later expressed opposition to the president's policies—leading to Republican charges of "waffling" on important issues. After the election, Kerry traveled around the country speaking to Democratic groups. But rather than focusing on major political issues, Kerry chose mainly to revisit the 2004 election and to decry what he characterized as unfair Republican tactics in that contest.[60] As in so many other cases, the heat of political battle seems to have transformed a principled political figure into a politician absorbed mainly with his personal successes and failures.

Why does personal ambition seem to grow among those who become involved in political contests? The answer to this question is probably to be found in human biology or evolution. Behavior, such as seeking power and status, that has a powerful biological basis will tend to be learned and repeated if an individual undertakes it.[61] Experimental psychologist Martin

Seligman employed the term "preparedness" to explain this phenomenon.[62] According to Seligman's theory, humans are prepared by evolution to learn particular things and to undertake particular actions more readily than other species. When stimuli fall into one of the categories for which an individual is biologically prepared, they can have an extremely potent and enduring effect.[63] Of course, individuals vary in the extent to which they are affected by any particular stimulus. Genetics and environment have made some more susceptible than others to the lure of political combat. Some individuals are able to walk away from the political battlefield. When asked by the Republicans to run for president in 1884, Civil War hero General William Tecumseh Sherman famously averred that if nominated he would not accept and if elected he would not serve.

For many others, though, the experience of political competition seems to awaken a drive for power and position that easily overwhelms whatever motives and principles might have initially led them into the political arena. Take Chicago's legendary Mayor Richard J. Daley, for example. Like Warren's fictional Willie Stark, though not lacking political ambition, Daley began his career in public life by seeking to help his poor Irish constituents. During his first term in the Illinois state legislature, Daley introduced bills to shift the state tax burden to business and wealthier taxpayers, to create a school lunch program for poor children, and to make it more difficult to evict poor residents from their homes.[64] After a few years in the political arena, however, Daley's sole focus became his own position and power. During his six terms in office, Daley took control of Chicago's electoral machinery and converted the city's bureaucracies into personal fiefdoms. He reduced the city council to a rubber-stamp legislature. "In the years he was here," said alderman Edward Burke, "we were useful to fill chairs and vote the way we were told to vote. That was the extent of it."[65] Politics had transformed Daley from a quiet, night-school-trained, working-class lawyer into "the Boss" who strove relentlessly to maintain an iron grip on the city even as municipal services deteriorated and middle-class citizens fled to the suburbs.[66]

INTERESTS AND PRINCIPLES

Although politicians work to promote their own political interests, they talk a good deal about political principles. During the 2006 national electoral campaign, Democrats often claimed to be deeply committed to protecting the nation's retirees from Republican efforts to undermine Social Security.

Republicans, for their part, said they were fighting to preserve public morality and respect for God by limiting stem-cell research. Both parties vowed to make certain that public officials adhered to strict rules of ethical conduct. Simply listening to politicians' claims, a credulous citizen might conclude that America's political class was an extraordinarily principled group.

Yet the principles espoused by politicians and public officials cannot simply be taken at face value. For the most part, principles must be understood as weapons of political combat rather than goals or purposes of political struggle. Politicians do not espouse principles or advocate issues simply as matters of personal belief or from an abstract philosophical perspective. Instead, politicians generally develop and champion issues that they hope will promote their political interests. Politicians and organized political forces are seldom willing to invest time, energy, and effort on behalf of issues they do not deem likely to enhance their power, status, or financial resources. Of course, all things being equal, politicians will tend to prefer issues that make sense philosophically and seem plausible as potential policies. Some politicians, to be sure, have advanced their careers on the basis of the most ludicrous claims. Who can forget Al Sharpton and the preposterous Tawana Brawley case that brought him to national prominence? For the most part, though, politicians who espouse plainly foolish issues run the risk of subjecting themselves to ridicule and to exposure as frauds.

Examples of the instrumental character of political issues include some of the great principles debated during the course of American political history—the argument between Jefferson and Hamilton over the nation's future, the subsequent conflict over slavery and sectionalism that nearly destroyed the Union, and the debate over government power versus individualism conducted in the 1930s. Often these clashing principles are presented to students abstractly, as if contending forces were merely arguing competing points of political philosophy. Yet, obviously, Jefferson and Hamilton were not academic philosophers. They spoke for competing economic interests in the fledgling republic—Hamilton for New England commercial forces and Jefferson for Southern planters. Similarly, the mid-nineteenth-century struggle over slavery was more a conflict about economics and political power than a debate over moral principle. Both Northern manufacturing interests and Southern commodities producers viewed control of the western territories by forces tied to their opponents as a mortal threat to their own influence over the nation's politics and policies. Because the Republican Party was closely tied to Northern business and vehemently opposed to the expansion of the Southern plantation economy into the territories, the election of a Republican president sparked Southern secession. It is worth noting that neither President Lincoln nor most Republicans viewed their conflict with the South as mainly involving a moral crusade against slavery. The "Great Emancipator" would never have launched a war merely for the purpose of freeing the slaves.

In the same vein, Franklin D. Roosevelt and the New Dealers viewed the welfare institutions and entitlement programs they constructed more in terms of political power than of moral principle. Welfare institutions and policies such as Social Security promised to tie the administration to an enormous popular constituency and enable it to cement its influence over the nation.[67] New Dealers could reasonably hope that tens of millions of Americans would look to President Roosevelt and future Democratic administrations as the great benefactors who continued to provide them with Social Security checks, civil service jobs, and other forms of government largesse. This would guarantee Democratic domination of America's government for decades after FDR's death.

A more contemporary example of the instrumental character of political principles is the GOP's emphasis on religious and moral appeals over the past quarter century. The Republican Party mainly represents particular segments of the American business community. So how did the party of business also come to be the party of religion? God and Mammon are not natural allies, after all. The Republican Party's concern with morality and religion began during the 1970s when GOP strategists sought issues that would attract white Southerners who were disenchanted with their traditional Democratic moorings because of the Democrats' liberal racial policies.

Issues such as abortion and school prayer and, later, gay marriage turned out to be important not only to conservative Southerners but to working-class Northerners as well. Moral and religious appeals, in effect, allowed the GOP to transform millions of Democratic workers into Republican churchgoers—a feat of political legerdemain that has helped elect three Republican presidents (against only one Democrat) since 1980. The GOP's magic is all the more remarkable when we consider that not all of these presidents have been notable for their personal religious commitments. President Ronald Reagan, for example, welcomed the support of religious conservatives but almost never attended church or participated in religious services. Reagan offered a variety of excuses when asked about the incongruity of a president courting religious voters while manifesting an apparent aversion to worship. President George W. Bush appears to be deeply religious, but, as a series of secretly taped interviews with the president indicate, Bush is hardly above manipulating his religious supporters for his own political benefit.[68] And other Bush administration officials seem to have private contempt for the religious followers whom they court in public.[69]

The GOP's successful emphasis on moral values and religion is even more remarkable considering how little Republican presidents and Congresses have actually done to ban abortion or restore the place of religion in public life. At the risk of being cynical, I might suggest that GOP strategists have little interest in actually achieving the goals they espouse. If, for example, abortion was actually banned, millions of lower-middle-class religious voters might have little further reason to support Republican candidates. Moses probably made the same calculation when he kept the children of Israel wandering in the desert for forty years seeking a promised land that was just a few days away. Politicians are keenly aware of the fact that sometimes, if a promised land is reached, citizens can see no further reason to follow the leaders who brought them there.

Politicians, to be sure, often do believe in, or at least do not strongly disagree with, the causes they espouse. Most are, at the very least, loathe to risk being charged with gross hypocrisy by taking positions with which they are known to have disagreed in the past. Hillary Rodham Clinton's recent statements supporting faith-based approaches to social problems are amusing exceptions.[70] Clinton's religious conversion in preparation for a 2008 presidential bid probably did not persuade religious conservatives of her godliness, but it certainly provided more grist for the GOP's attack mills.

If politicians believe in the principle they advocate, so much the better. Yet mere belief in a principle is seldom enough to induce political leaders to support it. It is quite unusual for politicians to back principles that run counter to their perceived political interests, even if they do happen to believe in them. For example, many members of Congress did not agree with President Bush's decision to attack Iraq in 2002. Few, however, were willing to take the politically risky step of opposing the president just because they thought he was wrong.[71]

Of course, when we do discover that a politician is espousing a cause in which he or she truly believes, we cannot assume that it was belief that led to action. In fact, belief often follows advocacy. Most individuals will tend eventually to agree with a point of view that they repeatedly advocate, even if the advocacy was initially less than sincere. Social psychologists call this phenomenon "self-persuasion."[72] Ancient biblical sages understood this concept when they argued that people did not need to believe in God before they prayed; belief, they said, would follow prayer.[73]

PRINCIPLES AS POLITICAL WEAPONS

Media accounts of battles over political issues seem to assume that these arise more or less spontaneously from popular needs and citizens' demands. Yet the truth is that most political issues are developed by intellectuals, political consultants, academics, and staffers in Washington's partisan "think tanks" such as the Brookings Institution, Heritage Foundation, American Enterprise Institute, Progressive Policy Institute, Cato Institute, and dozens of others. Indeed, "issues consulting" is a major Washington industry, with hundreds of experienced and would-be issue entrepreneurs peddling their ideas to public officials, political candidates, and interest groups. Sometimes these entrepreneurs create issues from whole cloth. That is, they offer a politician a potentially useful issue in which the public has exhibited no prior interest. For example, prior to the 1992 presidential election, consultants persuaded then senator and presidential hopeful Al Gore that he might enhance his standing among socially conservative Southern white voters by taking on the issue of sexually suggestive lyrics in rock music. This was not exactly an issue that had produced widespread popular concern. Indeed, the adults who might have been troubled by the problem could not understand the lyrics, while the teenagers who understood the lyrics probably liked them. Nevertheless, consultants convinced Gore that, once raised, the issue would attract popular notice and serve his political interests. Accordingly, Gore's wife, Tipper, made a series of speeches demanding that the music industry clean up its act and helped organize an effort to force the record industry to label albums containing offensive lyrics.

Rather than inventing issues based upon problems in which the public has exhibited no prior interest, issue entrepreneurs usually seek to identify potentially useful issues from among the many matters with which the public already has some concern. For example, issue specialists did not invent segregation or abortion. Instead, they found a vocabulary through which to frame and dramatize these matters, painting as evils needing to be rectified what some might have simply accepted as facts of life. An example is Dr. Martin Luther King Jr.'s strategy of leading groups of peaceful marchers into Southern towns such as Selma, Alabama, where they were sure to be attacked by the police.[74] By so doing, Dr. King demonstrated to millions of Northern whites, watching on television, that what they had previously ignored or downplayed as peculiar Southern "folkways" (to use President Eisenhower's characterization of the Jim Crow system) was a state of affairs fundamentally inconsistent with American values. Dr. King took a fact and created an issue.

One point to be noted about the use of issues as political weapons is that politicians and their advisers sometimes make mistakes. A politician will seek to make use of a particular issue only to discover that its effects were not exactly as he or she had hoped. Take Al Gore's issue of suggestive lyrics in rock music, for example. In making use of this issue, Gore and his wife forgot that the music and entertainment industry is among the most important source of funds for Democratic candidates. Gore's issue was seen by entertainment executives as an attack upon their industry, and they quickly made their displeasure known by refusing to contribute to Gore's presidential primary campaign while giving money to his opponents. The senator and his wife were forced to schedule meetings with industry moguls in which they apologized and explained that they had not really meant to castigate the record companies. Their criticism was only a carelessly conceived campaign issue.[75]

With these considerations in mind, let us assess the political uses of political issues. Speaking in general terms, issues are used for three broad political purposes: legitimation, coalition formation, and mobilization.

Issues and Political Legitimation

One of the most important instrumental uses of political issues is legitimation. *Legitimation* refers to the development of principles and claims through which politicians and political forces can present what may be self-serving conduct as fulfilling broader public purposes. A great deal of political activity takes place behind closed doors, hidden from the scrutiny of the media and the public. Presidents sometimes make momentous decisions in secret, consulting only a handful of trusted advisers. Contending political forces often pursue and accomplish their goals quietly in the offices of legislators (lobbying) and the hallways of assiduous agencies (corridoring). Often enough, though, politicians and competing political forces must make their cases in public. Politicians, of course, must periodically vie for election and appointment in public forums. And even the most powerful interest group may fail to secure its goals through a behind-the-scenes strategy and be forced, however reluctantly, to make its case in the open.

When they pursue private interests in a public setting, as we noted earlier, politicians and interest groups can seldom afford to be completely candid about their motives and purposes. Should presidential candidates appear on national television asking voters to support them because they have an overwhelming need for fame and power? This might be true but is not likely to be a successful electoral strategy. Should an interest group place advertisements in major periodicals seeking the public's help because its members hope to increase their wealth and prominence? This motive is quite likely to be true but quite unlikely to receive a warm popular reception. Rather than acknowledging their true purposes, politicians and political forces usually seek to paint a public picture of selflessness and community service. To this end, political interests continually endeavor to develop a repertoire of issues, principles, and stances that can provide a cloak of legitimacy as they pursue their interests.

The effort to legitimate political action can take a variety of forms. A simple tactic is *image polishing*. This refers to an attempt to portray a politician or group as an assiduous defender of some widely held political or social value. In recent years, groups have presented themselves as champions of peace, prosperity, security, freedom, equality, morality, the environment, and so on. The purpose of such efforts is to establish a sufficiently positive image of the political leader or group that the public will tend automatically to believe the group's claims and see its proposals in a favorable light.

One group that has employed a reasonably successful image-polishing strategy over the years is the higher-education lobby. Viewed objectively, most of America's thousands of colleges and universities could be seen as successful firms of varying sizes selling services at a very high price. Private college tuition can be as much as $35,000 per year with dormitory charges, books, and fees adding nearly another $10,000 to each student's annual bill. College faculty and staff members are not lavishly compensated. But, like their counterparts in other businesses, successful college administrators and managers—and even many mediocre ones—are handsomely paid, with some university presidents earning seven-figure salaries in addition to the usual perks of the corporate world such as houses, drivers, club memberships, and paid service on corporate boards. Universities may be not-for-profit entities according to the tax code, but, as is true of their counterparts in the charity business, this definitely does not mean that they are not run for the enrichment of their bosses.

Interestingly, however, most Americans do not view colleges as ordinary businesses. A survey published in a recent issue of the *Chronicle of Higher Education* revealed that although only 9 percent of Americans expressed a "great deal" of confidence in large corporations taken as a whole, more than 48 percent indicated a great deal of confidence in colleges and universities. This figure was comparable to the 44 percent proclaiming a great deal of confidence in churches and considerably more than the 26 percent who had a great deal of confidence in the health care profession.[76] What accounts for this relatively positive public perception of institutions of higher learning?

Obviously, Americans view education as the ticket to success for their children and are inclined to have a favorable view of the institutions that provide that ticket. However, the higher-education industry does not rely simply on spontaneous goodwill to bolster its cause. Instead, the industry has built a substantial lobbying and public relations apparatus. American colleges and universities are represented in Washington by more than fifty lobby groups led by the American Council on Education (ACE), which was founded in 1918. Larger institutions employ their own lobbyists as well. The University of California, for example, boasts a staff of twelve full-time lobbyists in its Washington office. Universities lobby for shares of the billions of dollars in research funds allocated by the federal government every year, and the industry as a whole lobbies for increased federal aid for higher education, especially in the form of increased federal loan and grant funding for students provided under the Higher Education Act and other pieces of federal legislation.

Building upon Americans' respect for education, the industry's public relations efforts emphasize the importance of providing access to higher education for all citizens, regardless of their financial means. The key to access, according to industry lobbyists and spin doctors, is an increase in federal subsidies to schools and students to make it possible for every American to afford college tuition. This approach, of course, is highly beneficial to the interests of the schools, which are guaranteed a steady stream of federally funded customers for their services. The equally obvious solution to the problem of access—slashing universities' lofty tuition costs and trimming their bloated managerial ranks—is certainly not presented as an option by industry spokespersons.

For the most part, Americans seem to support the education industry's viewpoint. Most Americans (roughly 70 percent) think Congress and the states should make more money available to the financially healthy higher-education industry.[77] By contrast, fewer than half favor providing federal support to prevent the nation's struggling passenger rail system from collapsing.[78] The difference reflects both the value Americans place on education and the effects of a century of successful image polishing. Taken together, these two factors have given the higher-education industry a strong base of popular approval upon which it can draw in the political arena.

Framing is another tactic designed to mask or cloak the pursuit of self-interest. The term refers to an effort to influence the way in which political events are perceived and interpreted. Any given event can be seen from a variety of different perspectives, and politicians and political forces will invariably present interpretations and explanations of their own actions that cast them in the most favorable light. For example, American policy in the Middle East is primarily aimed at ensuring privileged access to Middle Eastern oil. Other goals are secondary or tertiary. But if officials acknowledged the true character of U.S. policy, major domestic constituencies would be angered, and the government would be accused of shedding blood for oil. Accordingly, policy-makers endeavor to justify or frame their actions in more publicly acceptable terms. They claim to be engaged in nation-building or attempting to bring an end to tyranny or seeking to expand democracy. By affirming these lofty principles, policy-makers hope to legitimate their actions and thereby to secure and maintain popular support for them.

An important recent example of the use of framing in the domestic political arena is the issue of campaign finance reform. Proponents of reforming campaign spending practices generally assert that they are determined to cleanse the political process of special-interest influence. Many of these advocates of reform are undoubtedly sincere in their assertions. Often, however, the issue of political reform is used to hide self-serving efforts behind a mask that the media and the public reflexively accept as legitimate. This is certainly true of campaign finance reform, particularly the Bipartisan Campaign Reform Act (BCRA), enacted in 2002 in the wake of a number of campaign funding scandals. The act's main provisions prohibit the political parties from raising so-called soft money. Secondary provisions place limits on issue advertising by organizations and individuals. The concept of soft money arose from Federal Election Commission (FEC) rulings in 1978 and 1979 that freed individuals and organizations to make unlimited contributions to political parties. This type of contribution was dubbed "soft money" to distinguish it from the "hard money" contributions to individual federal candidates regulated by the 1971 Federal Elections Campaign Act (FECA). The parties used some of their soft money for voter registration and organizational efforts but spent most of it—hundreds of millions of dollars in the 2000 election cycle—to support their presidential, senatorial, and congressional candidates. Reformers argued that soft money contributions allowed wealthy individuals and powerful corporations to buy political influence and argued that BCRA would restore political power to ordinary Americans.

A secondary provision of BCRA placed limits on issue advertising. In its 1976 *Buckley v. Valeo* decision, upholding the FECA, the U.S. Supreme Court had said that the government could not impose financial restrictions on the independent efforts of individuals or groups to express their political views during a campaign. So long as these efforts were not coordinated with those of a candidate, they were deemed to constitute constitutionally protected free speech and could not be made subject to FECA spending limitations. In the aftermath of this decision, such independent spending often took the form of negative "issue ads," run during the several days before an election, urging the defeat of one or another candidate. BCRA's sponsors argued that these issue ads had become important vehicles through which moneyed special interests were able to exert undue leverage upon the political process. BCRA's authors inserted provisions in the new law prohibiting independent ads that named a federal candidate from being aired within thirty days of a primary election and sixty days of a general election.

Even though BCRA and more recent campaign reform proposals have been framed as "reforms," many members of Congress understand that their primary purpose is to protect congressional incumbents from political competition. Any limits on campaign spending help incumbents, who typically have the advantage of name recognition and the capacity to seek constituency recognition and draw media attention by introducing legislation, holding hearings, and presiding over public events. Incumbents also enjoy traveling on what are euphemistically called "fact-finding tours" to view floods, earthquakes, fires, and other natural and human-made disasters likely to attract television cameras. These and other built-in advantages of incumbency mean that insurgents must be able to raise and spend a great deal more than their incumbent foes just to level the playing field. BCRA's limitation on issue ads provided an additional assist to incumbents. One BCRA supporter had been the target of interest-group issue ads in the 2000 election and was determined not to repeat the experience. "After you've been a victim of soft money, you realize the magnitude of the problem," he said. "I'm determined to address this problem when we come back. It's really ripping at the fabric of our nation's political structure."[79]

Did this U.S. representative from Florida stand before his constituents and explain that he sought legislation that would prevent his political opponents from seeking to bring about his electoral defeat? He most certainly did not. Instead, he worked for campaign finance reform. In this way he could maintain the appearance of propriety while working to keep his opponents at bay.

Two other frequently used tactics of legitimation are *coattailing* and what is sometimes called the *nose-of-the-camel strategy*. *Coattailing* refers to the tactic of connecting two goals so that if one prevails, the other will be carried along in its wake. This tactic often allows a group pursuing a narrow interest to disguise its true purpose by championing a broad public interest. If the two goals are effectively linked, accomplishing one will also achieve the other, and the group will have attained its selfish purposes while presenting an image of selflessness. For example, in the 1970s, the International Brotherhood of Longshoremen opposed New York City's plan to replace the aging West Side Highway with a new road, dubbed Westway, that was to be built along the Hudson River. The longshoremen's union opposed the plan because it meant the demolition of old docks and piers along the Hudson. These piers had at one time been the heart of New York's shipping traffic, but for the most part, they were no longer used. For the union, however, the piers continued to be important. Years earlier, the union had entered into a "featherbed" contract with the Port Authority calling for its members to be paid for working on the piers whether or not there were ships to be offloaded. If the piers were eliminated by the highway project, the contract would be void, and union members would no longer be paid for not working.

Obviously, the union could not seek public support for its desire to put an end to a badly needed new road in order to protect its members' somewhat dubious livelihoods. But the union's leadership had a better plan. The union gave its financial support to a coalition of environmental groups that opposed Westway for a variety of reasons.[80] With the financial support of the union, one of these groups filed suit in federal court alleging that the destruction of the piers would adversely affect the habitat of the striped bass, a saltwater fish that spawns in the Hudson. The threat to the fish, environmentalists charged, would violate the National Environmental Policy Act and the Clean Water Act. Ultimately, a federal district judge and a federal appeals court agreed with the plaintiff and ordered an end to the highway project.[81] Along with the bass, the piers and the featherbed contract were saved. The union rode in on the coattails—or perhaps fins would be more apt—of the fish. Without ever having to campaign on behalf of their rather narrow and selfish interest, the longshoremen were able to prevail by linking their goal to the broader public interest of environmental preservation.

The *nose-of-the-camel strategy* is a common variant of coattailing. A politician or group employing this strategy will work for a principle it does not actually support in order to establish precedents favorable to the future implementation of principles it does support. Hence, the nose of the camel. If the initial principle slips into the tent, the others will follow. For example, during the 1950s and 1960s, several publishers of pornographic material—the best-known was Larry Flynt, the publisher of *Hustler* magazine—were the defendants in federal court cases that eventually applied First Amendment protection to sexually explicit material, making it difficult for governments to prohibit publications or films on the basis of their allegedly obscene content. In several instances, the defendants in these cases received substantial financial support from the mainstream print and broadcast industry. Why would respectable media enterprises help to defend rather sleazy pornographers? The answer is that mainstream publishers, filmmakers, and broadcasters calculated that court rulings extending First Amendment protection to blatantly obscene materials would make it virtually impossible for local, state, or federal government agencies to attack anything marketed by mainstream enterprises. One might say that *Hustler* was the nose and *Desperate Housewives* the body of the camel.

Interestingly, a similar strategy was employed by the media industry in the 1930s when the *Chicago Tribune* funded publisher Jay Near's Supreme Court appeal. Near's weekly paper, the *Saturday Press,* had been closed by Minnesota authorities after it published embarrassing stories about local politicians. The publishers of the *Tribune* had no particular love for Near's often scurrilous tabloid. The *Tribune* was, however, in the process of building a national wire service and was interested in establishing the principle that local authorities could not interfere with the press. The U.S. Supreme Court's decision in *Near v. Minnesota,* indeed, established this principle by holding that the First Amendment's guarantee of freedom of the press prohibited state authorities from exercising prior restraint upon newspaper publication.[82] Like Larry Flynt, Jay Near became the nose of a very large camel.

Issues and Coalition Formation

A second instrumental use of political issues is the creation and maintenance of political *coalitions.* Politicians, candidates for office in particular, almost invariably develop issues that they hope will win the support of popular constituencies. Many politicians, indeed, become closely associated with the issues they champion. George W. Bush espoused a strong national defense and a commitment to moral values. These two themes won the support of tens of millions of voters in two national elections. Bill Clinton won election twice on themes of economic prosperity and opportunity. Ronald Reagan was a vocal and successful proponent of tax cuts and economic reform. Politicians such as John Kerry or George H. W. Bush who fail to articulate a coherent set of issues are often accused by the media of lacking a clear message to attract voters.

America's most successful politicians, though, have done more than develop appealing issues. Political innovators such as Franklin Roosevelt and Ronald Reagan have devised issues that transformed political identities and created durable alignments of political forces. For example, FDR's

New Deal brought an entire generation of Americans into the Democratic Party. The New Deal consisted of a congeries of issues and programs, but none was politically more important than Social Security. Roosevelt's Social Security system, still in use today, is essentially a welfare program designed to provide a minimal level of support for the elderly poor and several other categories of needy individuals. Most Americans, however, see Social Security as a social insurance program rather than a form of public welfare. This misperception results from the fact that every wage earner pays into the program through payroll withholding and, after retirement, receives a monthly check regardless of financial means. Paupers receive checks, and so do the well-to-do. For this reason, Social Security is often called a middle-class entitlement.

A welfare program that provides benefits regardless of the recipients' means seems absurd. The program, of course, is actuarially unsound and penalizes impecunious young workers for the benefit of wealthy oldsters. But, however defective Social Security might be as a policy, politically the program was a masterstroke. Tens of millions of retired and soon-to-be-retired Americans firmly believe that they are entitled to a monthly check from the federal government, regardless of their actual level of need, because they paid taxes artfully disguised as insurance premiums. These current and anticipant beneficiaries, organized into a "senior lobby" by groups such as the American Association for Retired Persons (AARP), are prepared to fight tooth and nail for their benefits. And, for nearly three-quarters of a century, the Democratic Party has profited from this state of affairs. Social Security has firmly tied tens of millions of Americans to the political party that created and doggedly defends the system.

The political advantages the Democrats derive from Social Security help to explain the eagerness of the Republicans to substantially modify the system. Many Republicans favor at least partially privatizing Social Security and introducing means testing for beneficiaries. Privatization would permit individuals to invest their retirement funds in mutual funds or other financial vehicles whose value would be linked to the performance of the market. Means testing would eliminate or reduce the benefits paid to wealthier retirees. The GOP argues that these changes are needed to place the nation's retirement system on a firm financial footing, and perhaps they are. But just as the Democrats created Social Security on the basis of a political calculation, so do Republican proposals reflect the cold logic of politics. Privatization and means testing would cut the ties between pension recipients and the Democratic Party. Indeed, pensioners dependent upon market forces for their benefits would have reason to support the Republican doctrine of low taxes and economic growth. From the Republican perspective, a significant change in the nation's retirement system might help to bring about a change in the nation's political system as well.

As the example of the Social Security issue suggests, every individual is multidimensional. Every person has a race, a religion, an ethnicity, an economic status, an age, and a multitude of other salient characteristics that can become the bases for his or her political perspectives and partisan ties. For instance, racial issues may produce one set of coalitions and alignments, while appealing to precisely the same voters on the basis of economic status may lead to an entirely different coalitional pattern. Thus, defining the issue has extremely important political implications. In the case of Social Security, the existing pension system defines retirees as beneficiaries and links them to the Democratic Party. The retirement system proposed by the GOP defines retirees as investors and would potentially connect them to the Republican Party. But, of course, Social Security is not the only example of this phenomenon. Another contemporary set of issues that politicians have used to reshape political identities is the congeries of moral and religious appeals made by the Republican Party in recent years. These appeals, pioneered by Ronald Reagan and continued by his Republican successors, include opposition to abortion; support for school prayer; efforts to expand the role of religious groups as government-funded social service providers; and, most recently, opposition to stem-cell research and same-sex marriage.

As noted earlier, the GOP's moral values offensive was aimed, in part, at lower-middle- and working-class voters whose economic interests had tied them to the Democratic Party. Ronald Reagan and his successors sought to redefine these members of the Democratic working class as participants in the community of faith. Once individuals mentally left the working class to join this new group, they could be counted upon to cast their political lot with the GOP. On the whole, this Republican tactic has been successful. Blue-collar but religious Republican voters played a major role in President Bush's 2004 victory and could contribute to Republican strength until the Democrats find an issue that can redefine this group's political identity.

Issues play still another role in the construction of political coalitions. Issues can help to unite previously disparate—even mutually antagonistic—political forces under the same banner. By the same token, politicians can use issues to divide an adversary's supporters by driving wedges between former allies. One very important example of a contemporary issue used to unite former foes within the same coalition is abortion. For most of America's history, Catholics and Evangelical Protestants were bitter religious and political foes. Indeed, to many Evangelicals, Catholics were "Papists" and not truly Christian. In the 1970s and 1980s, though, conservative strategists, including Richard Viguerie, Howard Phillips, and Richard Weyrich, seeking to take advantage of the furor caused by the Supreme Court's prochoice decision in *Roe v. Wade,* made a determined effort to unite Protestant and Catholic conservatives within the Republican coalition. Such unity would enhance GOP strength and help to bring about the community of faith that was eventually to become a bedrock of Republican electoral strength. The issue of abortion played an important role in this endeavor. Opposition to abortion was an issue upon which leaders and members of both confessional groups could agree and which, with sufficient emphasis, could serve as the anchor of a new interfaith coalition. Republican activists brought together Catholic and Protestant religious leaders, most notably the late Cardinal Joseph O'Connor of New York and the Reverend Jerry Falwell of Lynchburg, Virginia, to serve as spokesmen for the nascent alliance and made opposition to abortion a major political theme. The result was a spectacular success, as this issue brought together ancient enemies and led conservative members of both faiths into the Republican camp.[83]

Another ingenious issue used by the GOP to unite formerly disparate groups is the matter of the so-called marriage tax penalty. Under the U.S. tax code, two wage earners filing federal income taxes as a married couple often pay more in income taxes than the two individuals would if they were single and filing separately. Repeal of this minor peculiarity of tax law has become a recurrent campaign theme for the GOP. Why does the Republican Party make much of what is essentially a small matter? The answer is that the Republican coalition includes fiscal conservatives who strongly favor cutting taxes and religious conservatives whose concerns include the sanctity of marriage. These two groups, drawn from disparate regions and social strata, are often uncomfortable with one another. The marriage tax penalty issue is a principle upon which they can agree, albeit for different reasons. Fiscal conservatives see it as another tax issue, whereas religious conservatives see the tax penalty as a deterrent to marriage. One religious broadcaster has gone so far as to suggest that the marriage tax is an effort by the devil to undermine the institution of matrimony.[84] But, whether the origin of the penalty is secular or satanic, the campaign to bring about its repeal stems from the very secular politics of coalition maintenance.

Issues are used not only to unite disparate groups but also to disrupt established coalitions. In this realm, too, a key example can be drawn from the tactics of the ever-resourceful GOP. Beginning in the 1960s and continuing well into the 1980s, Republicans used race as a wedge issue to destabilize the Democratic coalition. Since the 1930s, the Democrats had appealed to working-class black and white voters. Roosevelt's formula had been to avoid discussions of racial issues and to emphasize economic themes. During the 1950s, of course, with the emergence of the civil rights movement, this formula began to lose its potency. During the Nixon presidency, Republicans moved to take advantage of the Democrats' disarray. Nixon devised what he called a "Southern strategy."[85] This strategy entailed the use of racial rhetoric and symbols to hasten the flow of white Southern voters from the Democratic camp into that of the GOP.

In the Nixon era, Republicans emphasized their opposition to affirmative action programs and intimated that blacks were chiefly responsible for the nation's crime, drug, and welfare problems. Echoes of the Southern strategy were heard as recently as the 1988 presidential campaign, when George H. W. Bush accused his Democratic rival, Governor Michael Dukakis of Massachusetts, of having been responsible for the early release from prison of a black convict, Willy Horton, who went on to rape and murder a white woman. Posters depicting Horton as a dark and menacing figure and blaming Dukakis for his release were circulated to remind white voters of the importance of supporting the Republican presidential candidate. The Republican emphasis on race has diminished in recent years as GOP strategists have sought to bolster the party's appeal to upper-middle-class African American and Latino voters. For more than twenty years, though, the wedge issue of race helped to disrupt the Democratic coalition.

Issues and Political Mobilization

A third important use of political issues is popular mobilization. *Mobilization* refers to an effort by a group or politician to energize supporters and rally them for political action. Small-scale mobilization is a fairly common political tactic. For instance, the radio evangelist mentioned earlier exhorted his listeners one summer day to call their congressional representatives and demand that they vote for repeal of the marriage tax penalty. Several thousand responded, tying up congressional switchboards for an entire morning as they strove to exorcise the devil's handiwork from America's tax code.

In other instances, though, political mobilization has involved many more participants over a much longer period of time. In recent years, political leaders have been able to develop several issues that embroiled millions of Americans in protracted political struggles. During the 1960s and 1970s, the twin issues of civil rights and the Vietnam War sparked years of popular agitation. In response to these issues, hundreds of thousands of Americans signed petitions, wrote letters, joined boycotts and protests, and took part in marches and other demonstrations. A smaller number engaged in acts of civil disobedience and even violent protests.[86] In a similar vein, during the 1980s and 1990s, hundreds of thousands of Americans became involved in the effort to limit or ban abortion. They, too, marched, picketed, and protested. And, like their civil rights and antiwar counterparts, some antiabortion protesters turned to violence to halt what they saw as an evil practice.[87]

It is not always clear why some issues become sufficiently potent to sustain years of marches, protests, and political agitation while others seem to excite little popular enthusiasm. Clearly, issues that affect the basic economic interests of large numbers of individuals have the potential to become major foci for mass political agitation. During much of the nineteenth century, labor unrest and protest was a central fact of political life in every industrial nation. In recent years, though, a good deal of popular mobilization has had a moral rather than an economic basis. Americans have been urged to engage in moral crusades to do battle against evil rather than merely to seek more income. The politics of morality is often puzzling. Why do hundreds of thousands rally against abortion but only a handful protest the genocidal policies practiced for years by Sudanese Muslims against their black Christian countrymen? By what moral standard is the latter less reprehensible than the former?

Several factors influence the popular appeal and political potency of moral crusades. The financial and organizational resources available to a crusade's promoters are obviously important. Impecunious and unorganized prophets are no more likely to prevail than the unarmed variety disparaged by Machiavelli. The political power of the antiabortion movement, for example, derives largely from the organizational efforts of major church groups; religious institutions were also critical to the efforts of the civil rights movement. Proximity can also play a role. It is more difficult, though perhaps not impossible, to inspire followers to struggle against a distant evil than to oppose one that is nearer to hand and touches their own lives.

The promoters of successful issues have also been aware of the importance of young people—individuals in their midteens through early thirties—as a constituency. The civil rights, antiwar, and antiabortion movements, and many other great moral crusades of American history, grew in power as they captured the imaginations of the young. Younger readers may not appreciate the observation, but the young tend to be more credulous and more easily inspired to see the world in Manichaean terms than are their more mature counterparts. I once asked a middle-aged Persian friend who had fled Khomeini's Iran why he had not responded when the ayatollah handed out his famous "tickets to heaven." These cards were said to guarantee that if their bearers died fighting the revolution's foes, their souls would ascend directly to paradise. My friend replied that hundreds of thousands of young people had eagerly accepted the ayatollah's tickets, but he and other older Iranians had not shared their young countrymen's confidence that the destination printed on the tickets would always be honored. "No one could really say where Khomeini's tickets would take you," my friend remarked, "But I was very sure that my Swissair ticket would get me to Zurich."

Moral crusades can be extremely powerful political instruments. Forces that are able to excite and engage armies of supporters can harass, intimidate, and overwhelm their opponents. During the 1970s, liberal champions of the civil rights and antiwar causes were able to use the support mobilized through these issues to seize control of the Democratic Party and vie for power in the nation as a whole. In a similar vein, the antiabortion movement helped to bring thousands of zealous activists into the Republican Party and greatly expanded the GOP's electoral strength.

At the same time, though, moral crusades are dangerous. A powerful moral issue can take on a life of its own. Some of those who answer the call to fight for the cause can become so immersed in it that they believe any action taken in its name must be morally appropriate. Thus, some antiwar activists of the 1970s thought the pursuit of peace justified planting deadly bombs in university buildings. Similarly, some antiabortion activists appeared to believe that bombing clinics and murdering doctors demonstrated their respect for life. And obviously vicious terrorists and murderous suicide bombers are firmly convinced that they occupy the moral high ground. For the true believer, the line between moral crusade and murderous rampage is sometimes disturbingly thin.[88]

BECOMING REALISTICALLY CYNICAL

Once we see that politics is about self-interest and that political rhetoric is the weaponry of political struggle, we can begin to understand the sometimes cold and harsh reality of the political process. Politicians do not strive for office year after year because they are desperately eager to provide us with pension checks. Readers who are still of the opinion that politics is driven by an altruistic pursuit of the public good probably also believe in the tooth fairy and the Easter bunny and have total confidence in the claims of telemarketers.

2

Public Opinion:
Myths and Realities

Many of the same Americans who believe in the Easter bunny think that public opinion is a significant force in political life. Perhaps not all would accept James Bryce's famous assertion that popular support "has been the chief and ultimate power in nearly all nations at all times."[1] Most Americans, however, agree that citizens' preferences have a good deal of influence over the government and its policies. Nearly 80 percent of those responding to a recent national survey said that the government listened to the people most or at least some of the time. More than 90 percent agreed that elections made the government pay attention to public opinion.[2]

School textbooks, politicians' pronouncements, and even the supposedly cynical mass media contribute to this view of the political potency of citizen sentiment. Newspaper columnists and television commentators, for example, frequently link the power of presidents and other politicians to their popular standing. In 2005, when President George W. Bush's rating in the polls fell sharply, many pundits asserted that his loss of citizen support would erode the president's ability to govern. More generally, continual print and broadcast coverage of opinion surveys, the "mood" of the electorate, and the meaning of election outcomes certainly conveys the impression that public opinion and voting must be important phenomena. The media devote nearly as much attention to poll results and election analyses as they do to the celebrity gossip with which Americans seem endlessly fascinated. The implications of the extensive media coverage given these two topics could be viewed from similar perspectives. Year after year, unremitting news and feature coverage aggrandizes the significance of the cockamamie antics and vacuous views of America's gaggle of empty-headed television and film personalities. Perhaps incessant analysis of the meaning of minor shifts in public opinion and electoral behavior imputes to these matters more weight than they actually possess.

To be sure, citizens' perspectives are continually monitored and frequently evaluated by political elites and government decision-makers. Popular support is obviously essential to those seeking election or reelection to office. Nevertheless, public opinion, voting, and other aspects of popular political involvement are seldom the driving forces of national politics. Public opinion is not an autonomous and immutable force that politicians must discover and obey. The will of the people is, instead, a rather pliable phenomenon usually created by the very individuals and groups who claim to submit to it. Typically, forces seeking to achieve particular goals in the political arena, be they offices, programs, or policies, will endeavor to create a climate of opinion conducive to their efforts. Rather than satisfying citizen opinion, politicians and competing political actors ordinarily attempt to create opinions supportive of their own purposes and preferences.[3] Any resultant consistency between citizens' opinion and political or policy outcomes is more a reflection of the common origins of the two phenomena than a tribute to the power of public opinion. In 2002, for example, citing rather questionable intelligence data, the Bush administration was able to convince the public of the necessity of invading Iraq. By 2006, the administration's political foes were able to persuade a majority of Americans that U.S. forces should be withdrawn from Iraq, a sentiment contributing to Democratic victories in that year's House and Senate races. Neither the president nor his opponents acted in response to changes in public sentiment. Rather, changes in public opinion were responses to the campaigns of competing partisan forces seeking to build support for their own political and policy agendas.

Americans' citizen-centered view of public opinion as a potent force rests upon the implicit assumption that popular preferences are formed more or less independently of the efforts of contending forces to mobilize mass support. This assumption is a political counterpart of the concept of autonomy of consumer preferences in neoclassical economic theory and is vulnerable to the same criticism often leveled against that notion.[4] Consumers' preferences and choices are usually results of successful merchandising efforts and reflect the market power of competing firms more than the endogenous or autonomous judgments of individuals.

Certainly, public opinion can be a powerful force once formed. The formation of opinion, though, is typically a result of efforts on the part of contending interests, parties, and politicians to attract popular support and mainly reflects these groups' relative capacity to achieve visibility, to communicate cogent appeals, and to offer citizens solidary and material incentives sufficiently compelling to secure their fealty. Of course, all citizens cannot always be convinced of all things. Large numbers of Americans, however, have little knowledge of, or firm opinions about, most aspects of government and politics.[5] Consequently, their views are susceptible to frequent manipulation by politicians, advocacy groups, and political parties. Lincoln was surely correct when he said that all the people could not be fooled all of the time. But even Honest Abe knew that all the people could be fooled some of the time, and that at least some of the people might be duped all the time.

In their efforts to shape public opinion, politicians, interest groups, and advocates employ three main instruments: advertising, publicity, and measurement. The term *advertising* refers to commercial messages whose sponsors typically pay a fee to the newspaper, television station, or other communications medium presenting the material. An advertisement's readers or viewers usually know that the message was crafted by the individual or organization whose perspective it presents. Most do not conceive advertisements to be neutral or objective presentations. *Publicity* is information that politicians and advocates supply to journalists in a form designed to induce the media to disseminate it without charge as its own product. In some instances, the original source of the information is obvious; in other cases, viewers or readers may be led to believe that the material is an objective account of events crafted by impartial reporters. A good deal of the publicity to which Americans are subjected emanates from the government. This form of publicity is usually called *propaganda*. Government agencies, however, refer to official claims, exhortations, and efforts to manipulate the media as "public information." Virtually every agency has a well-staffed public information office that works to generate favorable publicity for the agency's leaders and programs. A third important instrument used by those seeking to manipulate public opinion is *measurement*. This instrument consists of opinion surveys, along with focus groups and other tools nominally used merely to enumerate and evaluate popular beliefs. The polls, however, do more than simply record the natural or spontaneous manifestation of popular belief. Instead, surveys are what are sometimes called *obtrusive measures*. As they measure, surveys interact with opinion to produce changes in opinion's character and identity. For this reason, measurement can be an important tool of opinion management.

Generally speaking, the ability of competing forces to make sustained and effective use of these techniques—their political "market power"—depends upon the social and economic resources they are able to deploy in the political arena. When groups that lack economic means or access to significant social institutions compete for public support with groups that possess such resources, the outcome, as critics of pluralist theories like to point out, is seldom in doubt. The poor and downtrodden are not really in a position to launch advertising campaigns or to commission opinion surveys. To be sure, less-fortunate groups can sway opinion if they can call upon allies and supporters from more privileged social strata. Such alliances, for example, played an important role in the success of the civil rights movement. And, as we shall see in Chapter 6, new digital and media technologies sometimes allow ordinary citizens to publicize views and events that those in power would prefer to keep hidden, as when an amateur videotape of Los Angeles police officers beating a black motorist in 1991 showed that police were lying in their account of events and forced a shake-up in the department. Normally, though, major institutions and the wealthy and powerful have a distinct advantage in the marketplace of ideas.

Often, of course, the various techniques of opinion management are used together in coordinated campaigns. For purposes of analysis, however, let us examine each individually and in turn.

ADVERTISING

Advertising is the most ubiquitous and perhaps the most obvious of the three instruments. Like the purveyors of goods and services, groups espousing programs, policies, and political candidates fill newspapers, billboards, magazines, television screens, and computer monitors with pitches for their products. Particularly during election years, ads sponsored by political parties, advocacy groups, and candidates for political office are a constant media presence. The mere fact that an advertiser's motives are often transparent certainly does not mean that advertising is ineffective. An advertisement's audience may be persuaded of the wisdom of some policy or virtues of a politician even when they know full well that the ad's sponsors are not exactly interested in telling the whole truth. In recent years, several advertisements have played important roles in national political struggles. For example, during the 1988 presidential election, George H. W. Bush's "Willy Horton" ad presented the glowering image of Horton, a convict who went on a rape-and-murder spree after his early release from prison. The ad charged that Bush's Democratic opponent, Governor Michael Dukakis of Massachusetts, had supported the early-release program and, by so doing, had demonstrated his inability to protect the nation from violent criminals. Millions of voters saw the ad, which helped to sink Dukakis's presidential bid. Another extremely effective advertisement was the "Harry and Louise" series sponsored by an insurance-industry trade group in 1993 to attack the Clinton administration's health care proposals. In the series of ads, a typical middle-class husband and wife expressed their fears that the Clinton program would undermine their health insurance protection. The ads were widely credited with turning public sentiment against the administration's plan.[6] One of the most controversial ads aired during the 2006 election cycle was used by Republicans to attack Tennessee Democratic senatorial candidate Harold Ford. Playing on racial stereotypes, the ad intimated that Ford, an African American, had had sex with a white woman. In the ad an attractive, scantily clad white woman averred that she had met Ford at the Playboy Club. "Harold, call me," the woman said in a suggestive voice. Ford lost his senatorial bid.

Most Americans deny that they are affected by advertising.[7] However, a number of studies compiled in a recent report by the Annenberg Public Policy Center indicated that advertising can influence attitudes even when citizens are unaware that their views have been shaped by repeated exposure to commercial messages.[8] For example, in a 2004 Annenberg survey, most respondents said they did not believe the commercials run during the presidential campaign, but when the same respondents were tested for knowledge of the candidates' positions on salient issues, their responses were often based upon misinformation that had appeared in the ads.[9] In a similar vein, studies of political issue ads run by corporations and interest groups, including oil companies, insurance trade groups, railroad corporations, and the nuclear energy industry, indicated that people exposed to such ads are significantly affected by their messages.[10] Clever or attractive ads can help identify problems, set the policy agenda, and even capture the attention of the national media, lawmakers, and government officials.[11] It is for precisely this reason that corporations and trade associations spend tens of millions of dollars promoting issues and polishing their images. "Corporations which engage in corporate advertising have a better image than those that do not," one major study concluded.[12]

Forms of Political Advertising: Institutional Ads

In the political arena, there are three main varieties of advertisements: *institutional ads, issue ads,* and *individual ads.* Institutional ads are those developed by interest groups, trade associations, corporations, and other entities aimed at the creation of a generally positive public image for the ad's sponsor. Institutional ads may be found in mass-circulation newspapers and on the television screen. Most often, though, institutional advertising appears in newsletters, magazines, and journals likely to be read by so-called opinion leaders—the more politically active and influential Americans whose views are likely to affect those of others. Most firms and trade associations engage in occasional image polishing to bolster their status with customers, investors, politicians, and the general public. Upscale periodicals usually carry ads from defense contractors, pharmaceutical companies, energy producers, and even cigarette manufacturers assuring readers of their sincere commitment to the public good.

Institutional ad campaigns are most likely to be launched by firms and industries that find themselves subjected to media scrutiny or political attack. For such enterprises, and the trade associations that represent them, an institutional ad campaign is a device through which to answer critics and create a climate of opinion in which lawmakers and regulators are less likely to look askance at the firm's activities. In other words, institutional advertising is typically used to buff images that have become badly tarnished. For example, in response to frequent public criticism of its low wages, lack of employee health care, opposition to labor unions, and propensity to hire illegal aliens, America's largest retailer, Wal-Mart, recently launched a multimillion-dollar institutional advertising campaign. Company ads in newspapers, in magazines, and on television proclaim that Wal-Mart brings good jobs and many benefits to American communities. The firm has even produced a video titled *Why Wal-Mart Works and Why That Makes Some People Crazy*. "To keep up with its critics, Wal-Mart has to run a campaign," said Robert McAdam, head of the firm's corporate communications staff.[13]

A typical example of an institutional ad can be found in a recent issue of *Congressional Quarterly Weekly Report,* a magazine read chiefly by members of Congress and their staffers as well as by journalists and academics. The back cover of the magazine featured a full-page message sponsored by the Southern Company, one of the Southeast's largest energy producers. Under a photo of a sapling in an idyllic forest setting, the ad's caption read, "We plan for something more than electricity—the environment." The ad went on to explain that the company is "committed to doing its part to help improve the quality of the environment."[14] Presumably, the ad was designed to induce the reader to equate the company with trees, birds, and forests.

In fact, the Southern Company is among America's largest polluters. Its energy production is heavily reliant upon old coal-fired plants that produce more nitrogen oxides, sulfur dioxide, carbon dioxide, and mercury emissions than those of virtually any other utility in the nation.[15] Southern's institutional ad campaign, coupled with litigation and lobbying activities, is the firm's response to efforts by the federal Environmental Protection Agency (EPA) to compel it to purchase and install billions of dollars' worth of pollution-reducing equipment. Vigorously advertising the company's concern for the environment is, undoubtedly, far less expensive than taking the action that would actually be needed to reduce the environmental damage inflicted by Southern's generating plants. In a similar vein, another recent issue of *Congressional Quarterly Weekly Report* featured a full-page ad sponsored by the Federal Home Loan Mortgage Corporation, an enormous purveyor of financial services known as "Freddie Mac." Under the caption, "The Most Valuable Egg in the American Nest," the ad explained that Freddie Mac had helped over 44 million Americans purchase their own homes by keeping mortgage rates stable and low. The ad ended with Freddie's trademark slogan: "We make home possible."[16]

This ad is one small piece of Freddie Mac's continuing campaign to generate the impression that it is a beneficent, public-spirited enterprise working to make the dream of home ownership a reality for every American. Freddie's own dream, however, is to continue earning very substantial profits at the expense of America's beleaguered taxpayers. Freddie, along with several sister institutions such as Fannie Mae (Federal National Mortgage Corporation) and Sallie Mae (Student Loan Marketing Association) is a government-sponsored enterprise (GSE). These GSEs, which we will examine in more detail in Chapter 4, are privately owned but government-sponsored "quasi-public" entities, each created by Congress for some specific purpose. Their quasi-public status allows Freddie and Fannie to borrow money at a reduced rate and exempts them from the hundreds of millions of dollars in state and local taxes they would pay as private corporations. All told, their reduced borrowing costs and tax-exempt status are worth several billion dollars a year to the two banks.[17]

Congress created Freddie and Fannie to expand the secondary market for residential mortgages and thus to make more mortgage money available to home buyers. But when it established the two enterprises, Congress gave them substantial autonomy. Both entities see themselves as being primarily responsible to their shareholders rather than to the government. Hence, their chief goal is profitability rather than some congressionally mandated purpose. For example, despite pressure from the government, neither Fannie nor Freddie has been eager to make mortgage money available to minority or working-class borrowers. And both Fannie and Freddie have shifted many of their operations from the mortgage market to potentially more profitable venues, such as financial arbitrage.[18]

In recent years, both Fannie and Freddie have been frequent targets of criticism from community organizations, academics, and federal officials up to and including former Federal Reserve Chairman Alan Greenspan. It is in response to attacks on their rather questionable practices that Fannie and Freddie spend millions of dollars each year on institutional advertising, to say nothing of lobbying activities and direct payoffs—in the form of grants—aimed at buying the silence of their most vocal critics.[19] In their institutional advertising, Fannie and Freddie seek to deflect attention from their actual business practices and hammer away at the increasingly false notion that their efforts are essential to maintaining affordable home mortgage rates. In one joint ad campaign, for instance, Fannie and Freddie imaginatively labeled critics of their shift of resources out of the mortgage market "a coalition for higher mortgage costs."[20]

In a similar vein, the American Red Cross engages in a good deal of institutional advertising. The Red Cross is frequently criticized for seemingly spending more money on administrative expenses, executive salaries, and perks than on its nominal mission. The organization raised tens of millions of dollars for Hurricane Katrina relief but infuriated hurricane victims by providing little in the way of actual service to them. When it comes to advertising, however, the Red Cross is second to none. Between 2003 and 2006, for example, the charity spent more than $500,000 to recruit Hollywood stars for its "Celebrity Cabinet," to promote its name to television and film producers so that it would be included in story lines, and to brand its chief executive as the face of the Red Cross. The "branded" chief executive unfortunately resigned in 2005. However, several stars did join the Celebrity Cabinet, and a Red Cross emergency vehicle appeared in an episode of *The West Wing*.[21]

Institutional advertising is not limited to firms and other domestic enterprises. Even countries engage in this practice. For example, in a recent issue of the *New Republic*, a magazine read mainly by upper-middle-class professionals and intellectuals in New York, Washington, and Boston, the Kingdom of Saudi Arabia sponsored a full-page ad touting its efforts to combat terrorism. Under the caption, "Strong Allies. Committed Friends," the ad featured an American flag next to a Saudi flag and asserted that terrorism stems from "deviant thoughts and misguided interpretations of our great religion and its noble message." The advertisement went on to outline the steps allegedly taken by the Saudi government to combat these "deviant thoughts," including changes in the educational system, monitoring of radical preachers, and dismissal of imams thought to be inciting violent jihad from their pulpits.[22] A reader might, indeed, come away with the strong impression that Saudi Arabia was helping the United States to fight global terrorism.

In point of fact, however, the Saudi government's long-standing practice has been to subsidize and support Islamic radicals so long as they do not make trouble within Saudi Arabia itself.[23] Many of the most radical religious schools, or madrasas, in the Middle East and Europe—schools where students are immersed in Wahhabism, a form of Islam that emphasizes anti-Western and anti-American perspectives—are financed directly or indirectly by Saudi sources. Indeed, over the past quarter century, the Saudi government has spent tens of billions of dollars to subsidize the dissemination of Wahhabi ideas throughout the world.[24] And, of course, many leading terrorist figures, including al-Qaeda leader Osama bin Laden as well as most of the 9/11 hijackers, have been Saudis. In a sense, Saudi Arabia has purchased a measure of peace at home by exporting its terrorists abroad. The Saudi ad campaign is designed to gloss over this rather embarrassing and politically inconvenient fact.

Issue Advertising

Even more ubiquitous than institutional advertising is material focusing on existing or proposed governmental programs and policies. In recent years, advocacy groups have launched ad campaigns dealing with issues of social policy, foreign policy, economic regulation, education, telecommunications, environmental policy, and a host of other concerns. Issue ad campaigns are usually undertaken in conjunction with either legislative or electoral efforts. Legislative issue ad campaigns are designed to win the support (or mobilize the opposition) of citizens and government officials for some policy proposal pending before Congress or the executive branch. Electoral issue ad campaigns, on the other hand, typically seek to link a candidate to policies likely to be favored by voters or to identify the candidate's opponent with policies most voters are thought to eschew. Such ads typically have the dual purpose of touting a candidate and promoting an issue.

Legislative issue advertisers make use of the print and broadcast media as well as direct mail and the Internet. According to the Annenberg Public Policy Center, between January 1, 2003, and December 31, 2004, some 914 organizations or coalitions sponsored 67,553 print and broadcast ads in the Washington, DC, metropolitan area alone.[25] These organizations literally spanned the alphabet from A (American Association for Retired Persons) to

Z (Zionist Organization of America) and collectively spent more than $400 million. The overwhelming majority of ads were sponsored by corporations and trade associations. Business-oriented groups accounted for $320 million, or about 80 percent of the dollars spent on issue advertising in this period. One corporation, Fannie Mae, spent $87 million to run nearly 11,000 ads promoting its views. Total spending on the part of consumer, environmental, and other citizen advocacy groups, by contrast, amounted to only $58 million. In addition to Fannie Mae, other major corporate issue advertisers were the multinational pharmaceutical company GlaxoSmithKline (2,596 ads costing $33 million), the telecommunications giant AT&T (1,409 ads costing $26 million), Boeing Aircraft Corporation (8,300 ads costing $17.7 million), and British Petroleum (3,624 ads costing $13.1 million).

Many of these thousands of corporate ads are designed to build support for federal spending on programs and products sold by their sponsors. Thus, for example, a dramatic ad sponsored by defense contractor Lockheed Martin Corp. depicted a missile leaving its launch pad. An announcer asked, "What if an enemy missile had just been launched? What would it take to stop it?" The ad went on to praise the virtues of Lockheed's missile defense technology and ended with the slogan, "Lockheed Martin: We never forget who we're working for."[26] Just in case some cynic might think the company works for its executives and shareholders, the ad showed a picture of a grateful military officer as the corporate slogan was announced. Along with several other major defense contractors, Lockheed hopes to earn billions of dollars from government spending on missile defense technology and hardware.

Other issue ads aim to bolster opposition to the enactment of rules and regulations that might adversely affect their sponsors' profits. For example, in 2003, as Congress worked to amend the Fair Credit Reporting Act, a coalition of credit-card companies and retailers organized to protect the act from revision. The act generally favored retailers and creditors and offered few protections to consumers. Organized as the Partnership to Protect Consumer Credit, the retailers and credit-card issuers produced a series of ads promoting their views. One of the most amusing of these ads seemed to identify a threat to the institution of marriage perhaps even more insidious than the much-maligned marriage tax penalty. "If Congress fails to renew the Fair Credit Reporting Act (FCRA)," the ad warned, "the resulting bureaucratic nightmare of bureaucratic red tape would make financing big-ticket items, such as an engagement ring or honeymoon trip, slower and more difficult.... That's why Congress needs to protect the national consumer credit system we already have."[27]

In a similar vein, a 2003 report by the Federal Reserve Board recommended that Congress reduce or altogether eliminate the de facto multibillion-dollar subsidy received each year by Fannie Mae, Freddie Mac, and the other GSEs. As Congress moved to consider the report in 2004, Fannie and Freddie unleashed an enormous barrage of issue advertising to defend their subsidies. "We built something special in America," intoned the announcer in one of Fannie's television ads. "The finest home financing system in the world.... And we're committed to expanding home ownership to millions more, because we believe that every American family deserves a special place they can call home. At Fannie Mae we're proud with our partners to have helped over 50 million American families become home owners."[28] The ad, of course, neglected to mention the Federal Reserve report demonstrating rather conclusively that Fannie, Freddie, and their ilk contribute little or nothing to expanding home ownership or to lowering consumer mortgage costs. Presumably this bit of reality would be inconsistent with that "special something" Fannie has worked so hard to build. Perhaps a more honest ad could show Fannie and Freddie, renamed Bonnie and Clyde, robbing the U.S. Treasury.

Whether issue ads are truthful or not, their sponsors assume that the ads are more likely to be believed if their self-serving character is at least slightly hidden from view. To this end, corporations and trade associations sponsoring issue ads often use aliases to hide their identities. Thus, for example, the "Committee to Protect America's Health Care" is a coalition of for-profit hospitals that runs ads calling for increased federal funding for those entities. "Voices for Choices" was the alias used by a coalition of telecommunications companies that unsuccessfully advertised on behalf of continued regulation of local phone services. "Project Protect" was the alias for forest-products companies who advertised the benefits of logging. The "Partnership to Protect Consumer Credit" was, as we saw, an alias for credit-card companies running ads against legislation that would have offered more protection to consumers. Both "Americans for Balanced Energy Choices" and the "Coalition for Affordable and Reliable Energy" sponsor ads promoting the virtues of coal as an energy source. "Some of us invest lots of time and money into making the world cleaner," announced the pitchman for Americans for Balanced Energy Choices. "And one thing that's helping is electricity from coal."[29] By the logic of these aliases, a coalition of strip-mining interests might call itself "Citizens for a Cleaner Earth," and a coalition of health insurers, companies notorious for raising premiums but refusing to pay subscribers' claims, might operate under the alias "Citizens Against Costly Medical Services." A Senate bill proposed in

2006 would have required lobby groups using such aliases to disclose their true identities. Many groups treated this proposal as a vicious attack on their freedom of speech. Wayne LaPierre, president of the National Rifle Association, suggested that this sort of disclosure requirement would have thwarted the activities of Tom Paine and, perhaps, undermined the American Revolution.[30] The proposal ultimately died in committee.

Like legislative issue ads, electoral issue ads appear on radio and television broadcasts, are printed in the pages of newspapers and magazines, and are distributed via the Internet and direct mail. Legislative ads run mainly when Congress is in session. Electoral ads tend to be concentrated during the two or three months prior to important electoral contests. Because their goal is to persuade an audience of the virtues or vices of some policy, legislative ads generally present an argument or rationale, however improbable, for the positions they advocate. Electoral issue ads, by contrast, are designed mainly to appeal to voters who already have a position on the issue in question and need no further persuasion. Instead, these ads seek to give such voters the impression that the candidate being touted shares their views or that his or her opponent does not. Typically, the add will present a popular position and assert that a particular candidate strongly supports it. Alternatively, the add will present what its sponsors take to be an unpopular view and endeavor to associate it with the opposition candidate. Many of these ads are brief—thirty seconds of television time—and present few facts and little or no evidence. Often, to skirt federal limits on campaign spending, the ads do not even ask viewers, readers, and listeners for their votes. Electoral ads rely for their impact on simple classical conditioning: the frequent repetition of two stimuli in conjunction with one another until an association is formed between them in the minds of audience members. Such conditioning apparently occurred in Pavlov's famous experiment, when dogs learned to associate the sound of a bell with food and drooled whenever they heard the bell.

Thus, in the 2000 presidential election, the Gore campaign aired the same TV ad hundreds of times in sixteen "battleground" states. Against a backdrop depicting a senior citizen said to be named Bob Darthez, apparently dismayed by high drug prices, the announcer intoned, "Al Gore is taking them on. Fighting for a prescription-drug benefit for seniors like Bob Darthez." The Bush campaign apparently disagreed, airing a thirty-second ad thousands of times in twenty-two battleground states in which the announcer asked portentously, "Whose economic plan is best for you?" He answered his own question, earnestly averring that "Al Gore's deficit spending plan threatens America's prosperity." What exactly was Al Gore's spending plan, or, for that matter, his drug plan? These ads were not very specific. The goal of the Democratic ad was to compel viewers to associate Al Gore with prescription benefits for seniors. The Republicans, on the other hand, hoped that sufficient repetition would lead viewers to regard Al Gore as a big spender. In the Pavlovian world of issue advertising, too many facts might interfere with the sound of the bell.

Individual Advertising

In addition to institutional and issue advertising, Americans are the recipients of scores of individual ads, particularly during election campaigns. Although candidates' virtues are often trumpeted through issue ads, numerous pieces of advertising never refer to issues. They simply exhort Americans to "vote for Smith" or "vote for Jones" without offering any reason whatsoever for so doing. Such ads, printed and distributed at considerable expense, appear in newspapers, on billboards, in mailings, and in the form of signs and posters covering every empty wall and festooning countless lawns in the weeks prior to national and state elections.

Such advertising has a twofold purpose. First, it is designed to enhance a politician's name recognition. The presumption is that citizens are more likely to cast their votes for a candidate whose name seems familiar than for one whose name they do not recognize. Second, the signs and posters, particularly those decorating hundreds of thousands of lawns, are calculated to create a bandwagon effect. Seeing one after another of their neighbors' lawns sporting "Vote for Smith" signs, the uncommitted voter is supposed to believe that he or she should vote for Smith, too. It is for this reason that campaign officials are eager to persuade home owners to accept their lawn signs. And it is for the same reason that unscrupulous campaigners often use the cover of darkness to steal the opposition's lawn signs.[31]

PUBLICITY

Like advertising, publicity is a technique used by politicians and advocacy groups to present information to an audience for the purpose of shaping individuals' attitudes toward some institution, public issue, or political figure. In the case of advertising, advocates pay the media to disseminate information and claims. Most readers or viewers of political advertisements know that the message they are receiving has been crafted by an interested party for self-serving reasons. Of course, millions of Americans every year seem to be swayed by commercials for worthless products, duplicitous politicians, crooked charities, and foolish ideas. Nevertheless, audience awareness of an ad's source and the intentions of its sponsors undoubtedly reduces the message's plausibility and effectiveness.

The goal of publicity is to enhance a message's credibility by creating the impression that it has been independently crafted by the news media rather than some self-serving politician or advocate. Rather than pay a newspaper or television station to carry their message, as they would in the case of an ad, the promoters of a publicity campaign seek to induce journalists and commentators to disseminate the group's message, through news and commentary as though it were their own idea or product. If publicity is well-planned and skillfully constructed, few viewers, readers, or listeners will be aware that they are being presented with information initiated by advocates rather than an account developed by putatively impartial journalists.

Its appearance of objectivity can make publicity an extremely effective instrument for shaping political beliefs. For example, a spate of news accounts has persuaded many Americans that a number of the detainees imprisoned at Guantanamo Bay are innocent victims rather than terrorists. Most Americans do not realize, however, that some of the accounts promoting this view were part of a publicity campaign organized and financed by the Kuwaiti government.[32] Indeed, many political "facts" unequivocally accepted by most Americans can be traced to successful efforts by advocates to publicize some issue or cause. Or take the famous 1956 news photo of Rosa Parks, the African American woman from Montgomery, Alabama, whose refusal to yield her bus seat to a white man helped to spark the civil rights movement. The photo shows Parks sitting in a front seat of a bus. Behind her is a white male who appears to be glaring at the diminutive black woman who defied the South's apartheid system. The news media dubbed this individual the "angry white man."

Reporters and editorial commentators portrayed Parks as a tired seamstress who spontaneously refused to give in to the South's Jim Crow laws. This image evoked a sympathetic response, especially among white Northerners. But actually, Parks was a longtime National Association for the Advancement of Colored People (NAACP) activist who had studied at the Highlander Folk School, a Tennessee institution originally established to train trade-union organizers. Parks was one of several women sent by the NAACP to publicly challenge Montgomery's policy of segregated bus seating. One of these women had already been arrested before Parks's famous bus ride, but when they learned that the other woman was expecting an out-of-wedlock child, NAACP tacticians decided Parks would make a better focus for publicity. And as for that angry white man giving Parks such a hard-eyed stare in the photo, his name was Nicholas Chriss, and he was a UPI reporter covering the story. Two *Look* magazine photographers asked Chriss to sit behind Parks as they carefully staged what soon became a celebrated photograph.[33]

Publicity Events

Politicians and advocates can make use of several instruments in their efforts to garner favorable publicity. The first of these is the creation or dramatization of events designed to illustrate or highlight a particular perspective. As in the Rosa Parks case, a dramatic event, properly portrayed, can attract the attention of the mass media and inspire stories and photos that ultimately influence the attitudes of millions of readers and viewers. As the Parks case suggests, leaders of the civil rights movement were especially adept at the use of the news media to gain widespread popular support for their cause. Dr. Martin Luther King Jr., in particular, learned to use television to illustrate to Northern audiences that the Southern Jim Crow system was brutal, evil, and fundamentally un-American.[34]

In his efforts, King was supported by an alliance of Northern white liberals, segments of the business community, and important elements of the national news media. The media not only saw a powerful story but also saw an opportunity to castigate the conservative coalition of Southern Democrats and right-wing Republicans that had tormented journalists and broadcasters over their alleged Communist ties during the 1940s and 1950s. This alliance gave King extraordinarily good access to the nation's television screens and helped him to sway public opinion in favor of his cause.

One of the most famous events organized by King was the April 1965 protest march at Selma, Alabama. King targeted Selma for a concerted campaign of protest activity partly because racial discrimination in Selma and the surrounding Dallas County was so starkly obvious. For example, because of systematic black disenfranchisement, only 2 percent of the county's registered voters were black, even though blacks made up 58 percent of the county's residents.[35]

Selma was chosen, however, not only because of its record of discrimination but also because King was confident that state and county political leaders were fools. He expected them to respond to peaceful protests with violence and, in the process, imprint themselves upon the collective consciousness of a national television audience as the brutal oppressors of heroic and defenseless crusaders seeking freedom and democracy.[36] Alabama and Dallas County authorities played their assigned roles convincingly. With network cameras watching, Alabama state troopers launched a vicious attack against protesters on the Raymond Pettus Bridge, leaving forty demonstrators seriously injured in what the media dubbed "bloody Sunday."[37]

From the perspective of protest leaders and the national media, Dallas County Sheriff Jim Clark might have been sent by central casting to play his part in the drama. Clark displayed a violent temper on camera, wore a "Never" button in his lapel, and armed his deputies with electric cattle prods. Clark unwittingly contributed so much to King's efforts that the protesters made him an honorary member of the Southern Christian Leadership Conference (SCLC) as well as the Student Nonviolent Coordinating Committee (SNCC) and the NAACP.[38] Clark certainly deserved his awards. Nationwide revulsion to the violence unleashed upon peaceful protesters generated enormous sympathy for the civil rights cause and helped create the setting for the enactment of the 1965 Voting Rights Act. In terms of the publicity it generated, the Selma protest became one of the most successful events in recent American political history.

Publicity Through Investigations

In recent years, a particularly important form of publicity event has been the official investigation. Since the Watergate investigation of the 1970s that drove President Richard Nixon from office, each political party has made use of heavily publicized investigations to harass and embarrass its foes in the other party. Thus, for example, in the 1980s, Democrats launched the Iran-*contra* investigations that damaged the Reagan administration. In the 1990s, Republicans did enormous political damage to President Bill Clinton with the Whitewater investigations. And, since 2000, Democrats have sought to initiate investigations of the Bush administration's ties to Washington lobbyists and the possibility that top administration officials leaked the identity of a covert CIA operative whose husband was critical of the president's policies in Iraq. In 2006, one influential Republican lobbyist, Jack Abramoff, negotiated a plea agreement with the Justice Department that seemed likely to lead to embarrassing disclosures about his ties to prominent congressional Republicans. In addition to these major investigations, each side has also initiated a score of lesser investigations of cabinet secretaries, judicial nominees, White House staffers, and others. After Democrats won control of both houses of Congress in the 2006 elections, they began planning investigations of the Bush administration's policies in Iraq and the president's domestic antiterrorism programs.

It is, of course, true that many of these investigations revealed evidence of serious wrongdoing in high places. In most instances, however, the actual purpose of the investigation was to publicly humiliate a political opponent by publicizing sensational charges of official and/or private misconduct. Often the charges simply involved embarrassing or inappropriate behavior, or minor infractions that hardly presented threats to the safety of the republic. Thus, during his confirmation hearings, Justice Clarence Thomas was accused, amid much fanfare, of engaging in inappropriate sexual banter with a former subordinate, and Judge Douglas Ginsburg was compelled to withdraw his name from consideration for the Supreme Court seat to which he had been nominated when it was revealed that he had smoked marijuana in college. Several Republican and Democratic cabinet nominations had to be withdrawn when it was revealed that the nominees had neglected to pay the so-called nanny tax for former household employees. And, of course, President Bill Clinton was humiliated by revelations of sexual escapades in the Oval Office. Other nominees, staffers, and officials were embarrassed by charges that they had made inappropriate comments, engaged in improper dalliances, or, worst of all, received poor grades at Yale.

In a number of instances, these stories were based upon leaks from disgruntled staffers or information that emerged during the routine course of news gathering. Many of the most embarrassing revelations, however, were uncovered by investigators employed by politicians specifically for the purpose of ferreting out potentially damaging information about their opponents. Each political party makes extensive use of experts in what has come to be called "opposition research." Some opposition research is done on a part-time basis by congressional staffers and political consultants. In the city of Washington alone, however, there are dozens of firms that specialize in this art. For a fee, opposition researchers will conduct computer searches; interview subjects' acquaintances; conduct surveillance; and read subjects' books, articles, and speeches to search for material that can be used against them.

One famous opposition researcher, Washington detective Terry Lenzner, specializes in searching subjects' trash—a practice known as "dumpster diving." Indeed, Lenzner wrote a magazine article on dumpster diving, which he characterized as a "very creative" means of securing information.[39] Lenzner first attracted attention during the Clinton impeachment battles in the 1990s, when he was employed by the president's allies to obtain information that might be used to discredit the various women who were making allegations of sexual improprieties against Clinton. Later, Lenzner was retained by the Oracle corporation to collect information about Microsoft that might be useful in Oracle's legal and political struggles against its giant rival. Microsoft charged that Lenzner had twice approached the night cleaning crews who serviced an office building used by one of its lobbying arms and offered to purchase the company's trash.

The effectiveness of dumpster diving and other forms of opposition research depends, in part, upon the willingness of the news media to publicize the information that is uncovered. Generally speaking, liberal newspapers, periodicals, and television networks are happy to report the misdeeds of conservative politicians, and conservative papers, periodicals, and broadcasters are delighted to devote time and attention to allegations of misconduct on the part of liberals. Thus, liberal publications such as the *New York Times* and the *Washington Post* were the first to publicize accusations of misconduct on the part of Richard Nixon, Ronald Reagan, former Republican House Majority Leader Tom DeLay, and other conservative politicians. In a similar vein, revelations of sexual improprieties on the part of Bill Clinton were initially publicized by the *American Spectator*, a conservative news magazine, and were given enormous play by *Fox Network News* and scores of conservative "talk radio" programs. Once a story has gained momentum, however, ideological factors seem to diminish in importance. Rather like piranhas sensing blood in the water, media of all ideological stripes revel in the struggles and, especially, the death throes of the unfortunate subject of a campaign of revelations. Reporters never tire of these political dramas; hence, contending political forces work to provide the media with a steady stream of new dirt with which to discredit their opponents. Dumpster diving is definitely a profession with a promising future.

Publicity Stunts

Some events have substantive importance beyond their publicity value. Martin Luther King Jr. had a valid and legitimate reason for protesting the treatment of African Americans in Dallas County, Alabama. There, as elsewhere in the South, blacks were subjected to discrimination and violence that ultimately sparked protest and counterviolence. A number of recent congressional and criminal investigations have uncovered important instances of wrongdoing on the part of senior public officials. Other staged events, though, seem to have little or no substance beyond their public relations role. Such events are often called "publicity stunts" to indicate the absence of a more meaningful purpose. One federal agency that has become notorious for staging particularly expensive and dangerous publicity stunts is the

National Aeronautics and Space Administration (NASA), the government entity charged with administering America's space program.

NASA is an agency whose culture was formed during the heady days when America raced against the Soviet Union to launch men into space and President John Kennedy dedicated America's resources to putting a man on the moon. That era reached its climax in 1969 with the Apollo 11 lunar landing. Since that time, political leaders have not seen space exploration as a top priority, and public interest in space has waned. Working closely with major defense contractors, NASA was able to secure funding for the construction of a small number of space shuttles, but the agency found its budgets constantly under attack and its efforts to promote interest in more ambitious exploratory programs generally thwarted. Indeed, most space scientists have urged NASA to scale back its endeavors, arguing that most of the cost and risk of NASA's program involves the difficulty of keeping human beings alive in space, and virtually all the scientific payoff could be achieved with much cheaper unmanned flights. For NASA executives, though, human spaceflight is the agency's raison d'être, and issues of cost and scientific value are secondary.

To stimulate support for its ongoing commitment to human spaceflight, NASA has resorted to publicity stunts, sometimes with disastrous consequences. In 1985, the agency invited America's schoolteachers to compete for a spot in the space-shuttle program. Agency executives reasoned that conducting a contest to send a teacher into space would generate enormous interest in the space program, particularly among millions of schoolchildren and their parents. Indeed, on the day that Christa McAuliffe, the winning teacher, was launched into space on the *Challenger* shuttle, televisions in classrooms throughout the country were tuned to the event. NASA executives were thrilled. Unfortunately, NASA's publicity stunt turned into a major public relations disaster and human tragedy when the *Challenger* exploded, killing six astronauts as well as the unfortunate teacher.

Undeterred, the agency has continued to seek ways of dramatizing its human spaceflight program. In 1998, for example, NASA sent the aging Senator John Glenn into orbit on the *Discovery* space shuttle. Three decades earlier, Glenn had been the first American to orbit the earth and had continued from his seat in the Senate to serve as a visible champion of the space program. NASA administrators hoped that sending such a legendary figure back into space would heighten public interest in human spaceflight. Criticized for spending nearly $500 million—the cost of a shuttle launch—on a publicity stunt, NASA bosses countered that the mission had a valid scientific purpose, namely, to investigate the effects of spaceflight on aging. Even if this somewhat fanciful explanation were true, it is not precisely clear why it would be useful to understand the effects of spaceflight on the aging process. Perhaps NASA plans to recruit a corps of senior-citizen astronauts, or, alternatively, the agency may have a secret plan to expand its revenue base by constructing retirement villages on Mars.

Nothing seems too bizarre for the fertile imaginations of NASA publicists. NASA publicity has been sufficiently effective that even after another space-shuttle explosion killed seven astronauts in 2003, most Americans continued to support the space program. Asked by CBS in 2003 whether the shuttle program should go forward, 75 percent of Americans said yes. In the same survey, only 27 percent said too much money was being spent on the space program. Only 11 percent said the space program did not contribute much to science—the answer that would be given by most space scientists.

How Advocates Write the News

Staged events can be effective publicity tools. Politicians and advocates, however, cannot always be certain that the media will afford them the coverage they seek or the interpretation they desire. Many commentators, for example, derided NASA's "senator in space" mission as a foolish waste of taxpayers' resources. To make certain that they receive precisely the media coverage they seek, advocates often develop strategies for actually writing rather than merely staging the news. Some techniques employed for this purpose are visible and obvious, whereas others may involve various forms of disguise and camouflage.

Perhaps the most obvious are speeches, press conferences, and other televised appearances in which prominent advocates articulate their views before national audiences. Members of the audience are likely to be aware that what they are watching is closer to a partisan communiqué than an objective account of events. Nevertheless, the fact that the media treat the event as news enhances the credibility of whatever claims are being presented. A skilled advocate, moreover, may be able to present compelling arguments that will sway popular sentiment. Indeed, even an unskilled but apparently sincere advocate can often be quite convincing. In late 2005, for example, President Bush delivered a number of speeches and held a nationally televised press conference to defend his administration's policies in Iraq. Though Bush is not exactly a modern-day Cicero, he does convey sincerity and conviction. In the wake of his publicity offensive, the president's poll standing temporarily rose more than ten points.

Other overt techniques of publicizing information and advocating points of view include the publication of magazine articles, weblogs, books, and films. For example, recent issues of the *New Republic,* a journal of liberal opinion, have featured articles critical of Republican social programs, GOP tax proposals, and President Bush's Supreme Court nominees and have offered a guide to "GOP D.C.—today's Republican-controlled, scandal-plagued Washington."[40] In a similar vein, recent issues of the *Weekly Standard,* a conservative magazine, have included articles supporting the Bush administration's efforts in Iraq, attacking the domestic and foreign policy ideas of congressional Democrats, and defending limits on stem-cell research. Films have been an important political medium for decades. During the 2004 election, for example, each side screened its own cinematic agitprop. Democrats swooned over *Fahrenheit 9/11,* which purported to document George W. Bush's ineptitude, and Republicans were thrilled with *Stolen Honor,* which sought to debunk tales of John Kerry's wartime heroism. Humorous sketches on such programs as *Saturday Night Live, The Daily Show,* and *South Park* can be potent political weapons.

Conservative political forces also rely upon a number of Washington think tanks, such as the Heritage Foundation, the Cato Institute, and the American Enterprise Institute, to publicize the ideas of the political right. Funded by major corporate donors, these institutions played an important role in promoting the agenda of deregulation, tax cuts, and commitment to free markets that effectively replaced Keynesianism as the nation's dominant economic perspective during the 1980s.[41] For their part, liberal political forces can always depend upon the American academic community to promote and publicize the current political ideas of the political left. Since Franklin D. Roosevelt and the New Dealers launched what became the "grants economy" that currently supports their research endeavors, American academics have been firmly attached to the liberal political camp. Few conservatives can be found among the arts and sciences professors at major American universities. Indeed, professors known to have a conservative political orientation will seldom be recruited for positions at top schools.[42] This liberal political orientation is, perhaps, especially evident among professors of education. According to the *Chronicle of Higher Education,* some education scholars have actually been evaluating students on the extent to which they are deemed to value social justice, acknowledge white privilege, and agree to become agents of change in fighting against sexism, racism, and homophobia.[43]

Of course, it is not clear that the liberal bias of the faculty has much influence on the college student population. Students' natural indolence, indifference, and propensity to skip class offer them considerable protection against ideological contamination.

Writing the News Covertly

Speeches, books, films, and other overt means of publicizing some set of facts and ideas can be persuasive even when their purpose is clear. Often enough, though, advocates can be even more persuasive when they write their own publicity while hiding its actual source. This public relations sleight of hand can take many forms, including the news leak, the press release, and the video news release.

A leak is the disclosure of confidential information to the news media. Leaks may emanate from a variety of sources, including whistle-blowers, lower-level officials who hope to publicize what they view as their bosses' improper activities. In 1971, for example, a minor Department of Defense staffer named Daniel Ellsberg sought to discredit official justifications for America's involvement in the Vietnam War by leaking top-secret documents to the press. The so-called Pentagon Papers were published by the *New York Times* and the *Washington Post* after the U.S. Supreme Court ruled that the government could not block their release.[44] In a similar vein, in 2005, President George W. Bush was infuriated when he learned that a still-unidentified source, presumably a whistle-blower, had leaked information concerning the president's secret orders authorizing the National Security Agency (NSA) to conduct clandestine surveillance of suspected terrorists without obtaining authorization from the special federal tribunal created for this purpose. Bush ordered the Justice Department to launch a probe of the leak. In 2006, a still unidentified source leaked part of a secret intelligence summary that seemed to contradict the administration's claims of progress in the war in Iraq. The president was furious and claimed the leaked portion of the report did not accurately reflect the full report. The administration proceeded to declassify portions of the report that seemed to support its claims about the war.

Most leaks, though, originate not with low-level whistle-blowers but, rather, with senior government officials, prominent politicians, and political activists. Such personages often cultivate long-term relationships with journalists to whom they regularly leak confidential information, knowing that it is likely to be published on a high-priority basis in a form acceptable to them. Their confidence is based upon the fact that journalists are likely to regard high-level sources of confidential information as valuable assets whose favor must be retained. For example, Lewis "Scooter" Libby, Vice President Cheney's former chief of staff, was apparently such a valuable source of leaks to so many prominent journalists that his name was seldom even mentioned in the newspapers, despite his prominence in Washington and his importance as a decision-maker.[45] The more recipients of leaked information strive to keep their sources secret, the more difficulty other journalists will have in checking its validity.

Through such tacit alliance with journalists, prominent figures can manipulate news coverage and secure the publication of stories that serve their purposes. One recent case that revealed the complexities of this culture of leaks was the 2005 Valerie Plame affair. Plame was an undercover CIA analyst who happened to be married to Joseph Wilson, a prominent career diplomat. Wilson had angered the Bush White House by making a number of statements that were critical of the president's policies in Iraq. In an apparent effort to discredit Wilson, one or more administration officials informed prominent journalists that Plame had improperly used her position to help Wilson. In so doing, these officials may have violated a federal statute prohibiting disclosure of the identities of covert intelligence operatives. The subsequent investigation revealed that the story had been leaked to several journalists, including the *Washington Post*'s Bob Woodward, who did not use it, and the *New York Times*'s Judith Miller, who did. Miller initially refused to name her source and spent several weeks in jail for contempt of court after refusing to testify before a federal grand jury looking into the leak. Though Scooter Libby had been widely blamed for the leak, it emerged that the actual culprit was former State Department official Richard Armitage. Nevertheless, in 2007, Libby was convicted of lying and obstruction.

Also seamlessly incorporated into daily news reports each year are thousands of press releases. The press release, sometimes called a news release, is a story written by an advocate or publicist and distributed to the media in the hope that journalists will publish it with little or no revision under their own bylines. The inventor of the press release was a famous New York public relations consultant named Ivy Lee. In 1906, a train operated by one of Lee's clients, the Pennsylvania Railroad, was involved in a serious wreck. Lee quickly wrote and distributed to reporters a story about the accident that presented the railroad in a favorable light. Many papers published Lee's slanted story as their own objective account of events, and the railroad's reputation for quality and safety remained intact.

Consistent with Lee's example, today's press release presents facts and perspectives that serve an advocate's interests but is written in a way that mimics the factual news style of the paper, periodical, or television news program to which it has been sent. It is quite difficult for the audience to distinguish a well-designed press release from an actual news story. For example, a recent posting on Pharma Watch, a weblog monitoring the pharmaceutical industry, identified an article published in the *New York Times* Science section that rehashed a news release issued by Pfizer, the giant pharmaceutical corporation. "A lawyer in New York, has had to deal with what is politely referred to as 'bladder control' for as long as she can remember," the article began. "Even as a teenager she woke up at night feeling the urge to urinate but not always making it to the toilet in time." Fortunately, thanks to the press release it copied, the article was able to propose a solution. "Urge incontinence is often treated with drugs like tolterodine, sold as Detrol."[46] Not surprisingly, the drug touted in this helpful news story is sold by Pfizer.

To take another example, an April 2005 article sent to thousands of newspapers by the Associated Press (AP) was headlined "Fed Unveils Financial Education Website." Apparently written by an AP reporter, the article discussed the various ways in which a new site developed by the Federal Reserve could help consumers make informed decisions. The article did not mention that it was basically a slight revision of a press release that could be found on the Fed's website.[47] In a similar vein, a recent *San Francisco Chronicle* story on teacher training claimed that students taught by teachers provided by Teach for America and other nontraditional sources performed significantly worse on standardized tests than students taught by traditionally certified instructors. The article failed to note that it was essentially a copy of a Stanford University press release touting the work of a Stanford professor who directs a traditional teacher-training program.[48] Or what about the June 2005 *Los Angeles Times* story titled "County Homeless Number 90,000"? This article claimed, without offering an explanation, that the number of homeless individuals in Los Angeles County had quintupled since the previous year. In presenting this shocking increase in homelessness, though, the article neglected to mention that the data came from a press release issued by the Los Angeles Homeless Service Authority, an agency whose budget is tied to the number of clients it serves. For the authority, more homelessness equals more money and staff. Indeed, on its own website, the authority indicated that it had undertaken its new count of homeless individuals in part to "increase funding for homeless services in our community."[49] These stories should not be seen as isolated examples. According to some experts, more than 50 percent of the articles in a newspaper on any given day are based upon press releases. Indeed, more than 75 percent of the journalists responding to a recent survey acknowledged using press releases for their stories.[50]

Journalists are certainly aware of the fact that the authors of press releases have their own agendas and are hardly unbiased reporters of the news. Nevertheless, the economics of publishing and broadcasting dictate that large numbers of stories will always be based upon such releases. Newspapers and television stations are businesses, and for many, the financial bottom line is more important than journalistic integrity.[51] The use of press releases allows a newspaper or broadcast network to present more stories without requiring them to pay more staff or incur the other costs associated with investigating and writing the news. As one newspaper executive said, the public relations people who generally write news releases are the newspaper's "unpaid reporters."[52]

In recent years, the simple printed press release has been joined by the "video news release," designed especially for television stations. The video release is a taped report, usually about ninety seconds long, the typical length of a television news story, designed to look and sound like any other broadcast news segment. In exchange for airing material that serves the interests of some advocate, the television station airing the video release is relieved of the considerable expense and bother of identifying and filming its own news story. The audience is usually unaware that the "news" it is watching is actually someone's canned publicity footage.

One recent example of a video news release was a pair of ninety-second segments funded by the U.S. Department of Health and Human Services (HHS) in 2004. After Congress enacted legislation adding a prescription-drug benefit to the Medicare program, HHS sent a video release designed to look like a news report to local TV stations around the nation. Forty television stations aired the report without indicating that it had come from the government. The segment was introduced by the local news anchor, reading from a government-suggested script. The anchor read, "Reporter Karen Ryan helps sort through the details," of the new Medicare law. Then, against the backdrop of film showing President Bush signing the law and the reactions of apparently grateful senior citizens, an unseen narrator, speaking like a reporter, presented the new law in a positive light. "The new law, say officials, will simply offer people with Medicare more ways to make their health coverage more affordable." The segment concluded with the sign-off, "In Washington, I'm Karen Ryan reporting." Viewers were not told that the entire "news" story had been distributed by the government.

Nor were viewers informed that Karen Ryan was not a reporter at all. She was an employee of the ad agency hired by the government to create the video release.[53] In response to criticism, an HHS spokesperson pointed out that the same sort of video news release had often been used by the Clinton administration and was commonly used by a number of firms and interest groups. "The use of video news releases is a common, routine practice in government and the private sector," he said. "Anyone who has questions about this practice needs to do some research on modern public information tools."[54]

Rent-a-Reporter

From creating phony reporters to read make-believe news stories, it is but a small step to hiring real reporters to present sham accounts. This step has been taken quite frequently by both the government and private advocates. A number of cases have come to light in recent years in which the government or some private concern has paid journalists to write favorable accounts of their activities and efforts. For example, late in 2005, the U.S. military acknowledged that contractors in its employ had regularly paid Iraqi newspapers to carry positive news about American efforts in that nation. The Washington-based Lincoln Group, a public relations firm working under contract to the federal government, said it had placed more than one thousand news stories in the Iraqi and Arab press over the past four years.[55] Iraqis reading the articles would have had no way to know that the material being presented to them was produced at the behest of the American authorities.

In a similar vein, the U.S. military and the U.S. Agency for International Development (USAID) operate or subsidize radio stations and newspapers in Afghanistan, staffed by local journalists who write or broadcast in local dialects. Every effort is made to maintain the impression that these media outlets are autonomous, Afghan-owned organizations with no connection to the United States. One USAID representative explained, "We want to maintain the perception that these [media] are in fact fully independent."[56] Needless to say, the U.S.-controlled media paint a rosy picture of American efforts in Afghanistan. Apparently, there is no bad news emanating from that impoverished and war-torn country. "We have no requirements to adhere to journalistic standards of objectivity," said a U.S. Army spokesperson.[57]

The government's practice of hiring journalists is not limited to operations abroad. In recent years, federal agencies have paid several journalists and commentators to report favorably on government initiatives and programs in the United States. The Department of Education, for example, paid commentator Armstrong Williams $241,000 to promote President Bush's No Child Left Behind law. Williams wrote favorably about the law in his newspaper column, commented positively about it during his cable television appearances, and urged other commentators to interview Education Secretary Roderick Paige.[58] Williams did not disclose his financial relationship with the agency whose programs he was touting. In a similar vein, HHS paid syndicated columnist Maggie Gallagher $20,000 to promote the administration's views on marriage. Gallagher wrote several columns on the topic without revealing her financial relationship with the administration.

Williams and Gallagher worked for the government, but the practice of hiring reporters is not confined to Big Brother. The private sector is also active in this area. Corporations, trade associations, and interest groups have also been known to provide gratuities to journalists. For example, in 2005, one well-known columnist was forced to resign from his position with the Cato Institute after it was revealed that he had accepted payment from a prominent Washington lobbyist in exchange for writing newspaper columns favorable to the interests of some of the lobbyist's clients. The lobbyist, Jack Abramoff, who in 2006 pleaded guilty to a number of violations of federal lobbying laws, paid the writer, Doug Bandow, to promote the causes of the Northern Marianas Islands, the Choctaw Indians, and other Abramoff clients. In one nationally syndicated Copley News Service column, Bandow defended the Choctaws' operation of gambling casinos, asserting, "There's certainly no evidence that Indian gambling operations harm the local community." Abramoff was arguing just this point to lawmakers. In another column, Bandow opposed federal "economic meddling" in the Marianas. This was precisely the position the Marianas government was paying Abramoff to advocate on Capitol Hill.[59]

There have been several other recent cases in which reporters and columnists were found to have received payment from industries and interests about which they wrote. In 2005, Indiana Wesleyan Professor Tom Lehman published a piece in *The Hill,* a magazine read by congressional staffers and members, praising so-called payday loans. It turned out that Lehman had accepted money from the industry that provides these high-risk loans to poor people.[60] In another case, syndicated columnist Michael Fumento praised Monsanto Co., a huge agribusiness enterprise, in his columns and in a recent book. Fumento, it turned out, received $60,000 from Monsanto, though he denied that the payment influenced his writing. Fumento's weekly column was canceled by Scripps Howard after the revelation.[61]

One group especially noted for paying writers and reporters for favorable coverage is the pharmaceutical industry. Many of the articles that appear in popular—and even scientific—journals reporting favorably on particular drugs are written by the drug companies themselves. In some cases, the writers are in the direct pay of the drug companies; in other reported instances, the writer cited in the story's byline is not the actual author of the account. Often a ghost writer employed by a drug company writes the story while the nominal author is paid for the use of his or her name.[62]

Perhaps it should not be surprising that the practice of paying writers for positive news has recently entered the blogosphere. At least one advertising agency, Tampa, Florida–based MindComet, pays bloggers to write nice things about its clients. The agency is currently in the process of creating a website that will link bloggers and sponsors. Advertisers will pay to post details they want bloggers to discuss about their product as well as a fee schedule. Bloggers will be able to sign up and arrange for payment.[63] Readers, of course, will not know that their favorite bloggers have become corporate shills.

Creating Media

Some politicians and advocates are content to hire journalists. Others are not satisfied unless they actually control their own newspapers or broadcast outlets. Most large firms, interest groups, and trade associations publish newsletters, magazines, and other house organs designed to publicize the group or firm's viewpoint and trumpet its virtues. Universities, for example, produce numerous proprietary periodicals. These always include an alumni magazine calculated to generate monetary contributions by stimulating feelings of nostalgia among the school's graduates. University publications almost always also include an administrative newsletter whose stories seem designed to convince employees and faculty of the amazing accomplishments of the horde of vice presidents, provosts, vice and associate provosts, deans, deanlets, deanlings, and ding-a-lings who seem to have taken over contemporary institutions of higher learning. The work of this gaggle of well-paid functionaries does not add much to the educational or research efforts of the university. Indeed, the vice provosts, deanlets, and deanlings spend their days attending an endless round of meetings, retreats, breakfasts, luncheons, and dinners where they consume excess tuition revenue while palavering aimlessly with one another.

Needless to say, the picture of administrative life usually painted by the university's house organ is quite different from this dispiriting reality. Here we read of the heroic accomplishments of the various provosts and deanlings, presented in a tendentious neo-Stalinist style. But just as truth could be found between the lines of the old *Pravda*, if closely read, a university rag can sometimes be unintentionally revealing—even incredibly funny. Take this story from Johns Hopkins University's administrative paper, the *Gazette*. Interviewed by a *Gazette* writer, Hopkins's newly appointed director of student involvement on the Homewood Campus shared his vision of academic life. Students, according to this functionary, need to learn more than academic skills. They also must be taught "the universal life skills that everyone needs to know." And what might be an example of these all-important proficiencies? According to this deanling, a premier example is event planning. "For many students, the biggest event they've ever planned is a dinner at home." But planning an event on campus might require "reserving the room, notifying Security, arranging transportation and lodging for out-of-town speakers, ordering food."[64] Armed with training in a subject as important and intellectually challenging as event planning, students would hardly need to know anything about physics or calculus or literature or any of those other inconsequential topics taught by the stodgy faculty.

Of course, some university administrators have evolved an academic vision too outlandish even for the editors of the house organ. Another deanlet at Johns Hopkins, the associate dean for academic programs and advising in the School of Arts and Sciences, proposed a curricular innovation that may actually have been too racy for the *Gazette*. This was the construction of a campus Slip 'N Slide. "We would set up tarps and hoses out on the campus and tell everybody to come with a bathing suit. It's something you could do every year. And you could look forward to a warm day in April when everybody gets half naked and has a good time."[65] No wonder tuition at prestigious universities is so high.

University administrators control media that reach a small and captive audience. National politicians and advocates have larger ambitions and often endeavor to create or control media that will be read or viewed by broad national constituencies. In the eighteenth and early nineteenth centuries, many newspapers were created by political parties or even by individual politicians to promote their political ideas and ambitions. And, before advertising revenues emancipated them, many newspapers depended upon government contracts and party subscriptions for their revenues, a dependence that allowed politicians to exercise substantial control over newspaper content. For example, in the early years of the republic, the *Gazette of the United States,* published by John Fenno, served as the semiofficial organ for Alexander Hamilton and his Federalist allies. The *Gazette* praised Hamilton at every turn and was, in its turn, the recipient of lucrative government printing contracts.

To counter the influence of Fenno's *Gazette,* Hamilton's archrival, Thomas Jefferson, undertook to found a rival newspaper. Jefferson secured the services of Philip Freneau, a talented poet and journalist, to establish a competing paper, the *National Gazette.* To help support the new venture, Jefferson gave Freneau a position as translator in the State Department. Needless to say, the new paper excoriated Hamilton while continually praising Jefferson. Freneau ceased publication after two years, but his *Gazette* was soon replaced by several new Jeffersonian papers, including the Philadelphia *Aurora,* edited by Benjamin Franklin Bache, a grandson of Benjamin Franklin. Bache's vituperative attacks infuriated the Federalists. He accused John Adams of corruption and even charged that George Washington had bungled Revolutionary War strategy.[66] The desire to silence the *Aurora* was one of the factors impelling the Federalists to draft the Alien and Sedition Acts. Bache was arrested in 1798 and charged with seditious libel but died in the yellow-fever epidemic of that year before his case came to trial. Several other Jeffersonian editors were convicted of sedition, but after Jefferson's election in 1800, the acts were allowed to lapse. Even as they attacked the Jeffersonian press, the Federalists continued to develop newspapers of their own, such as William Cobbett's *New York Evening Post,* to heap scorn on the Jeffersonians.[67] In the ensuing decades, the Jacksonians established a network of partisan newspapers, as did their partisan foes, the Whigs. The leading Whig editor, Horace Greeley, helped to elect William Henry Harrison in 1840. After the collapse of the Whigs, however, Greeley's *New York Tribune* became the chief organ of the new Republican Party, championing Republican opposition to the expansion of slavery.

Today's American newspapers are not formally linked to politicians or political parties, though this pattern continues to exist in other nations. In Italy, for example, one important politician, Silvio Berlusconi, owns or controls several television stations, a news magazine, and two newspapers that he uses to promote his party's ideas. But despite their nominal independence, many American newspapers have close ties to one or the other political party and generally champion its candidates and ideas. For example, the *New York Times* nearly always supports Democratic programs and initiatives, and the *Washington Times* is closely allied with the Republicans.

Many surveys, to be sure, indicate that the majority of national print and broadcast journalists identify themselves as Democrats.[68] And for several decades, Republicans have railed against what they see as liberal bias in the mainstream media, including the three traditional television networks: NBC, CBS, and ABC.[69] In response, Republicans have worked to develop a network of newspapers, periodicals, and broadcast media that, though not formally affiliated with the party, provide favorable coverage to the GOP's candidates and policy initiatives. These efforts have been quite successful. The abolition of the Federal Communications Commission's "Fairness Doctrine" in 1987 opened the way for increased on-the-air political commentary. A number of conservative broadcasters took advantage of this new opportunity and pioneered what came to be called conservative "talk radio" featuring such personalities as Rush Limbaugh and Sean Hannity, who preach conservative ideas and Republican politics to millions of listeners. At the same time, conservative billionaire Rupert Murdoch established the Fox television network, whose news and editorial content have a decidedly pro-Republican slant. Murdoch also financed the creation of the *Weekly Standard*, a conservative journal of opinion edited by William Kristol, former chief of staff to GOP Vice President Dan Quayle. The *Standard* has come to play an influential role in Washington policy debates. In these ways, Republicans have followed the example set long ago by the Federalists and Jeffersonians.

Of course, the Federalists and Jeffersonians could never have envisioned the latest front in partisan media warfare—the blog. Both Democratic and Republican activists have established Internet weblogs, or "blogs," to champion their parties' principles. Most of the millions of weblogs that currently form what is known as the "blogosphere" are little more than individuals' diaries. A number of political blogs, though, have a regular and substantial readership.[70] Democratic and Republican bloggers often provide material for partisan broadcasters and columnists, who then disseminate it to wider audiences. GOP bloggers, for example, have helped the party on a number of occasions. The most notable instance came during the 2004 presidential campaign when the CBS news program *60 Minutes* ran a story charging that George W. Bush had received preferential treatment from the National Guard in the 1960s. The Republican blog Power Line questioned the authenticity of the evidence cited by *60 Minutes* as well as the reliability of the story's main source. The subsequent furor led to an apology from CBS; the firing of a number of CBS news executives; the retirement of longtime CBS anchor and conservative bête noire Dan Rather; and the termination of media inquiry into Bush's military service, something that had been a rather embarrassing topic for the president.[71] All in all, not a bad day's work for a blogger.

Propaganda

As we have seen, the government employs many of the same publicity techniques used by private advocates. The government's efforts to shape public opinion, though, are often called *propaganda* and are somewhat different in kind and character from the activities of private advocates. To begin with, the government usually has the capacity to speak with a louder voice than almost any private concern. Important national officials—the president in particular—seldom have any difficulty attracting the attention of the media for their speeches and press conferences. Every government agency, moreover, includes a public information office staffed by a bevy of public relations professionals. The Department of Defense, for example, employs an enormous public information staff in the Defense Department Press Office and the Armed Forces Information Service. These offices, under the direction of the assistant secretary for public affairs, conduct press briefings, organize talks by military brass, maintain numerous websites, disseminate a daily blizzard of press releases, and operate broadcast and film facilities. The individual military services conduct their own public information efforts along similar lines.

The uniformed services, as well as several other government agencies, also maintain liaison offices in Hollywood, where they endeavor to influence the content of feature films. In exchange for access to military facilities, the free use of billions of dollars' worth of military equipment, and the availability of military personnel to serve as extras, the military seeks favorable cinematic treatment and, sometimes, final approval of the script.[72] One well-known film produced with the cooperation of the U.S. Navy was *Top Gun,* starring movie idol Tom Cruise. The navy donated the use of a fleet of F-14 jet fighters and their pilots, two aircraft carriers, and access to Miramar naval air station, charging the film's producers only for jet fuel. "The Navy gave us tremendous cooperation," said the film's director. Whenever a problem developed, "we contacted [the Secretary of the Navy]. He was very supportive."[73] In exchange for its cooperation, the navy received a popular feature film that portrayed the service in a very favorable light. After reviewing the script, navy public information officers did object to the pilots' use of salty language—apparently a practice in which real navy fliers never engage. After some discussion, however, the four-letter words were retained in the interest of cinematic realism.

Other recent feature films in which Hollywood and the military worked together include *Windtalkers, Pearl Harbor,* and *The Sum of All Fears.* In that last film, the producers agreed to change the original screenplay, in which an aircraft carrier was destroyed, after the navy objected to the depiction of one of its ships as vulnerable.[74] The military hopes to expand its cooperation with the film industry. "We want the opportunity to communicate directly to the American public through that powerful medium," said Philip Sirub, Defense Department special assistant for entertainment media.[75]

In addition to possessing a louder voice than most private advocates, the government is better able to manipulate media access to information. In some instances, citing such factors as national security interests or executive privilege, government officials and agencies can legally prevent the dissemination of information that might cause them embarrassment. Thus, early in the Bush presidency, Vice President Cheney invoked executive privilege in refusing to disclose the details of his meetings with energy industry executives—meetings in which the industry may have had significant behind-the-scenes influence over the administration's energy policies. And since the beginning of the Bush administration's war on terror, the government, claiming national security requirements, has held prisoners in secret facilities around the world where it is impossible for journalists to obtain information about their status or treatment. Private advocates have considerably more difficulty preventing coverage of a topic, though reporters charge that some important constituencies have occasionally been able to block reportage to which they objected.[76]

At the same time, when it believes its interests will be served, the government can provide journalists with access to remote and dangerous, but extremely newsworthy, locations where they might have extraordinary difficulty traveling on their own. During the 2002 Iraq War, for example, the U.S. military allowed selected reporters to go into battle with the troops. These embedded journalists, or "embeds," as they were called, rode into battle in tanks and armored personnel carriers, enjoying spectacular firsthand access to the combat zone. The DoD calculated that journalists who lived with small groups of soldiers under conditions of hardship and danger would be thoroughly co-opted by the experience and would write positive accounts of American forces in action. For the most part, this was precisely what happened. By giving journalists extraordinarily good access to information, the DoD was able to generate extraordinarily good publicity for its endeavors. And, just as the government can block access to information it wishes to hide by classifying it, so can government officials give journalists access to secret information they believe serves their political interests by declassifying it. Thus, in 2005, Vice President Cheney apparently authorized his chief of staff to leak classified information that Cheney hoped would lend credence to the administration's case for having invaded Iraq.[77] For several years, the Bush administration's propaganda barrage convinced millions of Americans to support the president's futile policies in Iraq.[78]

Finally, in the realm of publicity, the government has an important asset that is not readily available to private advocates. The government generally can rely upon Americans' patriotic sentiments, inculcated through the family, years of civic education in the schools, and the media, to promote at least initial acceptance of its claims, particularly when they involve foreign relations or national security matters. Most Americans feel a sense of pride in their nation and its institutions even when they do not like the particular individuals in office. In a recent national survey, 56 percent of all respondents said they felt very patriotic; 35 percent described themselves as somewhat patriotic; and 89 percent said that, whatever its faults, the United States had the best system of government in the world.[79]

This reservoir of patriotism means that the government's allegations will often be given the benefit of the doubt even when they are not supported by much in the way of evidence, and sometimes even when they seem patently implausible. In some instances, in fact, those who question the contentions of government officials are castigated for their lack of patriotism. Thus, for example, individuals who questioned President Bush's avowals in 2002 that Iraq possessed weapons of mass destruction were often assailed as unpatriotic, with some broadcasters refusing to even give air time to groups seeking to dispute the president's claims.[80] Ultimately, of course, popular patriotism does not offer the government full immunity against the unmasking of its deceptions. But much can happen before reality overcomes patriotism and Americans see through their government's propaganda. Iraq, as is now generally acknowledged, turned out not to possess weapons of mass destruction. Yet, several bloody years later, American forces continue to do battle in that wretched land.

Measuring Opinion

A third major instrument of opinion management is measurement—in particular, opinion polling. Politicians, advocacy groups, and public officials sponsor thousands of opinion surveys every year to assess public sentiment on issues ranging from abortion to Social Security to war in the Middle East. Some pollsters have argued that opinion surveys provide the most scientific and accurate representation of public opinion. George Gallup, one of the founders of the modern polling industry, asserted that opinion polls, more than any other institution, "bridge the gap between the people and those responsible for making decisions in their name."[81] Polling, of course, has no official place in the American governmental schema. The Constitution does not require public officials to follow poll results. During the entire Clinton impeachment process, the president's standing in the polls remained high—as did Richard Nixon's until the eve of his resignation. Conversely, his declining standing in the polls throughout 2005 and 2006 did not compel George W. Bush to withdraw American forces from Iraq. In fact, Gallup's view notwithstanding, the virtual representation provided by the polls does little to bridge the gap between citizens and decision-makers. If anything, the polls render public opinion less disruptive, more permissive, and more amenable to government and elite manipulation.

Polling has become so ubiquitous that commentators make little distinction between poll results and public opinion, but they are not the same thing at all. Public opinion can be articulated in ways that present a picture of the public's political thinking very different from the results of sample surveys.[82] Statements from leaders of interest groups, trade unions, and religious groups about their adherents' feelings are a common mechanism for expressing public opinion. The hundreds of thousands of letters written each year to newspaper editors and to members of Congress are vehicles for the expression of opinion. Protests, riots, and demonstrations express citizens' opinions. Government officials take note of all these manifestations of the public's mood. As corporate executive and political commentator Chester Barnard once noted, before the invention of polling, legislators "read the local newspapers, toured their districts and talked with voters, received letters from the home state and entertained delegations that claimed to speak for large and important blocks of voters."[83] The alternatives to polling survive today. But when poll results differ from other expressions of public opinion, the polls almost always carry more credibility. The labor leader whose account of rank-and-file sentiment differs from poll results is not likely to be taken seriously. Nor is the politician who claims that his or her policy positions are more popular than the polls show. In 1999, for example, Republican congressional leaders claimed that the public opinion disclosed by letters and phone calls supported their efforts to impeach and convict President Bill Clinton, even though national opinion polls indicated that the public opposed Clinton's removal from office. Virtually every commentator took the polls to be correct and accused the GOP of disregarding true public sentiment.

This presumption in favor of the accuracy of the polls stems from their apparent scientific neutrality. Survey analysis is modeled on the methods of the natural sciences and conveys an impression of technical sophistication and objectivity. The polls, moreover, can claim to offer a more reliable and representative view of popular opinion than any alternative. People who claim to speak for groups frequently do not. The distribution of opinion reflected in letters to newspapers and government officials is clearly unrepresentative. Scientific samplings of public opinion provide a corrective for false or biased representations of popular sentiment.

Polling, though, is both more and less than a scientific measure of public opinion. The substitution of polling for other methods of gauging the public's views profoundly affects what is perceived to be public opinion. Polling is what statisticians call an "obtrusive measure."[84] Surveys do not simply record continuities and changes in a naturally occurring phenomenon. The polls also define how individual opinions are to be aggregated. In opinion surveys, the views of well-informed people usually carry no more weight than those of the clueless.[85] Pollsters also choose the topics for which public opinion will be tested. In other words, the data reported by the polls are not "pure" public opinion but the product of an interaction between the opinion holders and the opinion seekers. As surveys measure opinion, they also form opinion.

Forming Opinion

Polling changes the character of public opinion in at least three important ways.[86] First, polling subsidizes the cost of asserting opinions. In the absence of polling, the cost and effort required to communicate an opinion are normally borne by those who hold the opinion. Someone wishing to express a view about abortion, for example, might write a letter, deliver a speech, contribute to an organization, or attend a rally. Polls, however, organize and publicize opinion without requiring the opinion holders to exert themselves in any significant way. The great majority of those whose views are supposedly captured in a survey are never even interviewed. A survey claiming to reflect the opinions of 250 million Americans is typically based upon interviews with only 2,000 or 3,000 randomly sampled respondents. The remainder are statistically, or "virtually," represented. They need not even have endured the nuisance of an interview.

The displacement of costs from the opinion holder to the polling agency has important consequences for the character of the opinions likely to be expressed. In general, an individual's willingness to bear the costs of asserting political opinions is closely tied to the intensity of those opinions. If you have strong feelings about an issue, you are more likely to invest the time and energy needed to make your views known than are others who hold less intense views. One never hears, for example, of a march on Washington by those who are indifferent or undecided about U.S. policy in the Middle East. As the example suggests, people with strongly held views are also more likely than their less-zealous fellow citizens to be found at the extremes of opinion on any given question.[87] When the costs of expressing opinion are borne by opinion holders, the views are likely to be both intensely held and relatively extreme.

Polls undermine this relationship between public expression and the intensity of opinion. The assertion of opinion through surveys requires almost no effort on the part of opinion holders. The views of those who care hardly at all about an issue count just as much as the opinions of others who care deeply. For this reason, the distribution of opinion reported in surveys is typically both less intense and less extreme than the public opinion that concerned citizens would have expressed on their own.[88] Indeed, many of the individuals responding to surveys actually know nothing about the issue at hand and truly have no opinion. They are essentially responding randomly to the question.[89] In opinion polls, the voices of Americans with strongly held views are drowned out by the indistinct murmur of the often apathetic and uninformed mass public.[90]

This is not entirely a bad thing. The polls may make it more difficult for activists at ideological extremes to claim widespread popular support when they do not have it.[91] Columnist and presidential candidate Pat Buchanan, for example, presented himself as a spokesman for "brigades" of true conservatives in 1996 and 2000, but surveys indicated that his xenophobic views commanded the support of only 2 percent of the American public.

The polls, however, also enable governments and politicians to claim that they represent true public opinion even in the face of manifest public discontent. President Richard Nixon, for example, claimed to be governing on behalf of the "silent majority" of Americans who did not join protest marches to demand changes in American race relations and an end to the Vietnam War. The administration invoked a silent majority that spoke only through the polls to counter the political weight and credibility of the hundreds of thousands of noisy Americans—citizens who felt strongly enough to take action on controversial issues. The administration preferred to govern on behalf of this silent majority precisely because of its silence. It was silent because it had no particular views on controversial issues and therefore imposed no particular constraints upon the government's conduct. Poll results provided Nixon with an excuse to ignore people who actually had opinions.

Polling transforms opinion in a second way—by treating it as an attribute of individual citizens rather than a property of groups. Before politicians sponsored polls, their information about the attitudes of ordinary Americans often came from the leaders of associations and groups. Those interested in the views of working people, for example, might consult trade-union officials. To find out about public sentiment in a town or county, a politician might inquire of its leading citizens. In the absence of contradictory evidence, the recognition of these leaders as knowledgeable informants about grassroots opinion enhanced their own political influence and may have bolstered the apparent political coherence and strength of the groups they led. The leader spoke for the group as a unified force and, by so doing, increased the chance that others would regard it as such.

Opinion surveys, however, go directly to individual members of the public, bypassing the groups to which they belong and the people who lead them. Polling therefore tends to disclose disagreements among group members and between leaders and followers. This, too, is not all bad. Survey data may prevent the leaders of a group from accidentally or deliberately misrepresenting their members' views. For example, the views of political party convention delegates usually differ substantially from those of the average voter. Republican delegates are more conservative than GOP voters, and Democratic delegates are decidedly more liberal than typical Democrats in the electorate. The polls are a helpful reminder to party leaders that not all Democrats, say, would support the views articulated at the convention by gay-rights activists and that not all Republicans share the beliefs of the leaders of the party's religious right.

At the same time, however, by undermining the ability of group leaders and activists to speak for their members, the polls can undermine a group's influence. One significant example can be drawn from the history of the American labor movement. In 1947, organized labor bitterly opposed the enactment of the Taft-Hartley Act, which union leaders disparaged as a "slave labor" act. After President Truman vetoed the act, the presidents of major unions vowed to work for the defeat of any member of Congress who voted to override Truman's veto. While senators and representatives weighed their options, poll data showed that most union members, unlike the leadership, neither fully understood the act nor viewed it as the decisive consideration for the congressional voting preferences. These findings emboldened a number of legislators with large trade-union constituencies to vote for the bill, and Truman's veto was overturned.[92] Accurate information about the preferences of individual union members diminished the collective power of organized labor. The example of organized labor suggests an important principle. Political polling was introduced in the United States by Mugwumps, Progressives, and other conservative elites as a way of reducing the collective power of their working-class opponents, who depended heavily upon coherent and disciplined organizations to make up for their members' individual lack of resources and influence.[93] The conservative *Chicago Tribune* was a major sponsor of polls in the 1890s, and the Hearst newspapers were avid promoters of polling in the early twentieth century. Today, of course, all political forces make extensive use of polling. The fact remains, however, that polling reduces the political weight of precisely those groups whose most important resource is their collective weight.

The third way that polling changes public opinion is by restricting the agenda of topics. Writers of letters to the editor generally choose the topics on which to express their views. The organizers of protest marches define the purposes of their action. But respondents in opinion polls express themselves on issues that have been selected by someone else. Opinions filtered through the polls are not spontaneous expressions of the public's own concerns but rather a reaction to concerns chosen by the pollsters. This is why opinions on many issues seem to change from week to week and to be quite sensitive to minor variations in the wording of the question. For example, hundreds of surveys in recent years have asked Americans whether they supported or opposed stem-cell research. But, depending upon the precise way in which the question is worded, Americans can be shown to support stem cell research two to one or to oppose it by a similar margin.[94] The reason for this variation is that the issue is not high on most Americans' list of priorities, and as a result, they do not have solid opinions to express. Knowing this, advocates work to design poll questions likely to elicit responses that will allow them to claim public opinion is on their side. For example, a 2003 Zogby poll was carefully and deliberately worded so as to increase the percentage of respondents who would assert support for teaching "intelligent design" in the public schools.[95]

Given the commercial character of the polling industry, differences between the polls' concerns and those of the general public are inevitable. Polls generally raise questions that are of interest to the purchasers of poll data—political candidates, newspapers, government agencies, business corporations, and public relations and advertising firms. The questions they are interested in, such as the relative popularity of competing politicians or brands of toothpaste, may or may not reflect citizens' own needs, hopes, and aspirations. More important, polls are components in the technology of opinion shaping. Corporations poll to determine how to persuade customers to purchase their products. Candidates poll as part of a campaign to convince voters to support them. All of these users of the polls shape questions so as to elicit responses that will allow them to claim the support of public opinion.[96]

For their part, government agencies and officials poll not to find out what the public wants but, rather, to find out how best to persuade citizens to support the government's policies and decisions. As Althaus noted, one of the most common uses of polls by political elites is to devise "effective communication strategies for marketing decisions and ideas."[97] Or, as Richard Nixon put it, opinion polls "let us know what obstacles we confront in attempting to sell a policy."[98] This use of polling became especially evident during the two Persian Gulf wars. Prior to the 1990–1991 war, the Bush administration's poll data indicated that the public was dubious about the reasons for going to war. The data, however, suggested that the public would respond to claims that Iraq's nuclear ambitions needed to be checked. Heeding the advice of its pollsters, the administration changed its rhetoric and was able to generate additional popular support for military action.[99] In a similar vein, in 2005, President George W. Bush began to face sharply declining popular approval of his administration's policies in Iraq. Poll after poll seemed to indicate that Americans were quickly losing confidence in the Iraq War and in the president himself. To the president and his advisers, though, these poll data did not mean that the administration's policies should be changed. Instead, the president worked to reshape opinion. He turned to an academic polling expert, Duke University political scientist Peter D. Feaver. Survey data developed by Feaver apparently suggested that Americans would support the war if they believed the military effort would lead to victory. Impressed by these findings, the president began to emphasize the theme of victory in his speeches on Iraq. In one November 2005 speech, Bush used the word "victory" fifteen times against the backdrop of dozens of "Plan for Victory" signs.[100] The strategy worked, at least temporarily. The president's public approval ratings temporarily climbed, and the war continued.

Rather than communicate the opinions that citizens want political leaders to hear, polls tell elites what they want to learn about citizens' opinions. Politicians and other advocates, in the words of Jacobs and Shapiro, "use research on public opinion to pinpoint the most alluring words, symbols and arguments to move public opinion to support their desired policies."[101] The end result is that polling changes the public expression of opinion from an assertion of demands to a step in the process of persuasion. When all is said and done, polls are tools for the management of opinion.

Public Opinion and Public Policy

In the United States, as in other democracies, citizens expect their government to pay close attention to popular preferences. As we saw earlier, most Americans believe that the government does listen to popular opinion most or at least some of the time. This view is bolstered by a number of scholarly studies that have identified a reasonable correlation between national policy and public opinion over time. Alan D. Monroe, for example, found that in a majority of cases, changes in public policy followed shifts in popular preferences. Conversely, in most cases, if opinion did not change, neither did policy.[102] In a similar vein, Page and Shapiro found that much of the time, significant shifts in public opinion were followed by changes in national policy in a direction that seemed to follow opinion.[103] These findings are certainly affirmed by hosts of politicians who not only claim to be guided by the will of the people in all their undertakings but seem to poll assiduously to find out what that will is.

But, once we accept the notion that there is some measure of congruence or consistency between public opinion and public policy, we should not take it to mean that the public's preferences somehow control the government's conduct. Most citizens do not have strong autonomous preferences with regard to most public issues. And many lack the basic information that might help them to understand and evaluate policy choices and governmental processes. For example, 40 percent of the Americans responding to a recent survey did not know that each state has two senators; 43 percent did not know what an economic recession is; 68 percent did not know that a two-thirds majority in each house is required for a congressional override of a presidential veto; 70 percent did not know that the term of a U.S. House of Representatives member is two years; 71 percent could not name their own congressional representative; and 81 percent could not name both of their own state's senators.[104] These findings suggest that many Americans can barely describe, much less control, their government.

When it comes to major public issues, many Americans have too much difficulty grasping the substance of the issue and the potential alternative policies to have any serious or coherent preference. For example, during the 2000 election campaign, reform of the Social Security system became a major issue. George W. Bush had proposed partially "privatizing" the system by allowing individuals to invest some of their payroll taxes in personal retirement accounts whose value would be subject to market fluctuations. Bush made a number of speeches on the topic, the idea was highlighted at the GOP convention, and the news media devoted considerable attention to it. After all the attention Bush's proposal received, however, surveys revealed that most Americans knew little or nothing about it and had no meaningful preferences on the issue. In summer 2000, after the Republican convention, 73 percent of those contacted by Princeton Survey Research Associates said they knew "little" or "nothing at all" about Bush's proposal.[105] More than half could not say whether Bush's proposed plan would raise taxes or how it might affect their likely Social Security benefits. More than half, however, favored the proposal—whatever it was.[106] The same pattern is apparent in surveys dealing with several other recent political issues.[107]

Many Americans' knowledge of contemporary political issues is limited to some half-remembered fact or claim they saw in an ad or heard on a newscast. And once they acquire some piece of information, many individuals will retain it long after it ceases to have any relevance. In a 2005 Harris poll, for example, more than a third of the respondents believed that Iraq possessed weapons of mass destruction at the time of the American invasion—this despite the fact that even President Bush had long since acknowledged that no such weapons had existed. Apparently these respondents hadn't been paying attention.

The unfortunate fact of the matter is that many Americans lack the cognitive tools or basic understanding of political and social realities to understand or to seriously evaluate competing political claims and proposals. Certainly, a minority of affluent, well-educated individuals—perhaps 20 percent of the public, according to even the most generous estimates—is knowledgeable about public issues and possesses the intellectual tools to evaluate them.[108]

The remainder are essentially what economists call "noise traders," that is, individuals whose actions are based upon faulty information and questionable reasoning. This is, after all, a nation in which, according to a 2004 CBS News survey, 55 percent of all respondents reject the theory of evolution in favor of the idea that God created humans in their present form. This is a nation in which, according to an October 2005 Fox News survey, 84 percent believe in miracles and 79 percent in angels. According to the same survey, 37 percent believe in astrology, 24 percent in witches, and 27 percent in reincarnation. Perhaps we should be relieved that only 4 percent believe in vampires, but, alas, 34 percent believe in ghosts. Some scholars have argued that, in the aggregate, the public can possess wisdom even though many, if not most, individuals are foolish. This argument, though, is based upon rather dubious statistical and logical assumptions.[109]

Their lack of information and basic political knowledge—and, frankly, lack of a simple capacity to distinguish fact from fable—makes many Americans quite vulnerable to manipulation by politicians and advocates wielding the instruments of advertising, publicity, and measurement discussed above. Though they give lip service to the will of the people, politicians and advocates are quite aware of the fact that most of the time many of the people have no particular will, or, for that matter, interest in or understanding of public issues. Their goal, as Jacobs and Shapiro noted, is to "simulate responsiveness" by developing arguments and ideas that will persuade citizens to agree with their own policy goals.[110] This effort begins with polling. As Clinton pollster Dick Morris affirmed, "You don't use a poll to reshape a program, but to reshape your argumentation for the program so the public supports it."[111] The effort continues with advertising, publicity, and propaganda, making use of the information gleaned from the polls.

What do these observations mean for the relationship between opinion and policy identified by Monroe, Page, and others? They suggest that opinion and policy are related primarily because of their common underlying origins. Rather than providing evidence that public opinion drives national policy, the correlation between the two derives from the fact that the same political forces seeking to shape national policy often find it useful to create a climate of opinion conducive to their goals.

Thus, for example, a coalition of forces that succeeded in bringing about the elimination of the estate tax in 2001 first made extensive use of polling and publicity over the course of several years to persuade the public that what they labeled the "death tax" was unfair and un-American. This public relations effort was a great success and helped smooth the way for the coalition's lobbying effort in Congress. As Graetz and Shapiro showed, while the federal estate tax actually affected only the wealthiest 2 percent of the populace, the intensive campaign for its repeal seemed to persuade many naive Americans that the tax actually affected them. One poll taken in the wake of the repeal campaign suggested that 77 percent of the populace believed the tax affected all Americans, and several polls indicated that more than one-third of the public believed they themselves would have to pay the tax.[112] When the tax was finally annulled, its elimination was supported by public opinion. But does this mean that a change in public opinion brought about the change in policy? Hardly. Instead, a particular set of political forces engineered a shift in opinion that helped them to persuade Congress to change national policy. A similar pattern was observed by Hacker and Pierson when they studied recent changes in tax policy. Citizens, they said, "proved vulnerable to extensive manipulation" as political elites framed a discussion that generated popular support for policy changes that served the interests of a small minority of wealthy Americans.[113]

So much for the primacy of public opinion in the American democratic order. Bryce was far off the mark when he called opinion the "chief and ultimate power" in all nations. Indeed, the notoriously cynical Austrian economist Joseph Schumpeter was much closer to the truth when he observed that the will of the people was the "product," not the "motive power," of the political process.[114]

3

Elections and the Limits of Popular Government

Voting is the only form of political activity in which substantial percentages of Americans routinely engage. More than 60 percent of those eligible—over 122 million people—cast ballots in the 2004 presidential election. The percentage who report participating in other forms of political action, even other electorally related activities, is relatively small. In 2004, only 13 percent gave money to a campaign, 7 percent attended a meeting, and barely 3 percent actually worked to help elect a particular political candidate.[1]

Most Americans think that voting gives them a measure of control over the government and its policies. This belief, like the more general idea that public opinion is important, is regularly affirmed by politicians, taught in the public schools, and frequently reiterated by the mass media. The schools endeavor to acquaint students with the importance of elections through classroom discussions and practical exercises. In their classroom history and civics assignments, students learn about the political power of the ballot box and the struggles waged by numerous groups of Americans to win the right to vote. These lessons are augmented by a variety of exercises, including periodic mock elections and contests to staff the largely ornamental class offices and student council positions that are found in nearly every school. The state of New York, for example, offered the following guidelines to teachers:

> To illustrate the voting process, present a situation such as: Chuck and John would both like to be captain of the kickball team. How will we decide which

boy will be the captain? Help the children understand that the fairest way to choose a captain is by voting.

Write the candidates' names on the chalk board. Pass out slips of paper. Explain to the children that they are to write the name of the boy they would like to have as their captain. Collect and tabulate the results on the chalk board.

Parallel this election to that of the election for the presidency.[2]

The media, for their part, continually urge Americans to vote. The broadcast networks and newspapers deploy armies of columnists, commentators, academics, and advocates to explore America's voting patterns and to explain their larger meaning and significance. Each election seems to provide new grist for these pundits' busy mills. In recent years, an unlikely covey of characters, including hard hats, soccer moms, Joe six-packs, and NASCAR dads, has been hoisted onto the political stage and poked, prodded, squeezed, and shaken to compel them to reveal their political secrets. Since most pundits accept the idea that voting is an important force in the political process, they often search for voter pathologies that might explain why the government seems so often to be on the wrong track. One recent writer, for example, appeared to suggest that what he believed to be the misguided policies of the Bush administration could be blamed upon the credulousness of such ordinary Americans as the benighted voters of Kansas.[3]

The idea that elections provide citizens with an important measure of political influence certainly seems plausible. Democratic elections, after all, permit ordinary citizens to select and depose powerful public officials. This electoral sanction compels candidates for office to vie with one another for popular approval and forces the nation's leaders to pay heed to citizens' wishes and welfare if they wish to retain their positions. As James Madison observed in *Federalist* 57, "the restraint of frequent elections" induces public officials to "anticipate the moment when their power is to cease … unless a faithful discharge of their trust shall have established their title to a renewal of it."[4] Indeed, as we saw in Chapter 2, elected officials do pay attention to the public—even if their goal is more often manipulation of citizen opinion than actual obeisance to the popular will.

Even if Madison is correct, the ballot does not necessarily enhance the political power of ordinary citizens. Though Americans tend to equate political participation and popular influence with voting, the ballot is hardly the only instrument citizens can employ to affect a government's conduct. Indeed, citizens engaged in activities designed to put pressure on their rulers long before the advent of elections. Popular political action in the absence of elections, to be sure, tended and still tends to take violent and disruptive forms—protest, riot, revolution, insurrection.[5] But, however dangerous and unsavory such forms of political action might be, there is little doubt that they can be effective.[6] The behavior of even the most rigid autocrat can be influenced by the ever-present possibility that his or her policies might provoke popular disobedience, clandestine movements, or mass violence.

Elections do not create a possibility of popular political action and citizen influence where none would otherwise exist. Instead, they offer a formal and institutional channel to take the place of the more impromptu tactics, including protest and violence, that might be employed by citizens seeking to force a government to listen to them. Despite official efforts to suppress popular agitation, the citizenry is seldom politically impotent in the absence of elections. Perhaps some regimes are sufficiently powerful and ruthless to stamp out most vestiges of popular dissent. But no government is all-powerful all the time. In recent years, much-feared authoritarian states, seemingly protected by enormous armies and powerful security forces, have disappeared overnight. Often it is precisely because clandestine or spontaneous forms of popular political activity are having too great an impact that governments seek to introduce electoral mechanisms or to expand existing voting rights and to persuade citizens of their value. As the late Walter Lippman observed, "New numbers were enfranchised because they had power, and giving them the vote was the 'least disturbing way' of letting them exercise their power."[7]

Two examples from recent American history appear to illustrate Lippman's proposition. One is the case of the Twenty-sixth Amendment, added to the Constitution in 1971, which lowered the U.S. voting age from twenty-one to eighteen. This amendment was adopted during a period of civil strife and disorder during which young people—college students in particular—engaged in sometimes violent protests over the Vietnam War, military conscription, race relations, social policy, and other aspects of American politics and society. Although student protesters made many demands, their agenda did not include voting rights for young people. But even though students may not have been especially interested in voting, many political leaders seemed eager to give them the right to do so.

Senate Judiciary Committee hearings on the subject indicate a belief among Democrats and Republicans alike that the right to vote would channel students' political activities from the street into the polling places. For example, Senator Jacob Javits (R–NY) said, "I am convinced that self-styled student leaders who urged such acts of civil disobedience would find themselves with little or no support if students were given a more meaningful role in the political process. In short, political activism ... is all happening outside the existing political framework. Passage of [the voting rights resolution] would give us the means, sort of the famous carrot and the stick, to channel this energy into our major political parties."[8] In a similar vein, Senator Birch Bayh (D-IN) said, "This force, this energy, is going to continue to build and grow. The only question is whether we should continue to ignore it, perhaps leaving this energy to dam up and burst and follow less-than-wholesome channels, or whether we should let this force be utilized by society through the pressure valve of the franchise."[9] Three years later, the resolution under discussion became a constitutional amendment.

In a similar vein, the Kennedy administration's focus on voting rights for African Americans was, in part, an attempt to divert civil rights activists away from their militant campaign for desegregation of schools and public facilities—a campaign that was engendering violent resistance throughout the South.[10] Suspicious of the administration's purpose, some black activists initially resisted participating in the voting rights effort. One faction of the Student Nonviolent Coordinating Committee (SNCC), an important activist group of the period, vehemently refused to take part in voter registration drives on the ground that they were simply an attempt by the national government "to cool the militancy of the student movement."[11] Eventually, however, the Kennedy administration told civil rights activists that it would help them secure voting rights but would not lend them its assistance if they focused on eliminating other forms of segregation.

VOTING AS A MEANS OF REGULATING POPULAR POLITICAL ACTIVITY

Perhaps citizens would be better off if they could make themselves heard effectively at the polls rather than having to undertake more arduous and, perhaps, risky forms of political agitation. But citizens also lose something when their political activity is confined to the voting booth. In the same sense that legalizing the sale of alcohol allows the government to regulate its distribution and consumption—a lesson learned from the violence associated with Prohibition—the construction of a formal electoral machinery permits governments to more effectively regulate and manage popular political activity. In the absence of elections, the timing and goals of popular political activity, as well as the identity of those who will take part, are determined by the participants themselves. But elections transfer control over these and other aspects of political action from the citizen to the state, thereby reducing the uncertainty and risk that citizen involvement in politics poses to the government.

For example, anyone who decides to do so can participate in protests or demonstrations. It is the government, however, that determines who is eligible to take part in elections. Of course, when democratic electoral institutions were initially introduced in Europe and the United States, governments sought to bar the participation of individuals whom they deemed to be undesirable. Race, religion, socioeconomic status, and a host of other factors became bases for exclusion from the electorate. Although these sorts of restrictions may have served the interests of particular political forces at particular times, they also reduced the value of elections as regulatory instruments. Other things being equal, governments have a stake in seeing to it that everyone engaged in political activity is channeled into the electoral arena, and most regimes eventually acceded to this fact. Accordingly, contemporary democratic governments impose few restrictions on voting rights. In fact, most seek to make voting quite easy, establishing numerous polling places and staffing and organizing an elaborate administrative machinery for enrolling voters, selecting candidates, and counting ballots. Among the Western democracies, the United States, with its antiquated registration rules, is probably the least facilitative of voting.[12] But even in the United States, voting is a relatively simple and painless task precisely because state, local, and national governments spend hundreds of millions of dollars each year to make it so. The administrative cost of the 2004 American national election, for example, was well over $1 billion.[13] More than 120 million Americans were able to vote because much of the cost of their participation was borne by various agencies of the state.

Ironically, electoral procedures that bring tens of millions of citizens to the polls can be seen as potent regulatory instruments. When participation involves difficulties, costs, and risks, only those with strong views and preferences are likely to be sufficiently motivated to take part. Because voting entails no risks and few costs, even those who lack firm opinions and have little interest in the outcome may be moved to respond to official and partisan exhortations and spend a few minutes at the polls. For example, every year on the anniversary of the Supreme Court's 1973 *Roe v. Wade* decision legalizing abortion, thousands of demonstrators have gathered in Washington. Some of these individuals come to affirm their support for the decision, whereas others come to voice their opposition. Not once in the more than three decades since the Court handed down its verdict have any demonstrators gathered to declare that they did not know or care much about abortion.

The don't-knows and don't-cares do, however, vote. In the electorate, as among those whose opinions are merely represented in the polls, individuals who do not have strong opinions usually outnumber those who do. As Philip Converse once observed, most voters' attitudes are, in fact, *nonattitudes.*[14] That is, they neither know much nor care much about most issues. By making electoral participation easy, governments can submerge those with strong views, almost always a minority, in a more apathetic majority. The virtue of this result, from the government's perspective, is that the don't-knows and don't-cares, like the "silent majority" President Nixon once found in the polls, don't impose much constraint on official actions. In a sense, through electoral institutions, governments transform political activity from a collective process for the assertion of demands into what often amounts to a collective statement of permission. Voting helps regulate political participation in other ways as well. Protesters organize themselves. Indeed, today, protesters organize themselves through the Internet. The French student demonstrators whose opposition to a proposed new labor law rocked the government and forced it to rescind its proposal in March 2006 communicated nationally via a website. The proposed new labor law, Le Contrat Première Embauche (The Contract of First Employment), was known by the acronym CPE, and hence, the website was called STOP-CPE.net. Protest leaders used the site to organize rallies and disseminate information.[15] Voters, though, are typically organized into districts or other electoral units by the government. Thus, though rioters are rather difficult to gerrymander, voters are subject to "electoral engineering" designed to affect the relative weights of various social groups and the outcomes of electoral contests. Protesters may target any facet of the political process they choose. Voters, however, are usually limited to the selection of representatives. Although a number of states do permit popular referenda on policy issues, at the national level, America's voters are not asked to make decisions about programs, policies, budgets, and institutional arrangements. In fact, even most public officials are not subject to popular election. Voters are limited to selecting those officials who hold what are legally deemed to be elective offices. In the United States, most judges and a score of high-ranking administrative officials are immune to direct electoral scrutiny.

Similarly, protesters and rioters can assemble whenever they want. Voting, however, takes place at regular intervals at times set by law. Between these intervals, elected officials serve fixed terms in office, and voters exercise no formal power. In *Federalist* 71, Alexander Hamilton explained that the purpose of limiting the frequency of popular participation and providing elected officials with fixed terms in office was to prevent the government from being forced to respond to "every sudden breeze of passion, or to every transient impulse which the people may receive."[16] Fixed terms are designed to allow elected officials to withstand the vicissitudes of public opinion and to make unpopular decisions without immediate fear of popular reprisal at the polls. Throughout the year 2005, for example, commentators noted that President Bush's popularity had dropped sharply, as had popular support for his administration's policies in Iraq. Some commentators asked whether the president, lacking popular support, would be able to continue governing effectively. President Bush, however, declared vehemently that he planned no change in policy. The president knew full well that he had no immediate reason to fear the national electorate, a body that comes into being only the Tuesday after the first Monday in November in even-numbered years and whose powers, like a mist, dissipate the next day.

Electoral institutions not only offer the government a measure of protection from the potentially negative consequences of popular political activity, they promise positive benefits as well. Just as governments derive income in the form of tax revenues from the lawful sale of alcohol, to continue the analogy, they stand to derive gain in the form of increased popular support from lawful citizen participation. Denying citizens an opportunity to participate in political life tends to alienate those who have political interests and ambitions. Indeed, the more the government attempts to harass or intimidate such individuals, the greater the chance that citizens who might have begun as mild malcontents will become full-fledged enemies of the state working, as Senator Javits noted, to spread their seditious ideas to others as well. The history of czarist Russia is replete with examples of this phenomenon.[17]

Providing those who wish to participate with a lawful outlet for their political energies, however, is likely to have the opposite effect, generating support for rather than opposition to the regime. A good deal of evidence suggests that an opportunity to participate in the decision-making processes of the institutions that rule them affords many individuals enormous psychic gratification that is not dependent upon their approval of the specific decisions that ultimately result.[18] This is true so long as the process is not seen as a complete sham, as in the case of, say, elections in the former Soviet Union. Thus, for example, employees are known to derive satisfaction from being consulted about company policies. From management's perspective, such consultation is a means of inducing employees to be more cooperative and to work harder.[19] Virtually everyone has encountered this management tactic at one time or another. The president of my university once called to ask my advice before he appointed a new dean of the College of Arts and Sciences. I was pleased to be consulted, and later neither I nor other senior faculty members voiced a word of opposition when the president made his choice.

Governments, for their part, have long been aware of the potential benefits of popular participation, though, to be sure, many national leaders have not been sufficiently enlightened or self-confident to risk their own defeat at the polls for the larger good of the regime. One group of notably enlightened statesmen, however, assembled in Philadelphia in 1787 to draft the U.S. Constitution. A number of the framers seemed clearly to understand that the new government they were proposing would be strengthened if ordinary citizens were allowed to participate in its affairs. James Wilson of Pennsylvania, for instance, said he supported the idea of popular election of the members of the House of Representatives because it would increase the new government's power. Wilson averred that he favored "raising the federal pyramid to a considerable altitude" and therefore wished to give it "as broad a base as possible."[20] Even delegates who feared excessive citizens' influence agreed that the election of at least some national officials would enhance the power and stability of the proposed new government by enhancing the popular "confidence" it was likely to inspire.[21]

Most often, governments need popular support during times of war and national emergency, and as a result, war, like civil disorder, has been a great incubator of voting rights. In the United States, both the Revolutionary War and the War of 1812 prompted state authorities to lower the barriers to voting in order to increase the martial enthusiasm of the militiamen upon whom the American military effort depended.[22] World War I was associated with suffrage expansion in both the United States and Europe. Indeed, the introduction of women's suffrage in the United States, Britain, and Canada was prompted mainly by these governments' desires to secure women's support for the war effort.[23] The relationship between war and voting rights is perfectly captured by a slogan coined during Sweden's nineteenth-century suffrage debates: "One man, one vote, one gun." In recent years, of course, this slogan has been abbreviated and its original meaning nearly forgotten.

The benefits they hope to derive from popular voting, coupled with their desire to avoid more disturbing forms of popular political action, has impelled many governments and national political elites to encourage citizens to vote while discouraging them from engaging in other forms of political activity. Their goal is not to stimulate participation per se. It is, rather, to make certain that those who are moved to participate are channeled into the electoral arena. In the United States, as we saw earlier, the virtues of voting are taught in the schools, promoted by the mass media, and touted by a host of civic institutions and foundations. And every year, state and local governments spend hundreds of millions of dollars to operate the nation's electoral machinery. Voting is the only form of popular political activity that receives this type of governmental subsidy. Those who wish to lobby or litigate must foot the bill themselves. And those who endeavor to express their views via protests, sit-ins, or demonstrations are likely to incur the displeasure of the authorities. This was what Senator Javits had in mind when he referred to the combination of carrot and stick. It is this combination that impels most Americans to confine their political involvement to voting and a small number of other electoral activities.

THE LIMITS OF VOTING

Demonstrations, protests, and political violence can have an enormous impact upon a government's personnel, politics, and institutional structure. In recent years, popular unrest helped to bring down the Stalinist regimes of Eastern Europe. Popular protests in Latin America have undermined American efforts to establish a hemispheric free-trade regime. During the past four years, massive popular demonstrations forced transfers of power and major policy shifts in Belize, Bolivia, Georgia, Ukraine, and French Polynesia. Even in China, a nation whose authorities are not noted for their forbearance, in 2006, rural protesters forced the government to alter its land expropriation policies, fire a number of local officials, and discipline a powerful provincial party secretary.[24] And political violence has certainly had a greater impact than voting upon America's occupation government in Iraq.

Frequent riots and demonstrations, to be sure, probably do not do much good for a nation's economy and certainly interfere with the order and stability many individuals seem to crave. The government, the business community, the media, and other established institutions never fail to point this out when they urge citizens to express their views via the ballot box and to forbear from engaging in more disruptive political activities. Thus, in 2005, investment analysts warned French political protesters that their actions were threatening investor confidence in the entire Euro zone.[25]

Although the virtues of civil peace and public order cannot be denied, it is important to understand that maintaining order by limiting popular political activity to the electoral arena comes at a price. Confined to voting, citizen participation is hardly a driving force in the political process. Protests or, for that matter, nonviolent forms of citizen-initiated political action often arise spontaneously and are typically controlled by the participants. The individuals taking part in a protest or other grassroots activity generally determine the agenda and goals of their participation. This is not true in the case of voting, where choices and alternatives are decided by external forces, not by voters themselves.

Indeed, what Schumpeter said about public opinion generally clearly applies to voting in particular. Voter opinion and voting behavior are products of the political process, not its "motive power." What Schumpeter meant, as we saw in Chapter 2, is that citizens' opinions are not formed independently but are, instead, generally the result of efforts by contending groups and forces to shape opinion for their own purposes.

By the same token, voters' views of competing candidates are seldom developed independently of the efforts of politicians to market themselves to the electorate. The driving forces in electoral politics are the resources and tactics of competing political forces, not the autonomous choices of ordinary voters. Few voters have any personal familiarity with any of the candidates for significant offices. Perhaps a small number of voters, like some especially intelligent or cautious consumers, might engage in independent research, seeking out objective information about the records and positions of the politicians who interest them. As is the case among consumers of other products, however, the percentage of voters who engage in systematic market research is small. Most voters are passive rather than active consumers of political information. And much of the information they passively receive is crafted by public relations consultants and presented by candidates and their supporters in the form of advertising and public relations campaigns via such communications media as television, radio, direct mail, billboards, and the Internet. Indeed, many voters seem to obtain a good deal of their political information from the much-derided thirty-second television spot ads that have become so ubiquitous in the weeks before every national election.[26]

Of course, many Americans deny that they are influenced by advertising, and some perhaps are not. Committed partisans, for example, can seldom be convinced to vote for the other party's candidate, though even they often need to be reminded by advertising and publicity to vote for their own party's standard-bearer.[27] The fact, however, that not all voters can be persuaded of all things does not undercut the argument that contending political forces, rather than voters, are the driving forces of the electoral process.

Long before voters can choose among them in primary or general electoral contests, the major contenders for important political offices have usually spent years raising money, building contacts and organizations, and making their names known to the public. At one time, perhaps, when American politics was dominated by political party machines, party leaders had an incentive to select candidates they deemed likely to please the electorate. In this way, preferences at least imputed to voters influenced the alternatives presented to the electorate. Today, of course, party leaders no longer have much power, though they do play some role in candidate recruitment. For example, in 2006, Rahm Emanuel, head of the Democratic Congressional Campaign Committee, recruited several House candidates who went on to victory. For the most part, though, candidates are independent actors who enter politics in response to their own ambitions rather than a call from the electorate. They are eager volunteers, not reluctant conscripts.

Some recent presidential candidates, including John F. Kennedy, Richard Nixon, Bill Clinton, and Al Gore, spent decades grooming themselves or being groomed by supporters for their eventual presidential campaigns. This process should be seen as the product-development stage of a political marketing effort. Generally speaking, politicians who do not invest in this longer-term marketing effort will never come to the public's attention and will never be among the alternatives available to the electorate. When they make their choices at the polls, even voters who are resistant to the particular claims presented in television commercials and other campaign media are seldom in a position to do more than respond to the options offered to them. Their choices are always constrained, even if not always driven, by the political market power of contending forces.

It is the politicians, their supporters, and the interests that fund political campaigns who dominate the electoral arena. Voters' choices are products of their efforts, not the result of autonomous deliberations by individual citizens.

POLITICAL MARKETING

Nineteenth-century American party organizations deployed enormous armies of patronage workers to maintain electoral loyalty and mobilize voters on election day. With the demise of these party "machines," campaigns have come to bear a good deal of resemblance to the merchandising efforts usually associated with commercial goods and services. Indeed, today's campaign strategies are usually developed by advertising and marketing specialists—individuals such as Democratic consultant Bob Shrum, who orchestrated the unsuccessful 2004 Kerry campaign, and Republican political operative Karl Rove, who directed the 2000 and 2004 Bush presidential campaigns.[28] Contemporary electoral marketing has several key elements, including grooming candidates, organizing campaigns, developing issues and tactics, and, of course, acquiring campaign resources. These elements are the political equivalents of the business world's notions of product development, communication, marketing, and investment.

The Well-Groomed Candidate

The first step in political marketing is the grooming of candidates. Grooming is the process through which ordinary citizens are transformed into candidates for office. At one time, political parties groomed the candidates. Today, ambitious individuals groom themselves or are groomed by supporters. One quaint bit of American mythology is the idea that any child can aspire to become president of the United States. In reality, only a tiny number of Americans can ever be serious contenders for the presidency or any other major political office. Generally speaking, those who make themselves plausible candidates for high political office follow one or a combination of three paths. These could be called *stepping stones, starting at the top,* and *coattails.*

Stepping stones. The first path, as its name implies, entails following a series of political steps from lower, less important offices to higher, more important ones. A politician may begin with local office, move on to statewide office, and from there seek some significant national position. For example, America's eighth president, Martin Van Buren, began his political career in 1813 as a New York state senator, then served as New York's attorney general, then as a U.S. senator from New York, then as secretary of state, then as U.S. minister to England, then as Andrew Jackson's vice president before being elected to the presidency in 1836. America's tenth president, John Tyler, stepped on many stones but then slipped and fell. Tyler began in 1811 as a member of the Virginia House of Delegates, then was elected to the U.S. House of Representatives, then to the Virginia Senate, then to the governorship of Virginia, then to the U.S. Senate, and then, in 1840, to the vice presidency on the Harrison ticket. General Harrison was known as "Old Tippecanoe," and the 1840 Whig campaign slogan was "Tippecanoe and Tyler too." When the old general died soon after the inauguration, Tyler succeeded to the presidency. (Tyler's new political nickname was "His Accidency.") So far, so good. Unfortunately, however, after Virginia seceded from the Union in 1861, Tyler stepped on one more stone, slipped, and permanently soiled his reputation. Tyler chose to run for a seat in the Confederate Congress and won, becoming the only U.S. president to serve as an official in the government of a hostile power.

In more recent years, Franklin D. Roosevelt was a president who rose to power through a series of stepping stones. FDR began his political career in 1910, shortly after graduating from law school, when he ran for the New York State Senate. In 1912, he was appointed assistant secretary of the U.S. Navy, and in 1920, Roosevelt became the party's vice presidential candidate behind presidential candidate James M. Cox. After recuperating from polio, Roosevelt was elected governor of New York in 1928 and became the Democratic standard-bearer in 1932. During the twenty-two years between his initial state senate campaign and his eventual presidential race, Roosevelt held or campaigned for four offices and performed numerous political services, including working for Woodrow Wilson at the 1912 Democratic convention and placing Al Smith's name into nomination with what became his famous "Happy Warrior" speech in 1928.[29]

Politicians following the stepping-stones strategy generally make use of whatever office they currently hold to enhance their public visibility and to expand their range of political contacts and allies. They regard any given office mainly as a platform from which to launch a campaign for higher office. For example, Senator Barack Obama (D-IL) seemed to view his seat in the Illinois legislature mainly as a launching pad for a U.S. Senate campaign, and his Senate seat primarily as a good place from which to mount a 2008 presidential campaign. His razor-thin legislative record appeared not to discourage millions of Americans from viewing the attractive and glib Obama as an excellent presidential prospect.

The premier modern example of a successful stepping-stones strategy is the career of the late John F. Kennedy. In 1955, then Congressman Gerald Ford asked his former House colleague, newly elected Senator Jack Kennedy, how things were going in the Senate. Kennedy replied that he had "bigger plans."[30] In particular, Kennedy was campaigning for the 1956 Democratic vice presidential nomination, which he saw as a logical step from the Senate to his ultimate goal, the presidency. To further those plans, Kennedy ignored most of his legislative duties and used his Senate seat to enhance his national visibility. Many congressional leaders regarded Kennedy as an ineffectual lightweight. While other senators worked on legislation, Kennedy logged more than 100,000 miles in his plane, flying around the country to give speeches and polish his image.[31] Democratic House Speaker Sam Rayburn often referred to his former House colleague as "that little pissant Kennedy." Kennedy's speaking abilities and literary efforts, however, gradually increased his public stature.

Kennedy's 1955 book, *Profiles in Courage,* which presented the stories of senators who had taken principled stands that ran counter to their political interests, was designed to transform the inexperienced senator into a recognized author, intellectual, statesman, and figure of national prominence. After the book's publication, Kennedy's father, Joseph P. Kennedy, was determined to secure a coveted Pulitzer Prize for his son. The elder Kennedy used his connections to convince the Pulitzer Prize committee to disregard its professional judges' recommendations and award John the Pulitzer Prize for biography. The fact that the book was written largely by historian and Kennedy aide Theodore Sorenson became an issue when columnist Drew Pearson went on Mike Wallace's ABC television program to allege that *Profiles* had been ghostwritten and that Kennedy's acceptance of the Pulitzer constituted a form of fraud.[32] In response to threats from Joseph Kennedy and his attorneys, however ABC dropped the allegations.[33] Wallace called the network's action a "craven" buckling to pressure from the Kennedys.[34] Theodore Sorenson was a gifted writer, and during the Kennedy presidency, the book became a staple of high school civics classes. Students were seldom told that President John F. Kennedy was not the real author.

Roosevelt and Kennedy were both members of wealthy and prominent families and made frequent use of their money and connections to move from stepping stone to stepping stone. Not all successful candidates, though, have such fortunate backgrounds. Presidents Nixon, Reagan, and Clinton, to cite recent examples, were impecunious but nevertheless managed to rise through the political ranks. The candidacies of all three of these men, and most individuals of similar backgrounds, were supported by wealthy and powerful interests whose resources more than made up for the candidates' own lack of wealth and family connections. Richard Nixon's first congressional campaign was funded and launched by prominent California banker Herman Perry. Ronald Reagan's 1966 gubernatorial bid was promoted by a group of wealthy California business executives. And Bill Clinton's initial political efforts, beginning with an unsuccessful 1974 House race followed by a successful 1976 campaign for the post of Arkansas attorney general, were backed by poultry billionaire Don Tyson.[35] Candidates may be propelled by personal ambition, but the path from stepping stone to stepping stone is smoothed by money and power. The more important the office, the greater the quantity of money and power needed to reach it.

Starting at the top. Not every individual who aspires to high political office finds it necessary to negotiate a series of stepping stones to reach his or her objective. Some are able to jump-start their political careers by capitalizing on the visibility, power, or prominence they achieved in some other endeavor. Such fortunate individuals can skip one or more of the usual steps and compete successfully for high political office without ever having held a lower office.[36]

One asset that often allows ambitious individuals to enter the political arena at a high level is fame. Since the founding of the republic, for example, many famous generals have sought the presidency, and six have actually won election: George Washington, Andrew Jackson, William Henry Harrison, Zachary Taylor, Ulysses S. Grant, and Dwight D. Eisenhower. Well-known generals who made unsuccessful bids for the White House include one-time NATO commander Wesley Clark and, of course, General Douglas MacArthur, who hoped that his wartime exploits would induce a grateful public to reward him with the nation's highest office. Washington, Jackson, and Harrison, to be sure, had held other significant elective and appointive posts before their elevation to the presidency. Washington had been a member of the Continental Congress and served as chairman of the Constitutional Convention. Jackson and Harrison had served in both the U.S. House of Representatives and the U.S. Senate, and both had been territorial governors.

The other three victorious generals, however, had no prior political experience whatsoever. Indeed, Taylor had never even been registered to vote and was not eligible to cast a ballot in support of his own election. Yet, these generals' fame and popularity were powerful political assets, allowing them to ignore lesser political offices and set their sights directly on the White House. Taylor and Grant were convinced to seek the presidency by party leaders seeking to make use of the generals' popular standing. Eisenhower, for his part, needed no prodding. Though "Ike" always denied harboring political ambitions, his biographer Stephen Ambrose noted that from the end of World War II, Eisenhower's actions "could not have been better calculated to put him into the White House. His numerous public appearances, his association with the rich and powerful, and the content of his speeches all increased the demand that he become a candidate. No professional politician could have plotted as successful a campaign for the general as the one he directed himself."[37]

Martial prowess, of course, is not the only form of fame that has allowed politically inexperienced individuals to start at or near the top of the American political hierarchy. John Glenn's renown as an astronaut, for example, helped him win a seat in the U.S. Senate from which he was later launched back into space. In recent years, a number of well-known entertainers and professional athletes have sought to parlay their celebrity status into political careers. Ronald Reagan, of course, was a film actor and television host who had held no public office before running for governor of California. And, in a similar vein, California Governor Arnold Schwarzenegger used the enormous fame he had garnered as the star of blockbuster movies such as *The Terminator* to launch a political career. Other entertainers who have successfully run for office in recent years include former California Senator George Murphy, former Tennessee Senator Fred Dalton Thompson, and former California Representative Sonny Bono. Television host Jerry Springer was previously mayor of Cincinnati, Ohio, and periodically considers running for the U.S. Senate.

The phenomenon of entertainers seeking political office is, of course, not limited to the United States. For instance, a well-known Indian actress, Jayalinthaa, used her fame to secure selection as governor of Tamil Nadhu province. What may be a uniquely American phenomenon, though, is the number of professional athletes who run for office. To cite just a few recent examples, former pro football quarterback Jack Kemp was elected to Congress and became the GOP's vice presidential candidate in 1996. NBA star Bill Bradley served as a senator from New Jersey and was a candidate for the Democratic presidential nomination. Hall of Fame pitcher Jim Bunning was elected to the Senate. University of Nebraska football coach Tom Osborne was elected to the House of Representatives, as were football stars Steve Largent and J. C. Watts. Former professional wrestler Jesse Ventura was elected governor of Minnesota, but it is not clear whether he should count as an athlete or an entertainer.

Some candidates who start at the top are rich rather than famous. Wealth is always a useful political asset. Nearly half the members of the U.S. Senate and perhaps a third of the members of the House of Representatives are millionaires, and hardly any of the others are poor. In recent years, the political importance of personal wealth has increased. To begin with, because of increased media expenditures, the cost of political campaigns has risen sharply over the past decade. For example, the average expenditure by a winning Senate candidate in 2004 was more than $6 million, more than twice the average cost of a successful Senate campaign in the 1990s. The average cost of winning a seat in the U.S. House of Representatives is rapidly approaching the million-dollar mark, even though many incumbents barely face opposition. At the same time, campaign finance laws have placed more and more complex and costly restrictions on contributions to political campaigns by individuals and interest groups. The result has been to increase the advantage to candidates who can finance their own campaign efforts.[38] Two notable recent examples of candidates with no political background who spent enormous amounts of money to win elections are John Corzine and Michael Bloomberg. Corzine, the multimillionaire former head of Goldman Sachs, one of the nation's most important investment banks, spent more than $60 million of his own money to win election to the U.S. Senate from New Jersey in 2000. Bloomberg, one of America's wealthiest men, spent more than $73 million of his personal fortune to win the 2001 New York mayoral election.

Of course, like fame, wealth does not guarantee victory. In 1998, for example, former airline executive Al Checchi spent $40 million of his own money in a losing bid to become governor of California. Similarly, in 2004, securities trader Blair Hull spent $29 million out of his own pocket in the hope of winning election to the U.S. Senate from the state of Illinois. Despite his money, Hull was not even able to earn a victory in the Democratic primary. Of course, Hull's opponent, Senator Barack Obama, was able to raise millions of dollars from Democratic contributors to counter Hull's personal wealth. Millionaires may lose, but they are seldom defeated by paupers.

A final sort of candidate who can sometimes start at the top is the leader of a new political movement or party. During the course of American political history, some new parties and political movements have been led by established politicians who failed to achieve their goals through conventional electoral processes. For example, former president Teddy Roosevelt formed his Bull Moose Party when it became clear that he would not be able to secure the Republican nomination in 1912. Other political movements have served as vehicles for political neophytes with a cause. For instance, James B. Weaver, Greenback Party candidate for president in 1880 and Populist standard-bearer in 1892, was a champion of the eight-hour workday, the progressive income tax, and a host of other causes. Weaver had served briefly in the House of Representatives but could never have aspired to higher office through conventional party politics. A more recent example of an individual who used a political movement to start at the top is H. Ross Perot. In 1992, the billionaire entrepreneur, who had held no prior political office, launched a presidential bid at the head of his own political movement, which he called "United We Stand America." Perot spoke fervently on behalf of a number of causes, including a balanced federal budget; the introduction of electronic town hall meetings that would allow citizens more voice in policy matters; and defeat of the then pending North American Free Trade Agreement (NAFTA), which Perot said would produce a "giant sucking sound" as American jobs rushed to Mexico. Perot spent $57 million of his own money on the campaign and won 18.9 percent of the national presidential vote, making his the most successful American third-party movement since the formation of the Republican Party in the late 1850s. Perot sought to revive his movement, renamed the Reform Party, for the 1996 presidential campaign, but his share of the vote dropped sharply. By 2000 the Reform Party had all but disappeared, and Perot himself seemed to have lost interest in politics.

Coattails. Some individuals who reach high office do so by clinging firmly to the coattails of a powerful and successful sponsor. The sponsor may be a friend, a political ally, or even a parent or spouse. Vice President Dick Cheney rose in politics by clinging tenaciously to the coattails of one of Washington's most powerful politician-bureaucrats, former Defense Secretary Donald Rumsfeld.[39] Several U.S. presidents have been the political protégés of former presidents or other important politicians. James Monroe, for example, was handpicked by his predecessor, James Madison. Similarly, Martin Van Buren was Andrew Jackson's chief political lieutenant and was chosen by Old Hickory to succeed him in 1840. Lyndon Johnson had been the protégé of powerful House Speaker Sam Rayburn, who helped secure Johnson's spot on the Kennedy ticket in 1960. Most vice presidents have not been the protégés of the presidents with whom they served. Many, however, have hoped that their years of service in the president's shadow would pave the way for their own presidential nominations. Indeed, five of the last eleven presidents—Truman, Johnson, Nixon, Ford, and the first Bush—had previously occupied the vice presidency. During the same period, two other former vice presidents—Walter Mondale and Al Gore—were defeated in presidential bids.

Family ties can also serve as powerful coattails. George W. Bush's political career was hardly hurt by his relationship to George H. W. Bush, whose own career had been promoted by his father, Senator Prescott Bush. The Kennedy family has been an important force in American politics for more than a half century. Ambassador Joseph P. Kennedy played an instrumental role in John Kennedy's rise to political prominence. John Kennedy, in turn, appointed his brother Robert to the post of U.S. attorney general, a position for which he had no obvious qualifications beyond his family ties. Robert was subsequently elected U.S. senator from New York and, had he not been murdered, might have won the presidency in 1968. Another of John Kennedy's brothers, Edward, continues to serve as senator from Massachusetts, and a variety of Kennedy cousins have run for office on the strength of their family connection. Another example of the importance of familial coattails is, of course, the case of Hillary Rodham Clinton, wife of former president Bill Clinton. The former first lady's prominence and connections helped her win election to the U.S. Senate from New York and are among her strongest assets for a 2008 presidential bid. The Clintons' political coattails have also helped their daughter, Chelsea, as interests seeking favor with the parents have found reason to employ the daughter. Recently, Chelsea Clinton was hired at a six-figure salary by Avenue Capital Group, a hedge-fund management firm founded by Marc Lasry, a major Democratic contributor. Lasry was, in effect, making a campaign contribution to Hillary Clinton, but not a contribution that would be covered by federal election law.

Coattailers occasionally turn out to possess considerable political talent of their own. Robert Kennedy, for instance, was a very astute politician whose rhetoric could sometimes inspire even cynical realists. Other coattailers, though, seem lost when they are left to their own devices. One of the most inept campaigners in recent American history was Robert's daughter, Kathleen Kennedy Townsend, who went down to an abysmal defeat to Republican Robert Erlich in the 2002 Maryland gubernatorial race, even though Maryland is a state where registered Republicans are about as rare as Eskimos. Like fame and fortune, coattails are not a guarantee of success.

But whether they involve coattails, stepping stones, or starting at the top, the processes through which political candidates are groomed are driven less by the preferences of voters than by the ambitions, tactics, and resources of politicians and their supporters. Voters' choices may determine the ultimate outcome, but competing candidates and political forces control the alternatives.

Organizing a Campaign

Candidates present themselves to the electorate by organizing political campaigns. In the nineteenth century, campaigns were planned and directed by party bosses employing the services of hundreds of thousands of patronage workers whose government jobs depended upon their willingness to engage in political activity on the party's behalf. Contemporary political campaigns are led by political consultants utilizing activist volunteers, paid campaign workers, lawyers, and sophisticated communications technology.

Campaign leadership. Leadership in the modern campaign is usually provided by professional consultants. Most consultants began their careers in the world of advertising or marketing. A small number actually have degrees in campaigning from such programs as George Washington University's Graduate School of Political Management. Consultants generally develop the campaign's overall strategy, frame issues, commission focus groups and opinion polls, recruit campaign workers, raise money, maintain useful relationships with the mass media, plan direct mail campaigns, seek damaging information about the opposition, and, in short, undertake all the activities needed for political success. Some consultants have become political celebrities. George Bush's chief strategist, Karl Rove, was a powerful figure in Washington for eight years. Bill Clinton's longtime adviser Dick Morris was viewed as a political genius until his relationship with a prostitute forced him to retire from the political arena. James Carville and Mary Matalin were not America's most successful consultants, but the fact that one is a Democrat and the other a Republican and that the two are married is sufficiently amusing to give both a good deal of radio and television exposure. Some consultants work only for Republicans and some only for Democrats, but a number of consulting firms boast partners from both camps and sell their services to the highest bidder. "This is not a political club, it's a business," said one well-known Washington political strategist.

Campaign workers. With the disappearance of patronage employees, campaigns turned to volunteers and paid employees to work as staffers and fund-raisers. Some candidates are better able to attract grassroots volunteers than others. Candidates associated with the religious right, organized labor, or senior citizens' groups such as the AARP can rely upon their allies to provide foot soldiers for the political trenches. Candidates who are not so fortunate often must rely upon paid fund-raisers and campaign workers. Prior to the 1980s, Democratic candidates were far better able than their Republican rivals to recruit volunteers. Organized labor provided the Democrats with workers, as did environmental and peace groups. During the 1980s, the balance of infantry power changed dramatically. During the Reagan era, the GOP forged an alliance with the Christian right and mobilized regiments of Christian soldiers for political warfare. Democrats have countered by increasing their efforts to recruit volunteers through feminist and student groups.

Campaign technology. Whether they depend upon volunteers or salaried staffers, contemporary campaigns do not employ the enormous armies of workers upon which nineteenth-century campaigns relied. Instead, modern campaigns rely heavily upon technology to win votes. Contemporary campaigns raise money through direct mail solicitation and the Internet. They organize campaign rallies via phone banks and websites. They probe voters' opinions though telephone and Internet polls and through focus groups. They communicate with voters through television and the computer.

The linchpin of contemporary campaign technology is a process known as "data mining," which has been employed in product marketing for years and is now being heavily used in the marketing of political ideas and candidates. Over the past several years, each political party has assembled an enormous database containing information about each of the 168 million registered American voters. The GOP calls its database Voter Vault; the Democrats call theirs Datamart.[40] Each database contains hundreds of pieces of information on every registered voter. The information is acquired from census reports; credit, banking, and store purchase records; warranty cards; magazine subscription lists; memberships; travel records; answers to opinion poll questions; and a myriad of other sources. Using this information and sophisticated computer programs, consultants can infer a good deal about the attitudes, preferences, concerns, and likely political behavior of each voter. These inferences, in turn, allow campaigns to develop individualized advertising and fund-raising messages that can be sent to voters via phone calls, mail, and e-mail, a practice called "microtargeting." This tactic not only reaches the right voters with the right messages but also increases the efficiency of fund-raising. The cost of raising money can sometimes be so high that much of the money raised is spent raising money. For example, in 1994, Virginia Senate hopeful Oliver North raised $17 million through direct-mail campaigns. However, the cost of his fund-raising operation was $11 million, for a net gain after expenses of only $5 million.[41] One reason for the high cost of North's fund-raising effort was his scattershot approach. Thousands of solicitations went to individuals who had no interest in contributing to a conservative Republican. Had the North campaign been able to target only the most likely contributors, it would have saved millions of dollars in costs and netted more to spend on the actual campaign. Both parties believe that data mining and microtargeting are extremely effective. One experienced political marketer said, "Politics is just awakening to the tools that have dominated commercial direct market for decades. There is no question about whether this stuff works. We see it work every day in the commercial world."[42]

Since the 1950s, campaigns have relied mainly on television to deliver messages to voters. Gradually, however, the Internet has begun to supplant television as a campaign medium. Contemporary candidates make use of e-mail, blogs, interactive websites, and text messaging to communicate with voters, organize rallies, and raise money.[43] The Internet, used in conjunction with data mining, is potentially a far more efficient campaign medium than television, allowing candidates to precisely target their messages and appeals. Both political parties have found that blogs are particularly effective instruments for attacking the opposition. Often voters are unaware of the partisan leanings of particular blogs and are inclined to take at face value information that amounts to little more than partisan propaganda. Often, too, accounts presented by bloggers are picked up by the mainstream press and widely disseminated. Because of its growing importance, the two parties have been fighting vigorously for control of the blogosphere.

Election law. No contemporary campaign would be complete without the services of a phalanx of legal specialists. Fifty years ago, the courts seldom became involved in electoral processes, and few attorneys knew much about election law. Today, election law is a major legal specialty, and some large Washington law firms have created election-law groups to deal with an ever-growing case load. Three types of electoral issues often become the foci of legal battles. One is the drawing of legislative district boundaries. Electoral engineering, or gerrymandering, is a time-honored electoral practice in which the party in power seeks to fortify its position by drawing congressional and state legislative district boundaries that will reduce the number of districts its opponents might hope to win. This result can be accomplished either by concentrating opposition voters into as few districts as possible or by scattering them across so many districts that they will not constitute a majority anywhere. Traditionally, the courts would not rule on districting plans, calling them strictly political matters. Since the 1960s, though, the federal and state courts have heard many cases alleging that districts were intentionally designed to discriminate against African American and other minority voters. And more recently, a number of cases have been generated by the GOP's very aggressive redistricting efforts in Texas, Pennsylvania, and other states. Traditionally, states were redistricted once every ten years after the results of each new decennial census revealed changes in population patterns. Led by former House Majority Leader Tom DeLay, however, Republicans have sought more frequent redistricting in states they controlled to take fuller advantage of their power. Democrats, of course, have challenged these efforts, leading to protracted legal battles.

A second set of legal issues has been spawned by the campaign finance rules Congress enacted in 1974, 1976, and 2002. Finance laws govern many aspects of campaign fund-raising and spending. They are often complex and confusing, and even where they are reasonably clear, many politicians conceive campaign finance rules to be a challenge to be surmounted rather than a blueprint to be followed. In recent years, a number of prominent politicians or members of their staffs have been charged with campaign spending violations. For example, in 2005, Hillary Clinton's Senate campaign treasurer paid a large fine for filing false reports with the FEC. The reports hid the identity of one of Clinton's largest contributors, a convicted felon who was hiding in Brazil to escape a stock-fraud indictment. In a similar vein, Tom DeLay was indicted in 2005 for campaign-law violations in Texas. Following the indictment, DeLay was forced to relinquish his post as majority leader.

A third set of campaign-related legal issues concerns the accuracy of vote counts. Since the 2000 Florida presidential election, which was, of course, decided in the courts after a statewide recount, every serious campaign has placed lawyers on retainer ready to challenge an unfavorable election outcome, especially if the election was close, or to defend against such a challenge. Hundreds of attorneys were waiting in the wings, ready to attack or defend close outcomes in every state, during the 2004 presidential election and 2006 congressional races. Issues that can be raised to attack an election result include the eligibility of voters, the validity of ballots, the accuracy of counting procedures, and the propriety of the instructions given to voters. For example, Republicans argued that the state's counting methods were flawed when they mounted a court challenge to the outcome of Washington's 2004 gubernatorial race. Eventually, the count was upheld, but not without an expensive court battle.

President Bush's attorney Benjamin L. Ginsberg called the 2000 Florida election struggle the "greatest peacetime mobilization of lawyers in American history." If so, the lawyers have never been fully demobilized.

Campaign Themes and Tactics

In principle, democratic elections permit voters to make any choices they please. In practice, voters' choices are constrained by the options offered to them. The late V. O. Key once called electoral choices "echoes in an echo chamber."[44] The options offered to voters include not only the candidates themselves but also the policy choices or other alternatives they present to the electorate. If the competing candidates discussed mainly foreign policy, voters would be hard pressed to base their decisions on their own concerns about social security. And, similarly, if candidates devoted their energies to attacking one another's personal integrity, voters would be likely to try to choose the more honest of the two.

Candidates can propose a seemingly infinite variety of choices to the electorate. In recent years, campaigns have focused on war and peace, public morality, candidates' personal integrity, social issues, the economy, and a host of other concerns. But although the possibilities may seem endless, there are essentially only three major themes that can be presented to the electorate individually or in some combination. Campaigns may emphasize issues; they may focus on character; or they may concentrate on questions of social, cultural, or ethnic identity. Each of these themes, moreover, is usually an expression of a particular campaign goal or strategy. Issue campaigns are usually employed for the purpose of political *activation*. That is, candidates seek to develop issues that will engage their supporters' attention and bring them to the polls in sufficiently large numbers to overwhelm the opposition. Campaigns focusing on character and personality, on the other hand, are usually aimed at *deactivation*. That is, they are designed to undermine the enthusiasm of the opposing side's normal supporters and discourage them from coming to the polls. This is the chief purpose of "opposition research," or dirt digging, designed to secure information that will discredit a candidate with all but his or her most vehement supporters. And, although appeals based upon identity may be employed for a variety of purposes, they figure most importantly in a campaign of *conversion*. That is, identity can be used to shift the political moorings of designated blocs of voters.

In any given electoral contest, to be sure, the voting choices of millions of Americans are barely affected by the issues and events of the campaign. These voters' choices are dictated, instead, by a long-term commitment to one or the other political party. Although many partisans are sufficiently open-minded to switch their votes in response to campaign appeals, tens of millions of Americans identify so strongly with either the Democratic or Republican Party that they evaluate issues, candidates, and sometimes even potential marital partners through the lenses of their partisanship.[45] Partisanship is not unrelated to issues and identities. Typically, particular groups develop ties to one or another party on the basis of its stands on important issues or its efforts to cultivate the group's allegiance during some period of economic or political crisis.[46] In the 1930s, for example, Franklin D. Roosevelt and the Democrats used labor and social programs to win the support of unionized workers and members of urban ethnic groups whose prior partisan allegiances had been shaken by the Great Depression. Many African Americans and Jews, in particular, were drawn to the Democratic Party because it provided them with political opportunities that they had previously been denied. Once established though, partisan identification, like a brand preference in the marketplace, can become "sticky" and take on a life of its own. For many Americans, partisan loyalty is a lifelong commitment that they even seek to pass along to their children.

An individual's partisan identification can change. Most white Southerners were staunch Democrats until the 1960s. But the Democratic Party's support for the civil rights movement weakened their allegiances and opened the way for the GOP to create Republican majorities in most states of the old Confederacy. Nevertheless, partisan ties can be quite resilient once established. Most Jews, for example, continue to loyally support the Democrats even though, as a generally wealthy group, Jews tend to benefit from Republican economic policies. One prominent Jewish GOP activist told me that the first time he voted for a Republican candidate, he felt as though he had abandoned his religious faith and converted to Christianity.

Issues. In Chapter 1, we examined the use of political issues as tools of political legitimation, coalition formation, and mobilization. Recent national campaigns have sought to devise issues that served each of these purposes. For example, the 2004 Bush presidential campaign emphasized the importance of "extending the peace" by spreading democracy and human rights around the globe. The theme of democratization should be understood as an effort to provide a legitimate-sounding rationale for the administration's decision to invade Iraq and topple the government of Saddam Hussein. The original reason given for invading Iraq—ending the threat posed by Iraqi weapons of mass destruction—was undercut by the administration's inability to find evidence that such weapons actually existed. The Iraqi weapons program had apparently collapsed years earlier. In casting about for a way of explaining what turned out to have been a colossal policy error, the Bush administration concluded that it could legitimate its actions by asserting that the elimination of Saddam's regime and the installation of a democratic government in Iraq would be beneficial for the Iraqi people and would ultimately serve the cause of world peace.

Though it may have made good campaign material, this pleasantly altruistic explanation of the administration's actions is, of course, false. U.S. policy in the Middle East is dictated mainly by America's need for oil and fear of terrorism. The administration regarded Saddam as a threat to oil supplies and a potential supporter of terrorism and decided that regime change was in order.[47] Like most great powers throughout history, the United States is generally indifferent to the internal politics of other nations except insofar as they affect American interests. Successive American governments have had no qualms about supporting repressive, even brutal regimes in Egypt, Saudi Arabia, and a host of other nations so long as they were believed to promote American economic and security interests. Most politicians, of course, believe that this harsh truth would not be accepted by America's voters. Hence, the talk of "democratization," a term designed to bestow political legitimacy and perhaps enhance electoral support for a foreign policy driven by oil and fear. Indeed, within a year of the election, the Bush administration had all but eliminated funding for organizations nominally seeking to build democratic institutions in Iraq.[48] Apparently Iraq had already achieved the requisite level of democracy.

For its part, the 2004 Kerry campaign sought to develop issues that would bolster and expand the Democratic Party's political coalition. The Democrat Party seeks votes, activism, and financial support from a disparate coalition of forces that seem to have little in common with one another except that all benefit or seek to benefit from the government's domestic social and regulatory programs. These include such groups as unionized workers; African Americans; feminist, prochoice, and gay-rights activists; upper-middle-class intellectuals; environmentalists; and senior citizens. They also include a number of business interests that profit from the government's domestic undertakings and elements of the legal profession, such as trial lawyers, who have convinced the Democratic Party to oppose reform of tort law and other legal practices that are costly to business but provide enormous profits for lawyers.

Tying these diverse concerns into one package, the main slogan of the Kerry effort was "A stronger America begins at home." Taken literally, of course, this slogan was somewhat disingenuous. Knowing that America's seniors were receiving adequate pension benefits would probably not frighten Osama bin Laden or convince al-Qaeda to refrain from launching attacks against the United States. But of course the slogan was not meant to be taken literally. It was, rather, designed to serve as a signal to often-feuding Democratic constituencies that, whatever their differences, they shared a common interest in shifting the nation's spending priorities to domestic programs. Thus, whatever its literal implications, viewed from the perspective of coalition maintenance, Kerry's slogan was very appropriate. In effect, the slogan's true meaning was "A stronger Democratic Party begins at home."

The 2004 Bush campaign offers another excellent example of the use of issues for political mobilization. For more than three decades, Republicans have declared their opposition to abortion and their support for "family values" to distinguish themselves from the allegedly libertine Democrats. Moral issues have swelled the GOP's ranks with religious conservatives who helped to elect four Republican presidents—Nixon, Reagan, and the two Bushes. In 2004, the G. W. Bush reelection effort made special use of a particular moral issue—opposition to same-sex marriage—to mobilize religious conservatives in key states. The issue had arisen because of a series of legal and political efforts by gay-rights activists seeking to compel the states to recognize the right of same-sex couples to marry. Religious conservatives were incensed by what they viewed as an attempt to undermine the traditional family and to force the states to condone immoral conduct.

Republican campaigners saw an opportunity to convert this moral indignation into votes for the president. To this end, Republicans sponsored referenda on the issue of gay marriage to appear on the November 2004 ballots in a number of closely fought battleground states such as Ohio and Florida. The effect of the referenda was to energize religious conservatives and to bring them to the polls in large numbers to strike a blow against immorality. While at their polling places, they also voted for President Bush. These efforts were critical to the president's 2004 victory. Religious voters gave Bush the margin of victory in Florida, Ohio, and Missouri. On a national level, 22 percent of all voters cited moral values as the issue that meant most to them. Of these individuals, 82 percent cast their votes for Bush. Mobilizing voters through same-sex marriage and other moral issues did much to give President Bush a second term in the White House.

Although every political campaign presents a host of issues to the electorate, except under unusual circumstances, politicians seldom expect to win more than a relative handful of new votes on the basis of the issues they articulate. Most voters evaluate candidates and issues through their own partisan lenses and will reflexively regard with suspicion positions asserted by the opposing party's candidates. A highly salient issue or unusual political circumstances may force new information past voters' partisan defenses, but for the most part, voters are disinclined to listen to those with whom they are predisposed to disagree.[49] To be sure, if politicians can raise issues that add even a small number of new voters to their coalition, this may help to turn the tide in a close election. Yet this scenario presupposes that candidates can count upon receiving the bulk of their support from existing sympathizers. For this reason, most campaign issues are designed to maintain the allegiance of the candidate's established supporters and to inspire them to go to the polls.

Consider the major issues raised by the two candidates in the 2004 presidential election. Whether their aim was legitimating past policy decisions, holding together disparate coalitions, or energizing supporters, the intended audience for most issues addressed by Bush or Kerry consisted

of each man's established partisan adherents. The Bush campaign emphasized opposition to abortion and same-sex marriage, the need for tax cuts,
mandatory testing in the schools, elimination of some pollution controls,
renewal of the U.S. Patriot Act, and the continuing need for U.S. military
engagement in Iraq. The Kerry campaign focused on raising the minimum
wage; strengthening environmental regulations; maintaining Social Security;
and protecting affirmative action, abortion, and gay rights. Essentially, each
campaign emphasized positions designed to resonate with its established
partisans while giving short shrift to issues that would mainly be of interest
to uncommitted or hostile voters. Bush campaigned to reassure his supporters of the legitimacy and validity of his decision to go to war in Iraq.
Kerry campaigned to unify the Democrats. Bush campaigned to energize
Republican evangelicals. For both, issues served mainly as tools for activating their partisan base.

Presidential character.   Many Americans view good character as an essential
attribute of political leaders. Most candidates for political office present
themselves as honest, courageous, intelligent, and possessing good moral
values. If they can, they will endeavor to suggest that their opponents manifest the opposite qualities. In 2004, the Bush campaign made two principal
contentions about the president's character. The first was that he was honest. "I say what I mean, and I do what I say," was the president's frequent
refrain. This claim was designed to distinguish Bush from politicians such
as Bill Clinton, whose personal integrity was somewhat suspect, to say the
least. Second, the president was presented as a strong and courageous leader
who had rallied the nation in the aftermath of 9/11 and undertaken decisive
action against the perpetrators of the attack and their supporters.

Democrats worked to challenge both these claims. The first was called
into question when Democrats asserted that the president had not been
fully candid about his Vietnam-era service in the Texas Air National
Guard. Like the children of many prominent families, Bush had been able
to secure a guard appointment. Since the guard was not assigned overseas
duties in the Vietnam era, this appointment virtually guaranteed that Bush
would be spared the rigors of combat in Indochina. Though this fact was a
bit embarrassing for a president who now presented himself as a wartime
leader, it was not politically fatal. The National Guard is a politically potent
institution. Democrats could not afford to antagonize hundreds of thousands of former guardsmen by intimating that their service was somehow
less than honorable, particularly in view of the fact that the guard did play
an important combat role in the two Gulf Wars.

Because of this consideration, Democrats focused instead on allegations that Bush had shirked many of his guard duties while his commanding officers looked the other way to avoid offending his powerful father. These allegations had been circulating in the media for some time but were given special prominence by a CBS news documentary narrated by longtime network anchor Dan Rather. The report averred that Bush had failed to report for guard duties, had failed to carry out assignments, and had generally treated his service in a cavalier manner. The potential for political damage to the president was enormous, but in the days following the program, sources sympathetic to Bush revealed that CBS's main source of information had been a longtime Bush adversary who could not prove any of his allegations. It appeared, moreover, that in its eagerness to present the story, CBS had failed to demand confirmation or evidence of the major charges being presented, in violation of the network's own rules. The resulting tumult led to the firing of a number of CBS executives and to Rather's precipitous "retirement." Although the allegations against Bush were not factually disproved, they had been politically discredited, and they were of little further value to the Democrats.

Democrats had a bit more success with their effort to undercut Bush's claim to be a strong and decisive wartime leader. The principal vehicle they developed for this purpose was the National 9/11 Commission. In the spring of 2004, the commission examined events preceding the attack on the World Trade Center and the Pentagon, seeking to ascertain whether the president and other top officials had failed to respond appropriately to warning signs. Congressional Democrats hoped that a probe of the Bush administration's failure to anticipate the 9/11 attacks might embarrass the president in an election year and undermine public confidence in his ability to protect the nation's security—an area long seen as the president's chief political asset. Unfortunately (from the Democratic perspective), their party did not control either house of Congress and therefore lacked access to either the House or the Senate's formal investigative machinery. Democrats, nevertheless, demanded an investigation and, through public pressure, ultimately forced congressional Republicans to agree to the creation of an ad hoc, bipartisan investigative panel to be appointed by the leaders of the two parties in Congress.

There had been some expectation that the panel would consist of individuals with expertise in national security matters. Some panelists did, indeed, possess such backgrounds. But the Democrats placed on the panel several individuals whose expertise was prosecutorial rather than in the realm of national security. These included Richard Ben-Veniste, an attorney and

Democratic activist who had helped to prosecute Nixon in the Watergate investigation and to defend Clinton in the Whitewater probe. The choice of prosecutors rather than national security experts underlines the role congressional Democrats hoped the commission would play.

Recognizing the president's peril and seeking to limit possible political damage from the commission's findings, the GOP insisted that the investigation be completed and its report released by July 2004, some four months before the 2004 election. Because of the tight time limit, the commission was not as powerful an investigative instrument as a full-blown congressional inquiry might have been. Nevertheless, commission hearings in March and April 2004 suggested that the Bush administration had not been sufficiently attentive to the terrorist threat prior to September 2001. This finding deeply embarrassed the president.

The hearings highlighted the testimony of a former national security aide, Richard Clarke, who had just published a book criticizing Bush for his inattention to the threat of terrorism.[50] Commission Democrats led by Ben-Veniste praised Clarke while castigating the Bush administration's star witness, National Security Adviser Condoleezza Rice, whose testimony the commission had demanded despite presidential claims of executive privilege. Ben-Veniste interrupted Rice repeatedly, while Democratic commission member Jamie Gorelick, who had served as an assistant attorney general in the Clinton administration, delivered a lengthy statement critical of Rice's testimony.[51]

Indeed, long before the publication of the official report, members of the commission made numerous public and media appearances to present their own views critical of the president. Ben-Veniste, Gorelick, and the others fully understood that the main purpose of the 9/11 probe was to undermine Bush's political standing—not to develop new intelligence and antiterrorism policies. Democrats also mobilized a group of survivors of 9/11 victims—the so-called Jersey girls—to make television appearances during the hearings to express outrage at the presidential failures that had allegedly been identified by the hearings. And, as if to dramatize the commission's findings, left-liberal moviemaker Michael Moore produced a film titled *Fahrenheit 9/11*, which mocked President Bush and portrayed him as a clueless dope on September 11 rather than the forceful leader depicted by the White House.

Republicans launched a series of counterattacks. They demanded that Gorelick resign from the panel, charging that her own actions as assistant attorney general had hampered the FBI and now produced a conflict of interest with her service as a commission member. And Republicans mobilized their own 9/11 survivors' group to make television appearances in support of President Bush. Nevertheless, through the National 9/11 Commission and its ancillaries, Democrats did manage to call into question the validity of President Bush's claims of strength and decisiveness.

While Democrats attacked the president's character, Republicans launched their own efforts to impugn the character of Bush's opponent, Senator John Kerry. The first of the senator's two main claims was that, unlike Bush, he had shown courage by serving in Vietnam, where he had commanded a patrol boat and had been decorated for his heroism under enemy fire. Second, Kerry presented himself as possessing greater intelligence than the president, an individual whose alleged lack of intellectual ability had been the subject of thousands of television comedy routines. In his public appearances, Kerry frequently sought to demonstrate his knowledge of history, economics, and foreign languages. The latter certainly distinguished him from Bush, who often seemed confused even by the English language.

Republicans vigorously contested each of these claims. To dispute Kerry's bravery in Vietnam, GOP operatives organized a group of conservative Vietnam veterans who called themselves Swift Boat Veterans for Truth. These so-called Swifties traveled around the country asserting that Kerry had distorted and exaggerated his wartime record. Democrats countered, charging that the Swifties were simply part of a GOP smear campaign. As evidence, Democrats pointed to the fact that Bush attorney Benjamin L. Ginsberg was also the legal adviser to the Swifties. Ginsberg was forced to resign from both positions. Although Republicans were never able to prove that Kerry had overstated his heroism in Vietnam, they did manage to raise doubts and convert what had been widely viewed as a settled fact into a question.

To counter Kerry's claim that he was smarter than the president, Republicans sought to redefine the issue a bit from intelligence to judgment. Bush and his aides argued that Kerry demonstrated poor judgment by frequently "waffling" on major issues. In Republican campaign materials and even in the nationally televised 2004 presidential debates, Bush sought to give examples of instances, such as the decision to invade Iraq, when Kerry seemed to shift from one position to another. Democrats countered that Kerry changed his positions as events and circumstances changed and pointed out that the president's reluctance to change his mind might be seen as intellectual rigidity rather than moral steadfastness. Given the general view that President Bush was not the sharpest leader America ever produced, Republicans were usually not too eager to engage in debates over the candidates' relative levels of intelligence. If, however, GOP operatives had managed to secure copies of Kerry's college records before the election, they might have welcomed a test of wits. Bush's academic record at Yale, to be sure, had been abysmal. But Yale grades disclosed after the election showed that Kerry's had been even worse.

Although both campaigns saw issues as instruments for activating supporters, each saw questions of character mainly as means of dispiriting some of its opponent's adherents. Thus, each 2004 campaign made a number of claims designed to persuade some of the other side's potential supporters that their candidate lacked sufficient moral fiber or intellectual stature to deserve their support. The Kerry campaign attacked Bush's stature as a wartime leader and intimated that the president was something of a dunce. The Bush campaign suggested that Kerry had not really been a war hero and lacked the firmness of judgment needed by a president. Attacks of this sort are not likely to convince a candidate's most committed supporters of his or her lack of virtue. Empirical studies suggest, however, that negative ads and other forms of character attack can discourage less-certain and less-committed individuals who might have voted for a particular candidate from going to the polls at all.[52] After all, who but the most rabid partisan would vote for a shirker, a dunce, or an inveterate flip-flopper?

Mistaken identities.   Finally, politicians often appeal to voters on the basis of their social or political identities. Politicians typically make such appeals by emphasizing that they share or at least sympathize with some salient trait of the voters whose support they are seeking. Such traits include gender, ethnicity, race, religion, and various other physical or social characteristics that voters deem to be important. One well-known example of identity politics is the ethnically balanced ticket. In the nineteenth century, urban political machines typically enrolled voters from a variety of immigrant groups. To maintain voter loyalty, machine leaders always made certain that the party's slate of candidates included representatives from all the major groups. Even as recently as the 1960s, the Democratic Party's slate in New York City was led by candidates named Lefkowitz, Fino, and Gilhooley, which presumably reminded the city's numerous Jewish, Italian, and Irish voters that they had reason to support the Democrats.[53]

Occasionally a political party would identify a candidate who, in his own person, represented multiple ethnic identities. One of the best-known examples is former New York Republican Mayor Fiorello La Guardia, who served three terms between 1934 and 1945. La Guardia, whose first name meant "little flower," was the child of an Austrian-Jewish mother and an Italian-Catholic father, grew up in what is today Serbia, and was raised as a Protestant. La Guardia was fluent in Italian, German, Yiddish, and Serbo-Croatian and campaigned in the language spoken by the voters he was addressing. He could also demonstrate equal piety in a Catholic church, a Protestant church, or a Jewish synagogue. La Guardia was such a successful practitioner of identity politics that to this very day New York's Italians and Jews argue over whether he was the city's first Italian mayor or its first Jewish mayor.

Since La Guardia's time, many new groups have become politically important while some of the older ethnic groups have waned in significance. In addition to the Irish, Jews, and Italians, politicians must endeavor to appeal to African Americans, women, Hispanics, Asian Americans, senior citizens, persons with disabilities, and a number of other groups. Today's political tickets frequently reflect this new diversity. In many parts of America, indeed, political commercials are as likely to be aired in Spanish as in English. Not even a modern-day La Guardia could personify all the diversity of contemporary American society, though Illinois senator and presidential hopeful Barack Obama comes close.

In addition to balancing the ticket, contemporary politicians endeavor to balance their appeal by vigorously expressing their sympathy and admiration for groups to which they do not actually belong. Almost every New York politician, for example, is certain to make a political pilgrimage to Jerusalem, the Vatican, and Dublin, stopping en route at numerous senior citizens' centers, African Methodist Episcopal churches, and mosques. Many politicians have learned to speak a few words of Spanish or, like Florida's Governor Jeb Bush, happily publicize their ties by marriage to America's rapidly growing Hispanic community. And, of course, a variety of politicians hope to benefit from supporting affirmative action, women's rights, subsidized health care for seniors, and other programs aimed at cultivating the sympathy of one or another racial, social, or ethnic group.

Identity, though, is a slippery concept. Every individual has many identities and the potential for even more. For example, almost everyone has some measure of identification with others with whom they share an ethnic background or gender. But there is no inherent reason why ethnicity and gender should be politically important while other traits such as, say, height, intelligence, or even hair color should have less political significance. The political importance of a given characteristic depends upon consciousness and leadership, not destiny. To begin with, individuals possessing the characteristic must believe that it ties them to one another and imbues them with interests and values different from those of people who do not share the attribute in question. In some instance, such consciousness is a product of history. Blacks and whites in the United States could hardly be unaware of the historic differences in life circumstances that made America's racial divide, at times, seem unbridgeable.

But, as Karl Marx said of class consciousness, a group's self-awareness seldom emerges spontaneously. In most instances, group consciousness is created by social and political entrepreneurs who hope to derive some advantage from imbuing the members of a group with a sense of identity and common political purpose. For example, senior citizens have become an active and self-conscious force in contemporary American politics. Representatives of the senior lobby constantly demand that the government provide enhanced pension and health care benefits for the elderly, and because seniors are more likely than other Americans to go to the polls, politicians vie with one another to express their concern and admiration for America's older citizens. The self-consciousness and political prominence of seniors did not arise spontaneously. Since time immemorial, aging simply had been a fact of every person's life, not a trait that distinguished some individuals from others. Seniors became a self-conscious group largely because of the activities of the American Association of Retired Persons and other lobby groups during the 1960s.

Founded in 1958, the AARP was a small group led by a retired teacher named Ethel Andrus. Andrus's chief goal was to convince health insurance companies to sell policies to older consumers, who were deemed poor risks by the industry. Andrus developed an alliance with Leonard Davis, a broker for a Chicago insurance company that provided health coverage for the AARP's members, but the organization's real growth came after 1962, when the Senate rejected what later became the Medicare program. Hoping to build support for the enactment of Medicare by some future Congress, the Social Security Administration (SSA) encouraged the AARP to begin lobbying for the program. With the enactment of Medicare in 1965, Davis formed Colonial Penn Insurance and began marketing policies to supplement Medicare to AARP members. These so-called Medigap policies generated tens of million of dollars in profits for the AARP, which became, in effect, a paid marketing agency for Medigap insurance through its magazine and other publications. Building upon its success, the AARP began marketing a variety of other products and services to seniors.

To enhance its lobbying power and importance in the marketplace, the AARP worked tirelessly to encourage seniors to view themselves as a unique group with the AARP as its representative. The AARP's magazine, pamphlets, news releases, advertising, and local meetings work to build consciousness among seniors of their distinct interests, needs, and perspectives. AARP publications and meetings focus on health, social, employment, financial, and even sexual issues said to be particularly important to seniors. In these ways, the AARP helped make seniors conscious of themselves as a distinctive stratum and paved the way for the political attention seniors receive today. The development of group consciousness among older Americans has been electorally significant. In the past, as Americans aged, they either retained their preexisting partisan identifications or, as they became wealthier and more conservative in their thinking, tended to shift to the Republican camp. As self-conscious "seniors," however, older Americans have become members of the Democratic coalition. Voters over the age of sixty-five, who in the past had tended to support the GOP, have voted Democratic in three of the last four presidential elections.

As the example of seniors suggests, the creation of new identities can be a powerful political weapon. By making individuals conscious of an alternative identity, politicians can change their political perceptions, partisan ties, and voting behavior. Since the 1980s, for example, the GOP's emphasis on religion and morality has helped to make Christian fundamentalists conscious of themselves as a distinct group with distinct views and interests. Many of these individuals hold blue-collar jobs and, in their capacity as workers, certainly do not benefit from Republican economic and tax programs, which mainly serve upper-income groups. If these voters were primarily conscious of themselves as workers, they would probably be affiliated with the Democratic Party. Yet, by persuading these blue-collar workers to become conscious of themselves first and foremost as Christians, the GOP has been able to tie them to the Republican coalition. This feat of political magic, begun during the Reagan era, has helped to elect the last three Republican presidents.

Money and Politics

Some pundits are fond of declaring that money does not buy elections, but this is a naive view. As noted above, the average cost of winning a Senate seat is about $6 million, and the average cost of winning a House seat is approaching $1 million. Successful presidential candidates and their supporters spend hundreds of millions of dollars. In 2004, Bush and Kerry each raised more than $300 million for their presidential races. Another $500 million was spent in support of one or the other candidate by nominally independent nonprofit groups—the so-called 527s and 501(c)4s—that are currently not covered by campaign spending restrictions imposed in

2002 by the BCRA. These groups, named for the sections of the tax code under which they are organized, can raise and spend unlimited amounts on political advocacy so long as their efforts are not coordinated with those of any candidate's campaign. A 527 is a group established specifically for the purpose of political advocacy, whereas a 501(c)4 is a nonprofit group established for some other purpose that also engages in advocacy. A 501(c)4 may not spend more than half its revenues for political purposes, but many political activists favor this mode of organization because, unlike a 527, a 501(c)4 is not required to disclose where it gets its funds or exactly what it does with them. As a result, it has become a common practice for wealthy and corporate donors to route campaign contributions far in excess of the legal limits through 501(c)4s. The donor makes a legal contribution to the 501(c)4, which keeps a cut and donates the remainder of the money to a designated "grassroots" campaign on behalf of the politician.[54] Taking account of other federal, state, and local elections, more than $3 billion was spent by or on behalf of candidates in 2004.

In some instances, to be sure, candidates who spend lavishly come out on the short end. But even when this happens, they are usually defeated by opponents who spent almost as extravagantly. Though superior financial resources do not guarantee success, generally speaking, the candidate who raises and spends the most money wins. A 1996 study conducted by the Center for Responsive Politics found that 92 percent of the House races and 88 percent of the Senate races were won by the candidate who spent the most money.[55] The candidate without money, like Machiavelli's unarmed prophet, is usually doomed to failure.

The fact that campaigns cost a great deal of money is hardly surprising. Marketing any product is expensive. One major cost is television advertising. Producing a thirty-second television commercial can cost $500,000, and airing it on network television can cost anywhere from $100,000 to $2 million each time it is presented. Local television time is much less expensive, but repeatedly airing ads even during off-peak hours on local TV can entail hundreds of thousands of dollars in expenditures. Another major cost is staffing, particularly attorneys' fees. For example, in 1998, Senator Carol Moseley-Braun (D-IL) raised nearly $5 million for her reelection effort. Of this, the senator spent more than $1.1 million—20 percent of her campaign war chest—on lawyers' and accountants' fees.[56] The campaign finance reforms enacted in 2002 have forced politicians to hire even more lawyers and accountants. How ironic that new rules nominally designed to reduce the role of money in politics force campaigns to raise more money to pay for legal and accounting services needed to ensure compliance with the new rules, themselves. And, of course, fund-raising is itself an expensive enterprise—witness the case of Oliver North, whose fund-raising costs absorbed two of every three dollars his campaign was able to raise.

Some of the dollars raised by politicians come from small contributors making $25 or $50 donations in response to mail, phone, or Internet solicitations. In the 2004 presidential race, about one-third of the money raised by Bush and Kerry consisted of donations under $200.[57] Perhaps as many as two million Americans contributed small amounts of money to the Bush and Kerry campaigns.[58] The bulk of the money spent in the 2004 election, nearly $3 billion, came from wealthy donors and from corporate, labor, and ideological interest groups working through political action committees (PACs), 527s, and 501(c)4s. Some of the largest spenders were liberal organizations such as Emily's List, whose PAC and 527 spent nearly $20 million to help elect liberal women to office. But this was more than balanced by the hundreds of millions spent by over a thousand business PACs, such as the National Association of Realtors, the American Bankers' Association, the Beer Distributors' Association, and a horde of PACs linked to individual corporations. PACs sponsored by the United Parcel Service, Pfizer, FedEx, Wal-Mart, AT&T, Anheuser-Busch, Union Pacific, Bank of America, SmithKline Beecham, and HSBC were the top-ten corporate donors. The dependence of candidates upon these billions in contributions has important consequences.

Voters and donors. In principle, there are two reasons to think that elections might allow citizens some measure of control over the government's conduct. These are, to put it simply, choice and accountability. Elections permit citizens an opportunity to choose representatives who share their own interests and preferences. They also give citizens a chance to hold officials accountable for their actions by threatening to depose those whose conduct in office is inconsistent with popular wishes. These ideas certainly seem plausible. The problem, though, is that the behavioral presumptions underlying the choice-and-accountability model apply more aptly to the relationships among politicians and interest-group donors than to the connections between politicians and ordinary voters.

To begin with, as we observed earlier, most voters do not have autonomous preferences that lead them to search among possible candidates for the ones whose views are consistent with their own. Most voters, moreover, have relatively little information upon which to base their choices. To a considerable extent, voters rely upon candidates to supply them with information about themselves and allow their preferences to be formed during the campaign by the marketing efforts of politicians. Organized groups, on the other hand, are typically not very interested in candidates' campaign commercials. Corporate, labor, and ideological groups have well-defined interests and preferences and often employ staffers and lobbyists to identify the strategies through which their interests are most likely to be advanced.

In some cases, interest groups will simply provide financial help for politicians who they believe are likely to support their needs and goals. Typically, ideological groups support candidates who share their beliefs. For example, when he was a senator, former Attorney General John Ashcroft, a longtime champion of the religious right, received hundreds of thousands of dollars in contributions from conservative religious groups that expected him to promote their agenda.[59] In a similar vein, liberal groups spend a good deal of their campaign money supporting the election of their ideological comrades and attempting to defeat conservatives. For example, during the 2004 contest, the Media Fund, a liberal 527, organized a $5 million advertising campaign attacking President Bush. "President Bush," the announcer intoned, "remember the American dream? It's about hope, not fear. It's about more jobs at home, not tax breaks for shipping jobs overseas. It's about giving our children their chance, not our debt. It's about providing health care for people, not just profits. It's about fighting for the middle class, not special interests.... It's time to take our country back from corporate greed and make America work for every American."

Corporate groups and PACs, for their part, tend to adopt a more pragmatic contribution strategy. Rather than limiting their contributions to their existing allies, business groups continually seek to make new friends by giving money to candidates of all political stripes and sometimes to both candidates in the same race. Often politicians approach interest groups and lobbyists to demand money, and corporate interests will make contributions to keep friends and avoid making enemies.[60] Corporate donors even contribute to candidates who are fond of accusing them of seeking to subvert the political process. For example, in 2000, Senator John McCain loudly attacked special-interest politics as he campaigned for the Republican presidential nomination. He asked voters to help him "break the Washington iron triangle of big money, lobbyists and legislation that for too long has put special interests above the national interest."[61] But the very same special interests that McCain vilified were happy to contribute to his campaign and to raise money on his behalf. Firms were not about to allow a bit of populist rhetoric to stand in the way of maintaining a good relationship with the powerful chairman of the Senate Commerce Committee, and for his part, the senator was certainly not going to permit his own rhetoric to interfere with raising money. McCain's fund-raising events were often organized by some of Washington's most powerful special-interest lobbyists, who just happened to represent companies that had an enormous stake in legislation before McCain's committee. These included railroads, communications firms, wholesalers, soft-drink distributors, and others.[62]

Corporate interests endeavor to be strategic in their choice of lobbyists. Many of Washington's lobbyists also serve as campaign treasurers and major fund-raisers for political candidates.[63] Individuals such as Peter Hart, Tommy Boggs, Peter Knight, Ken Duberstein, and Vin Weber are influential, in part, because of their ability to raise money for politicians. Interest groups will often hire lobbyists who they know to be key fund-raisers for the politicians they hope to influence. In so doing, they are not making a campaign contribution that would have to be reported to the Federal Election Commission, but they are nevertheless seeking to make use of the fact that the lobbyist promoting their interests will be seen by the targeted politician as an important source of campaign money. For example, in 2003, a coalition of television networks seeking to loosen rules governing their ownership of local TV stations hired Gregg Hartley as their lobbyist. Hartley, formerly a top aide to powerful House Majority Whip Roy Blunt, is one of Blunt's top fund-raisers. Companies hiring Hartley to lobby for them are almost certain of receiving a positive reception from Blunt. Seventy-one members of Congress list lobbyists as treasurers of their reelection committees.[64] Seven members of the powerful House Appropriations Committee, five Republicans and two Democrats, have PACs headed by lobbyists with business before the committee.[65]

In some instances, too, corporate groups form strategic alliances with ideological or not-for-profit groups. As indicated before, a corporate interest may find it useful to hide its campaign contributions by laundering them through a not-for-profit. For example, in the late 1990s, a variety of gambling interests opposed a bill that would have prohibited Internet gambling. Members of Congress were reluctant to accept money directly from what might have seemed to be unsavory sources. At the direction of former Washington superlobbyist Jack Abramoff, the affected gambling interests made contributions to religious groups led by former Christian Coalition executive director Ralph Reed and Traditional Values Coalition founder the Rev. Lou Sheldon as well as tax-reform groups headed by Grover Norquist. In turn, these groups lobbied against the Internet gambling ban, providing laundered campaign funds for prominent members of Congress.[66] This tactic, called money-swapping, is fairly common. The Clinton administration allegedly engaged in extensive money-swapping with such organizations as the International Brotherhood of Teamsters. In one case, a foreign national hoping to influence the administration was advised that a direct contribution would be illegal. Instead, Democratic fund-raisers advised this person to make a contribution to Teamster President Ron Carey's reelection campaign. The Teamsters, in turn, made a legal contribution to the Clinton campaign.[67]

Interest groups are not only in a better position than mere voters or even small donors to employ a strategic calculus in doling out their support; they also are far better able than voters to hold politicians accountable for their actions in office. As David Mayhew has observed, the average voter has only the "haziest awareness" of what a congressional representative or senator is actually doing in office.[68] Most voters pay no attention, and even many of those who do have little understanding of the complexities of the legislative process. Even attentive voters who read the newspapers and watch televised discussions would be hard-pressed to distinguish between a member of Congress who actually works hard to promote a particular cause and one who merely makes speeches or issues press releases.[69] Interest groups are in a much better position to make such judgments. Their lobbyists and staffers attend hearings, meet with legislators and members of their staffs, and prowl the corridors of Capitol Hill exchanging information with one another.

Of course, even interest groups can be duped. Native American gambling interests made millions of dollars in contributions and apparently got little for their money. Nevertheless, Washington's more savvy interest groups know precisely what legislators are doing and can react furiously if they feel betrayed. Take, for example, the AARP, which employs twenty-two full-time lobbyists, a thirty-two-scholar think tank, and more than 2,000 volunteer organizers. AARP lobbyists monitor congressional activity on a daily basis and meet with members of Congress to present the organization's views and complaints. AARP organizers are prepared to touch off furious phone and letter campaigns in the districts of members whose attentiveness to senior issues is deemed lacking. In Washington, the AARP is nicknamed "Darth Vader," and members of Congress know they will definitely see the dark side of the force if they take the organization's money and fail to follow through on their commitments.[70]

It is sometimes said that money and lobbying do not buy legislation, they merely buy "access" to lawmakers. This is a naive perspective. Unlike some starstruck voters, organized groups are not much interested in being photographed with famous politicians. Their goal is to secure the enactment of legislation that serves their interests. And from all indications, they accomplish this goal on a regular basis. Consider the following recent news stories: Over the past several years, a coalition of sixty corporations, including Pfizer, Hewlett-Packard, and Altria, spent close to $2 million in lobbying fees and campaign contributions to persuade Congress to lower the tax rate on earnings from their foreign operations. The result was legislation signed by the president in 2004 that has already saved the companies about $100 billion in taxes.[71]

In a similar vein, after spending millions in campaign contributions and lobbying fees, corporations succeeded in bringing about the enactment of pension legislation in 2006 that allows them to sharply cut the amount they are required to contribute to the employees' pension funds. The savings to major corporations are expected to total as much as $160 billion over the next three years.[72] Similarly, the 2006 energy and Medicare bills contained billions of dollars in corporate benefits secured through millions of dollars in campaign contributions and lobbying expenditures.[73] The same pattern can be found at the state and local levels. For example, in 2006, after handing out $1.4 million in campaign contributions to Virginia legislators, a coalition of builders, contractors, developers, and real estate agents persuaded the state legislature to kill the governor's proposal for limits on suburban development.[74] In a similar vein, a coalition of labor unions was able to halt Wal-Mart's expansion into Maryland by making substantial contributions to the campaigns of forty-eight members of the Maryland General Assembly during the month prior to the vote. Wal-Mart had hired a dozen lobbyists to promote its agenda through argument and persuasion. The unions, though, had a better understanding of Maryland politics. They skipped the arguments and paid cash for the votes they needed.[75] So much for buying access.

Follow the golden rule. Of course, not all legislation is bought and paid for, though a good deal is. Not all bills serve special interests, though many do. In some instances, politicians may feel compelled to defer to grassroots sentiment on major and highly visible matters. Even the most venal office holders cannot ignore such matters as inflation, unemployment, high gasoline prices, and other issues likely to arouse even the most quiescent voters. Most of the time, though, elected officials have every incentive to pay a good deal of attention to the organized interests that fund their campaigns and far less attention to mere voters. Politicians follow the golden rule—not the biblical golden rule but the political golden rule, which, simply put, is that those who have the gold make the rules.[76] Often enough, voters are not aware that their elected officials are giving them the short end of the stick. How many voters understand the intricacies of the law governing taxation of profits earned abroad, or energy tax credits, or Medicare reimbursement rates? When it comes to these matters, politicians can serve corporate interests without even considering the views of ordinary citizens. Citizens can safely be assumed to have no views on these topics. But even when it comes to matters that citizens do care about, politicians will usually follow the golden rule.

Take the issue of immigration. Most Republican voters favor restrictions on further immigration. Business, however, favors unrestricted immigration in order to ensure a continuing flow of low-cost workers. Not surprisingly, the GOP's leadership sides with business on this issue. In the case of the Democrats, one could point to an even more dramatic illustration of politicians' inclination to privilege organized interests over ordinary voters. The Democratic Party strongly supports abortion rights because feminist and liberal forces are such important donors and activists in the Democratic coalition. At the same time, almost all the users of abortion services are poor and minority women whose children, if they matured and joined the electorate, would very likely become Democratic voters. It might be said that the Democrats are willing to sacrifice future generations of voters to obey the dictates of an organized interest. So much for the primacy of voting.

4

Private Interests and Public Policies

Many policy analysts assert that government action is often required to correct what they call "market failure." This concept refers to inequities, inefficiencies, or harmful externalities produced by the operations of private markets. The presumption underlying this idea is that government agencies and officials are motivated mainly by concern for the public's welfare and will intervene in the private sector in ways that are likely to promote broad public interests.

The reality, though, is that political processes are hardly guaranteed to produce fair and equitable results or to serve the general interest. Policymakers are often driven by self-interest, partisan predispositions, institutional concerns, and the demands of powerful constituency groups. Often, too, public programs are developed or administered by bureaucracies, courts, private contractors, and other entities whose decision-making processes lack transparency and are open to only a narrow range of participants.[1] Though every governmental program is of course touted by its proponents and sponsors as serving the public interest and correcting private problems and failures, the unfortunate truth is that many, albeit not all, such programs serve particularistic rather than general interests.

Though each has many variants, public programs frequently suffer from one or another of three pathologies that, collectively, might be dubbed policy failure, the political analogue of market failure. The first is *mobilization bias,* that is, the fact that well-organized groups with substantial resources and a high stake in a particular policy are more likely than ordinary individuals to engage in successful efforts to pressure officials to enact the policies they favor.[2] The second is *organizational bias.* Institutions and agencies charged with developing and implementing public policies often pursue plans that promote their own institutional interests even when the public interest might better be served by some alternative set of programs. The third is *private capture.* Many important public policies are administered not by government bureaucracies but by private contractors or other designees. In a number of cases this system has allowed private interests to use public power for their own purposes.

Mobilization Bias

Of these three forms of policy failure, mobilization bias is probably the most ubiquitous and certainly the most familiar because of frequent accounts in the mass media revealing instances in which policies were driven by the efforts of small groups rather than some larger public purpose. In virtually every domestic and policy arena, organized groups engage in a host of activities designed to influence the policy-making process. They seek to manipulate public opinion, influence politicians through campaign contributions, lobby Congress and the bureaucracy, and litigate in the courts. Ordinary citizens seldom have the knowledge, resources, or sense of involvement and commitment to compete successfully with organized and mobilized interests. The late Mancur Olson famously observed that small, organized groups were usually able to prevail against large, unorganized ones because the latter suffered from what he called collective action problems. "Unless the number of individuals in a group is quite small or unless there is coercion or some other special device to make individuals act in their common interest, rational self-interested individuals will not act to advance their common or group goals."[3] Indeed, every rational individual in a large collectivity will "free ride" in the hope that others will invest the time, energy, and effort needed to achieve collective purposes. For these reasons, public policies are more likely to serve narrow interests than the welfare of the general public.

Of course, even the most active and powerful interest groups never present themselves as motivated by self-interest or greed. Groups always characterize their proposals as designed to serve the general good—if only to provide plausible cover for politicians whose support they have acquired or hope to secure. Generally, however, mobilization biases are most likely to occur when the costs of an interest group's favored program are distributed so widely that no set of potential opponents will have much of an incentive to work against it. In these situations, a well-organized group may be able to purloin the keys to the public treasury without encountering more than a whisper of opposition. In other cases, an interest group may be able to design a self-serving program so cleverly that those who pay for it actually believe themselves to be beneficiaries. The fortunate recipients of what might be called stealth benefits do not have to steal the keys to the public treasury. Instead, the public eagerly turns over its hard-won cash to them. A contemporary example of the first sort of program is the federal government's effort to encourage the use of ethanol as a motor-vehicle fuel additive. An example of the second is the mortgage-interest tax deduction.

Fuel from Corn

Ethanol, or ethyl alcohol, is the most common compound found in alcoholic beverages. Ethyl alcohol is simple to produce through fermentation and distillation and has been used by humans as an intoxicant for thousands of years. In recent years, though, ethanol has also become an important fuel source in a number of countries. By itself, or mixed with gasoline to form a compound popularly known as gasohol, ethanol can power motor vehicles. All the motor fuel sold in Brazil, for example, contains at least 25 percent ethanol, and cars manufactured or sold in that country can run on ethanol, gasoline, or virtually any mix of the two. Ethanol can also serve as an oxygenate additive for gasoline in place of methyl tertiary butyl ether (MTBE), which has been commonly used for that purpose. Ethanol can be produced from the sugar or starch in a variety of agricultural crops, including sugarcane (its main source in Brazil) and corn (its chief source in the United States). Ethanol can also be produced from a variety of other crops, such as sugar beet, sorghum, switchgrass, barley, and potatoes.

Because ethanol can be made from a renewable resource—agricultural crops—grown in the United States, ethanol producers and their political supporters have argued that increased use of ethanol in motor fuel would help to preserve nonrenewable resources such as oil while lessening America's dependence upon energy suppliers in the volatile Middle East. Ethanol, its proponents say, also helps small family farmers by providing a new market for their corn crops. Brazil has been able to replace about 40 percent of its demand for gasoline with ethanol and has recently asserted that it is no longer dependent upon foreign oil. Many have claimed that increased use of ethanol in motor fuel could have the same result in the United States. In April 2006, President George W. Bush said, "For the sake of economic security, and for the sake of national security, we have got to get off of Middle Eastern oil, and the best way to do so is with Iowa corn."[4]

The U.S. government has been heavily subsidizing the production and use of ethanol since the 1970s. The Energy Tax Act of 1978 granted a four-cents-per-gallon exemption from federal excise taxes to motor fuels blended with a minimum of 10 percent ethanol. This tax break launched the "gasohol" market. Subsequent tax advantages were granted to ethanol producers in 1980, 1982, 1984, 1990, and 1992. In 1980, Congress appropriated several billion dollars to stimulate alternative fuel production, much of which was spent on ethanol technology. In 1994, the Environmental Protection Agency (EPA) issued regulations requiring that 30 percent of the oxygenates contained in fuels be derived from ethanol. This number was doubled by the 2005 energy law, which called for the replacement of MTBE with ethanol over a six-year period. All in all, ethanol production has received tens of billions of dollars in federal subsidies over the past thirty years.

If it was, indeed, the case that ethanol could become a renewable and domestically produced substitute for foreign oil, these billions in federal subsidies would have been well-spent. Unfortunately, however, the claims made by proethanol forces are based more upon political hype than economic and technological reality. The problem with ethanol as a source of fuel is quite simple: The energy cost of producing a gallon of ethanol from corn is greater than the energy that can be produced by that gallon of ethanol. Thus, ethanol production consumes rather than creates energy.

According to a study undertaken by David Pimentel of Cornell University and Tad Patzek of the University of California–Berkeley, making ethanol from corn requires 29 percent more energy than the ethanol fuel itself contains.[5] Pimentel and Patzek calculated that ethanol made from corn contains 76,000 Btu per gallon, but producing that ethanol from corn requires about 98,000 Btu. By comparison, a gallon of gasoline contains about 116,000 Btu, and the production of that gallon—including drilling the well, transporting, and refining it—requires only around 22,000 Btu. Pimentel also argued that when used to produce ethanol, corn is not truly a renewable resource. "Corn production erodes the soil about 12 times faster than the soil can be reformed, and irrigating corn mines groundwater 25 percent faster than the natural recharge rate of groundwater. The environmental system in which corn is being produced is being rapidly degraded."[6] Pimentel calculated that if an American automobile were fully fueled by ethanol, eleven acres of farmland would be required to grow the needed corn each year. On a national basis, this would mean that 97 percent of the total land area of the United States would be needed to grow the corn to fuel America's automobiles. Obviously, this is an impossibility and suggests the outer limits of ethanol's utility as a fuel even if, somehow, the energy requirements for its production were substantially reduced.

Pimentel and Patzek also calculated the costs involved in producing ethanol from agricultural crops other than corn and concluded that no matter what U.S.-based crop were used, the energy cost of producing ethanol would be greater than the yield. In the case of switchgrass, production of ethanol requires 50 percent more energy than is yielded; sunflowers 118 percent more; soybeans 27 percent more; and so on. The one exception to this picture of net loss of energy from ethanol production appears to be the case of Brazilian sugarcane. A gallon of ethanol produced from sugarcane contains more energy than is used in its production. However, the quantity of land needed to sustain an ethanol-based motor economy in Brazil is enormous, and sugarcane, a crop that requires a tropical climate, is not a viable source of ethanol in the United States.[7]

If ethanol is not the answer to America's energy problems, then why has the federal government invested billions to subsidize its production? The answer is simple. Ethanol producers are highly organized and concentrated in politically important agricultural states. The proethanol lobby includes such groups as the Renewable Fuels Association, the National Corn Growers Association, the American Coalition for Ethanol, the National Ethanol Vehicle Coalition, the Ethanol Producers and Consumers, the Illinois Corn Marketing Board, and a host of others. The campaign for ethanol subsidies and tax breaks is strongly backed by virtually all the members of Congress and governors representing agricultural states, particularly in the Midwest. Much of the farm lobby backs ethanol production.

And agribusiness, an important source of campaign contributions for members of both political parties, is strongly committed to the ethanol cause. Though proponents of ethanol frequently point to the small family farmer as the chief beneficiary of proethanol programs, the reality is that the ethanol industry is dominated by Archer Daniels Midland Co. (ADM), an agribusiness giant that produces 25 percent of the U.S. ethanol supply.[8] Other agribusinesses that have become major ethanol producers include VeraSun Energy of South Dakota and Cargill, Inc., of Minnesota. These powerful corporations are actively involved in the political process. Employees of ADM donate millions of dollars to political candidates during every election cycle. Indeed, former ADM Chairman Dwayne Andreas and his wife personally gave millions to both political parties and routinely flew candidates on Andreas's corporate jet.[9] ADM and the others have made continued government support for ethanol production a major goal of the lobbying efforts.

Opposing ethanol use are a small group of scientists who point out that ethanol will worsen rather than alleviate America's energy problems and a small number of consumer groups who assert that ethanol is already raising rather than lowering the price of gasoline. But these scattered opponents hardly carry much weight against the political power of the ethanol lobby. Perhaps if ethanol substantially raised the price of gas, the ensuing public outcry would give pause to ethanol's political friends. Government data, however, indicate that the direct cost to consumers of expanded ethanol use is only about four cents per gallon of motor fuel.[10] This direct cost of pennies per person is hardly enough to give ethanol's opponents the kind of incentive for political battle that ethanol's supporters receive from the prospect of earning billions in profits.

As a result of their chiefly unopposed efforts, ethanol producers expect to continue benefiting from government programs. Under the terms of the 2005 energy bill, ethanol will soon fully replace MTBE as a gasoline additive. The 2005 act also provides a ten-cents-per-gallon production credit for small ethanol producers and offers service-station owners a 30 percent tax credit for installing equipment that will dispense ethanol to motorists. In 2006, the Bush administration proposed spending $150 million on biofuels research, $160 million to build three biofuels refineries, and $188 million in loan guarantees to promote investment in ethanol. With the help of the federal government, the ethanol industry expected to put thirty-three new plants into operation by 2007, leading to the production of about five billion gallons of ethanol, up from a mere ten million gallons in 1979. Ethanol backers, however, are not satisfied. Illinois Congressman Jerry Weller wants to increase production to 25 billion gallons.[11] This would, needless to say, require additional tax breaks, more investment funds, and less regulation for the industry. Of course, another way to make more ethanol available to Americans might be to import it from Brazil. Not surprisingly, however, the ethanol lobby vigorously opposes any reduction in the steep tariff that currently keeps foreign ethanol out of the U.S. market. Apparently, increasing ethanol supplies is a good idea only if the ethanol is produced in Iowa.

Although its actual value as a fuel is, at best, dubious, ethanol's political prospects seem so bright that hundreds of small farmers are seeking to jump on its bandwagon. Throughout America's agricultural heartland, farmers and investors are making plans to grow more corn and build new ethanol plants. "Everybody in the corn industry is repositioning [for ethanol production]," said one Iowa farmer.[12] "We'll be the Arabs of the Midwest," said another.[13]

Subsidizing the Mortgage Industry

Ethanol's supporters prevail easily in the political arena because they are well-organized and highly motivated, whereas those who pay for the use of ethanol have little incentive to fight. In the case of the mortgage tax deduction, those who pay not only are unprepared to fight, they are actually convinced that they benefit from a federal policy that mainly serves the mortgage industry and costs the general public billions of dollars.

The mortgage-interest tax deduction has been an element of America's tax code since the introduction of the federal income tax in 1913. Under America's current tax law, individuals who file itemized personal income-tax returns may deduct the interest on as much as $1 million in mortgage indebtedness plus the interest on another $100,000 in home-equity loans. A family in the 35 percent federal income tax bracket could realize a savings of $350 for every thousand dollars of mortgage interest they pay during the year. A family in the 15 percent bracket might save $150 for every thousand dollars in mortgage interest they pay. This can result in a nominal savings of thousands of dollars for an upper-bracket taxpayer with a large mortgage. For example, an upper-income family with a $1 million mortgage currently realizes an average annual tax savings of about $21,000 per year.[14] The average deduction though, is only about $1,680 for home owners who itemize.[15] According to some estimates, the cost to the U.S. Treasury of tax deductions for mortgage interest was more than $70 billion in 2005 and will total more than $400 billion over the next five years.[16] This makes the home-mortgage deduction the nation's third-largest tax expenditure behind corporate deductions for employee pensions and health care premiums.

Proponents of the mortgage-interest tax deduction argue that its chief purpose is to encourage home ownership. Though there is not much real evidence to support this proposition, it is often argued that home ownership gives people a stake in the community and the nation, making them better neighbors and better citizens. Thus, the billions of dollars spent annually by the federal government to subsidize home mortgages is said to be a small price to pay for a more peaceful and contented society.[17]

Even if this proposition were true, the current mortgage-interest tax credit does not seem to be the appropriate vehicle for expanding home ownership opportunities. To begin with, nearly 80 percent of the benefits provided by the mortgage-interest deduction and other housing tax credits accrue to the wealthiest 20 percent of Americans. Less than 5 percent of these tax benefits are received by the bottom 60 percent of Americans. About half of all families with residential mortgages receive no tax benefit at all.[18] In other words, those families most likely to own homes without government help receive most of the government's largesse, whereas families who struggle to afford their homes receive little or no assistance from government subsidies. "The people who have the biggest homes, who make the most money are the greatest beneficiaries of this tax subsidy," said Nicholas Retrinas, director of Harvard's Joint Center for Housing Studies. "If you rent you don't get the deduction. Even if you own a home and have a modest income, you're likely to take a standard deduction, which means you don't get it."[19] Some analysts argue that rather than encouraging home ownership, the mortgage subsidy mainly inspires people who could already afford a home to purchase a more expensive one and to borrow heavily against it.[20] Indeed, a number of nations—including Ireland, Britain, Australia, Israel, Japan, and Canada—all have home ownership rates equal to or higher than those in the United States, but none allow mortgage interest to be deducted from their income taxes.[21]

Despite its dubious value as a tool for promoting home ownership, the mortgage-interest deduction is politically almost untouchable, as becomes evident every time its repeal or modification is proposed. In 2005, the presidentially appointed Advisory Panel on Federal Tax Reform proposed eliminating the mortgage-interest deduction and replacing it with a "home credit" that would allow families to reduce their taxes by a flat 15 percent of the interest they paid on their mortgage regardless of their own income. Under the proposal, interest could be deducted on mortgages less than or equal to 125 percent of the median home sales price in that particular county, up to a maximum mortgage of $412,000. The panel proposed making the deduction available to all home owners, whether or not they filed an itemized tax return. The panel also proposed eliminating the mortgage-interest deduction for second homes. Had the proposal been adopted, its effect would have been to provide mortgage assistance to less-affluent families who currently receive none while reducing the tax break available to wealthier home owners. This change would certainly seem consistent with the government's avowed goal of expanding home ownership opportunities. The social benefits of home ownership presumably can be realized on the basis of one home and do not require individuals to occupy two or three residences, as is now sometimes the case.

The panel's proposal, nevertheless, generated a storm of protest from the housing and home-lending industries. "It [the panel's proposal] would have a chilling and potentially devastating effect on home prices across the board," said Bob Davis, executive vice president of America's Community

Bankers, an industry trade association. "I just can't imagine that the support of home ownership for middle-class Americans will be abandoned, especially in the range where the proposed reduction would hit."[22] This sentiment was echoed by Rep. Steve Israel (D-NY), who said, "This is a full-scale assault on middle-class home owners, and we need even at this early moment to indicate to the president that we'll bear any burden to defend against it."[23] Israel represents an affluent Long Island district. After frantic lobbying by the National Association of Home Builders, the National Association of Realtors, the Mortgage Bankers Association, and other trade associations representing the lending and housing industries, the proposal sank without a trace.

Vehement industry opposition to the idea of eliminating the mortgage-interest tax deduction is not difficult to understand. The availability of a tax deduction encourages wealthier Americans to purchase second homes; to purchase more expensive homes; and to borrow against the value of their homes, not only for home improvements but for clothing, jewelry, vacations, and a myriad of other routine expenditures. From the perspective of the housing and lending industries, any cut in the mortgage-interest deduction would threaten their lucrative markets in second homes and home-equity lines of credit and might have a negative impact on home sales and prices, thereby reducing builders', Realtors', and lenders' profits.

The housing industry, though, is not alone in its opposition to elimination of the deduction. Depending, of course, on how the question is posed, surveys indicate that as many as 85 percent of all Americans oppose elimination or modification of the deduction, whereas only 6 percent favor such an action.[24] Such poll numbers helped the housing industry stop the 2005 panel's proposal in its tracks. "I haven't heard anyone on the Hill say it's a good idea," said one industry lobbyist.[25] Most Americans, even those who are not currently eligible for the mortgage-interest deduction, seem to think that they can benefit from its provisions—if not now, then at some future time. Those who are currently able to take advantage of the tax benefit of a residential mortgage fear losing it and fear also that the elimination of the tax benefit could have the effect of lowering housing prices and reducing the value of their home. This is precisely the argument continually made by the housing industry. "Limiting or eliminating tax benefits will have an adverse impact on housing markets and the value of housing," said a spokesman for the Mortgage Bankers Association.[26]

Of course, home owners are entitled to be concerned about the value of their investments, and there is no doubt that some—especially owners of expensive properties—would see a drop in the market value of their houses if the mortgage subsidy were eliminated. This pain for sellers, though, would likely be counterbalanced by the gain for buyers, and eventually the market would adjust to the new reality. The long-term losers from elimination of the deduction would be not home owners but the real estate sellers, mortgage lenders, and home builders who, in effect, currently pocket a multibillion-dollar taxpayer subsidy every year.

Americans think the mortgage-interest deduction is a savings to them, but it is not. The deduction drives up home prices by allowing purchasers to assume larger mortgages. If the subsidy had not existed, most Americans would probably have been able to purchase the same house they currently own at a lower price. The difference between the amount of money Americans borrow with the subsidy and the amount they might have borrowed without the subsidy is a gift from the American taxpayer to the housing industry. Hence, the mortgage tax deduction is a stealth benefit to the housing industry. Americans overwhelmingly support a program they think benefits them, but actually their taxes pay for a program to reward a wealthy industry.

Organizational Bias

Mobilization biases are common—perhaps the norm—in the American policy-making process. Organized interests carry far more weight in political life than ordinary citizens, and politicians will generally sacrifice the interests of the latter for those of the former. This is especially likely to be the case when the citizenry does not see the costs or is not fully cognizant of its stake in a program. Mobilization biases, though, are generally associated with programs developed by Congress. As more and more federal programs come to be products of bureaucratic rather than congresssional decision-making (a point to which we shall return in the next chapter), a second type of policy pathology—organizational bias—has increased in importance.

Bureaucracies are created to give effect to the will of the nation's elected representatives. However, over the decades, the practices of bureaucratic agencies have often reflected their own external or internal interests more than Congress's plans or some broader conception of the public purpose. Two types of organizational interests or biases are especially likely to drive the behavior of bureaucratic agencies. First, agency executives are always concerned with their budget, power, and autonomy vis-à-vis other institutions and political forces.[27] For example, as we saw in Chapter 1, since the creation of the DoD and the CIA in 1947, the secretary of defense and the director of central intelligence have engaged in continual bureaucratic struggle over control of the nation's intelligence assets and budgets. In the 1960s, the DoD created its own unified intelligence arm, the Defense Intelligence Agency (DIA), and ever since that time, the DoD has steadily encroached upon the CIA's turf.[28] In recent years, for example, the DoD has been able to win control of a major CIA asset, the National Reconnaissance Office, which collects intelligence data through satellite imaging and other technological means. President Bush's decision in 2006 to appoint a career U.S. Air Force officer and DoD official, General Michael Hayden, to head the CIA was seen by some agency executives as a further blow to the CIA's autonomy and standing in the intelligence community.

A second type of organizational bias often results from an organization's internal politics. Just as organizations vie with one another, so do factions within an agency compete with rival groups for money, power, and prestige. A particularly important factor in such internal struggles is the agency's definition of its central mission and core responsibilities. For any organization, much follows from the way in which its mission is defined. Alternative definitions of the organization's mission are likely to empower different groups within the agency. Usually, one or another faction within the organization bases its claim to power and preferment upon its particular ability to carry out the agency's core mission. A change in mission might threaten that power. For example, when aircraft carriers were developed, the top commanders of many navies resisted their introduction. These officers had generally built their careers on the command of battleships and other surface combatants and feared that a shift in naval missions and tactics would diminish their influence and empower a rival faction of officers—which was, indeed, what eventually took place.[29] The commitment of a bureaucracy's leaders to the mission that bolsters their own power within the organization is a major reason that bureaucracies often seem reluctant to change their practices and priorities in response to shifts in the external environment. The often-heard claim that armies are always prepared to fight the previous war expresses this idea.

Long-established bureaucratic agencies usually evolve priorities and procedures that advance both the internal and external goals of their leadership cadres. That is, agency executives will identify a mission and set of practices that justify their own agency's budgetary claims and power vis-à-vis other institutions while simultaneously reinforcing the established structure of power within the agency itself. Over time, this mission and associated practices can become so deeply ingrained in the minds of agency executives and staffers that adherence to it becomes a matter of habit and reflex. Students of bureaucracy refer to this set of established pattern of practices and beliefs about the organization's role and purpose as the agency's institutional "culture."[30]

James Q. Wilson has observed, "Every organization has a culture ... a persistent, patterned way of thinking about the central tasks of and human relationships within an organization. Culture is to an organization what personality is to an individual ... it is passed from one generation to the next. It changes slowly, if at all."[31] Agency cultures are sometimes born with agencies' original missions, the personalities of their early leaders, and the character of their earliest supporters. Once established, agency cultures can be remarkably resistant to change as agencies recruit employees and executives thought to be sympathetic to the agency's values and, for good measure, subject them to a lengthy process of training and indoctrination.

Military indoctrination—including the curricula of the service academies and the training practices of the so-called boot camps endured by new recruits—has become the stuff of folklore and the topic of many popular films. The new recruit, whether officer or enlisted person, is subjected to an intense period of indoctrination aimed, in large measure, at imbuing him or her with the culture and traditions of the service in question. Marine recruits are subjected to a week of "disorientation" designed to sever their ties to civilian life and then are taught the values of the corps. According to one authority, "To be in the Corps is to be in a state of mind that dictates one's relationship to the rest of the world."[32] Although civilian bureaucracies do not run boot camps, most conduct orientation programs, and some, most notably the U.S. Forest Service, approach military methods in their efforts to ensure the loyalty of new personnel.[33]

Many agencies seem incredibly dedicated to missions defined long ago. The U.S. Fish and Wildlife Service (USFWS), for example, was created in the nineteenth century to protect and conserve the nation's animal species and still does so today, generally disregarding other economic and social interests. In recent years, the USFWS has worked to return wolves and grizzly bears to the Northwest, even though these animals represent an economic and even physical threat to individuals engaged in ranching and recreational pursuits in the region.[34] Often a cataclysmic event is required to alter an agency's long-established culture or sense of mission. For example, during the early 1980s, the U.S. Coast Guard, which viewed itself as a quasi-military force, finally accepted the idea that boating safety and environmental protection were within the scope of its mission—but only after the agency was moved from the U.S. Treasury Department to the Department of Transportation and then to the Department of Homeland

Security, provided with new leadership, given a new statutory base, and subjected to several presidential orders.[35]

All agencies, civilian as well as military, are almost certain to resist efforts to compel them to undertake activities that are foreign to their institutional cultures and thus seem to pose a threat to their institutional autonomy or internal balance of power. Seidman averred that attempts to compel agencies to engage in such activities are usually futile. "Alien transplants," he wrote, "seldom take root" and are continually "threatened with rejection."[36] For example, numerous congressional efforts to compel Fannie Mae, a quasi-public government-sponsored enterprise, to provide loans to low-income families have failed to affect the agency's behavior. Despite its public charter, Fannie Mae conceives itself to be a commercial enterprise with a duty to operate in as profitable a manner as possible. Loans to poor borrowers who lack creditworthiness do not comport with this sense of mission and are constantly—and successfully—resisted by the agency in spite of congressional pressure.[37]

In the case of civilian agencies, top executives are, of course, appointed by the president, who may endeavor to use the appointment process to impose new priorities and even entirely new missions on established organizations. Nevertheless, presidential appointees whose ideas are inconsistent with an agency's culture and sense of purpose are almost certain to encounter stiff resistance, sometimes verging on mutiny, from their nominal subordinates. For example, Richard Nixon's efforts to appoint executives who would change the behavior of several domestic social and regulatory agencies, including the EPA, sparked a series of agency revolts that included leaks to Congress and the media by senior staffers. Nixon's attempt to plug these leaks with the creation of the "plumbers' squad" helped bring about the Watergate scandal and Nixon's ouster from office.[38]

Organizational Culture: The Case of the Military

The issues posed by organizational culture are especially pronounced in the case of military institutions. Although every bureaucracy has a distinctive culture and its own sense of mission, the cultures of the military services are likely to be more sharply defined and more resistant to change than those of their civilian counterparts. Military cultures are, in part, forged in battle and reinforced by distinctive uniforms and patterns of indoctrination. A former chairman of the Joint Chiefs of Staff, General David Jones, observed that the services "find it difficult to adapt to changing conditions because of understandable attachments to the past. The very foundation of each service rests on imbuing its members with pride in its mission, its doctrines and its customs and discipline—all of which are steeped in traditions."[39]

Critics, including military insiders, have often accused the Pentagon of rigidity and inability to innovate. Former Defense Secretary James Schlesinger, for example, described the military bureaucracy as a "remarkably efficient mechanism for the suppression of new ideas."[40] Although change may be forced upon the military during wartime, critics charge that the military services in times of peace are more concerned with order and discipline than with military effectiveness. The services, according to their critics, tend to promote officers who conform while frustrating those who show imagination or creativity. Admiral Elmo Zumwalt, a former chief of naval operations who was himself known as an innovator, once averred that officers who rose to the top ranks of the services tended to be those who accepted established orthodoxies rather than officers who had the temerity to question or challenge entrenched service doctrines.[41]

Despite these criticisms, it seems clear that the military services do continually modify their weapons, tactics, and force structures. Indeed, innovations that promote or at least do not challenge a service's long-established understanding of its mission have every chance of success in America's contemporary military environment. The military services have been extraordinarily innovative in recent years, developing and acquiring such a dazzling array of sophisticated new weapons that some analysts have claimed we are witnessing another "revolution in military affairs" driven by computers, precision-guided munitions, battlefield sensors, and remotely operated weapons.[42] As Richard Stubbing observed, far from resisting innovation, since World War II, each military service, "within its established doctrine and tactics, has been pushing for ever more advanced weapons and equipment incorporating state-of-the-art technology."[43]

If, however, a military service is confronted by demands from its civilian overseers or other internal or external forces to adopt policies, procedures, weapons, and tactics that are *not* clearly consistent with the service's understanding of its own role and mission, it is likely to resist. Such resistance will manifest itself even if the proposed innovation may serve broader military goals and national interests so long as the service's leaders view the external demands as threats to their organization's autonomy or internal balance of power. One fascinating contemporary example of this phenomenon is the case of the U.S. Air Force and the A-10 attack plane, a craft that served broad military interests but represented a serious threat to the bureaucratic autonomy, internal balance of power, and general organizational culture of the air force.

The organizational culture of the U.S. Air Force: victory through air-power. Nations are often affected by the condition of their founding, and perhaps the same is true for military services. The U.S. Air Force was created in 1947, when the Army Air Corps broke away from the U.S. Army. Much of the subsequent history of the air force is linked to its desire to maintain its hard-won autonomy, and especially to its intense focus on blocking anything that seemed to indicate a renewed subordination to the army.[44] Even today, air force officers complain bitterly if they perceive what they regard as external—especially army—interference with the use of airpower. For example, during the 2002 Afghan War, senior air force officers made public their unhappiness over the fact that an army general, Tommy Franks, leader of the U.S. Central Command, had the authority to make decisions about air force bombing missions in Afghanistan. Air generals claimed that Franks's interference had undermined the effectiveness of their bombing campaign, though some junior air force officers speaking off the record said this charge was inaccurate.[45] Air force leaders were also incensed that civilian CIA operatives were intruding on the air force's turf by launching their own air strikes against Taliban and al-Qaeda targets.[46] The CIA controls a fleet of Predator drone aircraft armed with Hellfire missiles that engaged in a number of combat sorties. "Something would happen and we would say, 'What was that?'" said one air force officer, complaining that his service should at least have been notified in advance if the CIA planned an air strike.[47]

The air force's concern for independence helps to explain its devotion to a particular military doctrine—the strategy of airpower. This doctrine asserts that command of the air is a necessary and sufficient condition for national military success. This doctrine was first put forward in the 1920s by an Italian military strategist, Giulio Douhet, who wrote, "To conquer the command of the air means victory; to be beaten in the air means defeat and the acceptance of whatever terms the enemy may be pleased to impose."[48] Douhet's ideas were elaborated and popularized in the United States by a Russian émigré, aircraft designer, and World War II Army Air Corps officer, Major Alexander de Seversky. De Seversky's book, *Victory Through Air Power,* became a best seller; a Disney film; and, along with Douhet's book, required reading for all air corps officers.[49] De Seversky wrote, "We cannot ... dream of conquering the enemy without first capturing dominance in the air—once we have a clearcut dominance in the air, all else becomes a secondary, subordinate, auxiliary operation."[50] De Seversky went on to argue that a separate air force was a "precondition for successful modern warfare."[51]

Douhet and de Seversky provided the theoretical underpinnings for the army air corps's demand for independence from the army and for the strategic doctrines developed by air corps leaders such as the famous Billy Mitchell, who demonstrated the efficacy of air attack against naval targets. The most important of these doctrines was the concept of strategic bombardment. During World War II, air corps leaders argued that heavy bombardment of the German and Japanese homelands would destroy both enemies' industrial bases and their will to carry on the war. Indeed, air generals such as Jimmy Doolittle, Hap Arnold, and George Kenney asserted that strategic bombardment by itself could defeat the Germans and Japanese and, accordingly, should become the chief American military strategy.[52]

During the course of the war, the heavy losses inflicted upon unescorted American bombers by German interceptors convinced the air generals that bombers needed fighter escorts to successfully carry out their missions. Fighters also, of course, served to intercept enemy bombers on their way to Allied targets. Thus were born the two main elements of today's air force—the strategic bomber, which may now be armed with cruise missiles rather than bombs, and the air superiority fighter designed to defeat enemy fighters in air-to-air combat as well as to destroy enemy bombers. This latter role became especially important during the early years of the Cold War, when the main threat facing the United States was deemed to be nuclear-armed Soviet intercontinental bombers. Eventually, within the air force, the swift and glamorous fighter came to have more importance than the ponderous bomber. Indeed, some observers suggest that the contemporary air force is run by a "fighter mafia," a group of generals who are former fighter pilots and view the air superiority fighter as the primary, rather than secondary, manifestation of airpower.[53]

Douhet and de Seversky continue to be read to this day by junior air force officers. Successive generations learn that the twin mission of the air force is strategic bombardment and the destruction of enemy air forces that stand in the way of American control of the skies. Interestingly, postwar studies strongly suggested that strategic bombardment was not a major factor in America's victory in World War II.[54] And in the Korean War and the Vietnam conflict, strategic bombardment was of marginal significance. The Strategic Air Command, to be sure, was very eager to find a role in the Vietnam War and flew a number of B-52 missions in South Vietnam and Laos. These bombing missions, however, had little military impact and, according to ground commanders, had a more profound effect upon local monkey and parrot populations than upon the enemy.[55] The air force's commitment to the doctrine of strategic bombardment, however, was too strong to be shaken by empirical evidence. The use of better aircraft and more powerful weapons, the generals averred, would prove Douhet and de

Seversky correct. Accordingly, in all of America's recent conflicts, including the two Persian Gulf wars, the campaign against Serbia—which was waged almost exclusively as an air campaign—and the war in Afghanistan, leaders of the air force have sought to make strategic bombardment—under their own control—the centerpiece of American military strategy.[56]

Close air support or duplicitous deployment? The case of the A-10. The air force's commitment to the doctrine of airpower unfortunately can become a military liability when it leads to lack of cooperation with civilian authorities and the other military services in combat operations. It is generally recognized that modern warfare requires "combined arms"—that is, a coordinated effort among different types of forces.[57] Coordination, however, can become problematic when the various forces involved have their own doctrines and chains of command. Prior to the seventeenth century, infantry, artillery, and cavalry typically operated in separate units under separate officers often drawn from disparate social strata. Each followed its own battle plans, coordinated, if at all, by only the most senior officers on the battlefield.[58] In the modern era, the most difficult problems of coordination have involved relationships between armies and air forces. In principle, airpower can vastly increase the effectiveness of ground troops by providing what is known as "close air support." This support consists of attacking enemy forces, including enemy artillery and tanks, to pave the way for the advance of ground forces. The effectiveness of close air support was demonstrated by the German attack on France in 1940. In this campaign, the Germans employed Stuka dive-bombers to attack French positions at the Meuse River in coordination with and in advance of German infantry and armor, disrupting French communications, suppressing French artillery fire, and allowing the Germans to move quickly without waiting for their own artillery and ammunition.[59]

Though the value of close air support seems undeniable, in practice, the necessary level of coordination between ground and air forces has been extremely difficult to achieve. Typically, ground and air forces have distinctive cultures and understandings of their missions as well as different command structures. Air generals know that close air support is among the most dangerous missions their pilots can undertake. To provide air support for ground forces, pilots are forced to operate at low speeds and at altitudes where they are exceptionally vulnerable to ground fire and often incur heavy casualties. For example, of the 115 aircraft lost by the Israelis during the 1973 Arab-Israeli War, most were shot down by surface-to-air guns and missiles while flying close air support missions.[60] Air generals also view close air support as a diversion from their true mission of strategic bombardment and the attainment of supremacy in the skies. Despite their success at the Meuse, this was true even for the Germans. Although German air and ground operations were more closely coordinated than has been the case in many other armies, the German army had no direct control over the operations of the Luftwaffe, which had its own doctrines and mission priorities.[61] A ground commander who sought air support was required to transmit his request up the chain of command. At the division level, the request would be forwarded to the air force, where it would be transmitted down the chain of command to the Stuka pilots who would actually fly the mission. By the time the Luftwaffe responded, if it did at all, the ground situation had usually changed substantially.[62]

Similar problems hampered the coordination of American air and ground units during World War II. Though still nominally part of the army, the air corps viewed its central mission as strategic bombardment of Germany and, later, Japan. Other priorities defined by the air corps included air superiority and interdiction of enemy supply lines. Close air support of American and Allied ground forces in contact with the enemy was given the very lowest priority for the assignment of air corps personnel and resources.[63] As was the case in the German air force, ground commanders seeking air support were required to forward their requests up the chain of command, where they were given to senior air corps leaders who would decide whether or not the requested mission represented an appropriate use of air assets. Response time to a request for air support could be several hours. The air corps strongly resisted army requests that the control of aircraft be decentralized and that ground commanders be given operational control of air missions. Some individual air corps generals, such as Elwood Quesada, who commanded the Ninth Air Force in France after the Normandy invasion, saw the importance of air-ground cooperation.[64] For the most part, though, the air corps high command was "fundamentally opposed to the role" of close air support, refusing even to develop and acquire aircraft specifically designed for that purpose.[65] From the perspective of the air corps, close air support subordinated the corps's role to that of the ground commander and thus was to be eschewed if possible.

The same issues surrounded close air support during the wars in Korea and Vietnam. By the time of the Korean War, the air force was an independent service and even more reluctant than before to subordinate its missions to the needs of army ground commanders. The air force insisted that army requests for close air support be forwarded to the command of a "numbered" air force. This level is more or less equivalent to an army's division command.

From this level, the request would be sent to a wing commander and then to a squadron commander for action. Average response time was forty-five minutes.[66] This air force insistence on centralized control meant that air strikes often were useless by the time they were actually undertaken. The marines, by contrast, did not face issues of interservice conflict and received excellent close air support. The marines relied upon their own service's navy and marine flyers operating from aircraft carriers stationed in the Sea of Japan. Unlike the air force, the navy decentralized control of air operations, allowing ground commanders to directly call air group (an intermediate level between an air force wing and squadron) or even squadron commanders for support. Marine and naval aircraft also maintained air patrols over the battlefield in order to be ready to provide a swift response to such requests. As a result, the average response time for a marine request for close air support was five minutes.[67]

Ironically, later in the war, the air force succeeded in placing marine air missions under its own centralized control. This change had the effect of increasing marine response time to the air force's forty-five-minute average. During the war, ground commanders developed enormous animosity toward the air force. For example, when General MacArthur launched his combined marine-army landings at Inchon in September 1950, he ordered all air force planes excluded from the airspace over the invasion area and gave exclusive close air support duties to Marine Air Group 33.[68]

In Vietnam, air force and marine operations paralleled the Korean War pattern. Marine and navy jets flew over combat zones in what were called "on-station, on-call" missions to provide support within minutes to marine ground force commanders.[69] The marines and navy also developed equipment and tactics providing all-weather and nighttime close air support capabilities. The air force, by contrast, assigned close air support a low priority and insisted that preplanned strikes against enemy positions were more effective than on-call, close air support at the request of ground commanders. The air force refused to keep jets on station and declined to provide its aircraft with all-weather air support capabilities. This lack of air force support was enormously frustrating to army ground commanders, who believed that it reduced their effectiveness relative to that of the marines.[70] The air force solution to this complaint was to demand that all air operations, including those of the navy and marines, be brought under its control under the concept of "single management." Although the air force was not interested in providing close air support to ground forces, it was vitally interested in the notion of air force primacy in the skies. After an intense political struggle, the air force convinced DoD officials and

President Lyndon Johnson to back its position.[71] After March 1968, single management became the rule. As in Korea, the result was an increase in response times for all air missions to more than forty-five minutes and a drop in the effectiveness of air support.[72] Frustrated by lack of air support, the army proposed that it be allowed to design its own aircraft for close air support missions and to control them in combat. The air force strongly resisted, insisting that it could do a much better job, and prevailed after a struggle in Congress. Later, one air force officer admitted, "We accepted those missions solely to keep them away from the army. We had no intention of sinking our budget into things we didn't like."[73]

Events in Korea and Vietnam, as well as the success of the marine corps, convinced the army that it would have to continue to search for its own sources of close air support despite opposition from the air force. The 1947 Key West Accords, defining the division of responsibilities among the military services, prohibited the army from operating fixed-wing combat aircraft. However, a new technological development opened the possibility of creating army-controlled close air support that did not depend upon fixed-wing aircraft. This development was, of course, the helicopter. In 1962, the DoD had commissioned a study under the direction of General Hamilton Howze to deal with issues of army aviation, including the problem of close air support. The army had hoped that the Howze commission would recommend abrogation of the Key West prohibition of fixed-wing aircraft. However, Howze, a former helicopter pilot, recommended instead that the army develop a fleet of rotary-wing helicopters—not covered by the Key West agreement—to meet its aviation needs. The army had used helicopters in Korea for air evacuation of wounded soldiers and, on a limited basis, for the transport of troops and supplies. Howze, though, recommended that the army arm its helicopters and build an air fleet capable of providing close air support for its own ground troops.[74]

In response to the Howze report and to its needs in Vietnam, the army began a massive buildup of attack helicopters, deploying thousands of armed UH-1 helicopters, which provided the army with a close support force of its own. The air force initially protested when the army began to arm its helicopters, asserting that this tactic represented a violation of the spirit, if not the letter, of the Key West agreement. However, the air force did not object too vigorously because it saw the clumsy and lightly armed UH-1s as essentially not worthy of an airman's interest. The UH-1 was slow and so vulnerable to ground fire that many were downed by North Vietnamese and Vietcong soldiers armed with rifles. From the air force's perspective, the UH-1 represented no threat to its own control of the skies. The army also recognized the limitations of the UH-1 and moved to develop a more effective attack helicopter. In the late 1960s, the army tested the Cheyenne helicopter, which proved a failure, and began development of the AH-64 Apache helicopter, a heavily armed, armored, and high-speed craft. The Apache was the first helicopter specifically designed for close air support and represented a qualitative leap over its predecessors.[75]

Improvements in army helicopter design and performance began to concern the air force. As army helicopters became more sophisticated, they began to pose a threat to air force air supremacy and to the air force's budget. Air force planners feared that Congress would give the army billions of dollars for helicopters that might have been awarded to the air force for its aviation programs. Accordingly, in 1970, the air force announced plans to develop a new ground-attack aircraft that would provide close air support more effectively and efficiently than the army's helicopters. The air force's friends in Congress pushed for funding, and the result was the Fairchild A-10, which came to be known as the "Warthog" because of its somewhat ungainly appearance.

First put into production in the mid-1970s, the A-10 was one of the most effective—and cost-effective—ground-attack aircraft ever built by the United States or any other nation. An A-10 is cheaper than an Apache helicopter and less vulnerable to ground fire or other aircraft. The plane operates at subsonic speeds to make it an effective ground-attack instrument. It has a long range and can "loiter" over the battlefield, waiting for ground-attack missions. The craft is heavily armored to withstand ground fire. Indeed, the pilot literally sits in a titanium tub designed to provide protection against the ground fire expected at low altitudes. The A-10's weapons include air-to-ground missiles and a 30-millimeter Gatling gun armed with depleted-uranium armor-piercing bullets that can penetrate the armor of any tank.[76] During the first Persian Gulf War, the A-10 proved devastating against Iraqi tanks, even though pilots complained that the air force doctrine of centralized mission control continued to prevent them from coordinating their attacks with the needs of ground commanders.[77]

The development of the A-10 would seem to be an example of successful military innovation. Despite its concerns about subordination to army missions, the air force developed and built a plane to provide close air support for ground forces. Yet appearances can be deceiving. The air force developed the A-10 because it was concerned about the success of the army's helicopter program, not because it actually wanted to provide close air support. In a sense, the enemy the A-10 was designed to defeat was the U.S. Army, not some foreign power. And unfortunately, from the air force's perspective, the A-10 was a dismal failure. The aircraft might have no difficulty destroying enemy tanks, but it was unable to block the use of U.S. Army helicopters. Although the army had proclaimed its satisfaction with the A-10 program, it was not prepared to place all its trust in the air force. So, despite the A-10, the army persuaded Congress to appropriate $10 billion for its Apache helicopter program.

The air force responded by attempting to rid itself of what it now saw as a useless weapon. Originally, air force plans appeared to call for ten or more A-10 wings, but only five were ever produced. One of these wings was quickly moved to the Air National Guard. Indeed, in an unprecedented move, the first seventy-two A-10s to come off the production line were sent directly to the Air National Guard.[78] Before the Persian Gulf War intervened, air force plans called for the other A-10 wings to also be sent to the national guard and reserves.[79] The A-10 performed impressively during the first Persian Gulf War, but the plane's proven effectiveness served only to increase the air force's fear that it would come under pressure from Congress and the army to acquire more Warthogs.[80] After the war, the air force lost no time in resuming its plans to shift all the A-10s out of the active-duty air force and into the reserves and guard units. During the second Gulf War, many A-10s were flown in combat by female reservists. Ironically, air force officials had long fought against allowing women to fly combat missions but were willing to allow women to fly close air support missions—arguably the most dangerous of all military duties. In a sense, the air force had put two of its problems in the same package.

In addition, the air force began reconfiguring its remaining A-10s for the mission of forward air control while claiming that modified F-16s—which the air force renamed A-16s—could provide any close air support needed by the army. The designation "A" indicates a craft designed for ground attack, whereas "F" denotes a fighter aircraft. The change of designation, however, did not make the F-(or A-)16 a suitable plane for ground attack. Close air support requires an aircraft that is capable of operating at slow speeds and low altitudes. Even in the era of "smart" bombs, munitions dropped from high altitudes can be inaccurate and may threaten friendly forces—as the "friendly fire" casualties incurred in Afghanistan and Iraq illustrate. Despite its new name, the A-16 was still a supersonic, high-altitude fighter. In response to this attempted sleight of hand, both the Senate and House Armed Services Committees accused the air force of ignoring the need to modernize its close air support capabilities.[81]

Eventually, the air force found a way to eliminate the A-10. It agreed to cooperate with the navy and the British Royal Air Force in the development of a new aircraft, dubbed the joint strike fighter (JSF). This aircraft was to meet the demands of the American and British militaries for a craft that would function as an interceptor, an air superiority fighter, a light bomber, and an attack plane. One version of the JSF, to be used by the marines, would be a two-seat aircraft, designed to fly at subsonic speeds and capable of vertical takeoff and landing like the British Harrier now used by marine pilots. For its part, the air force has asserted that the JSF will replace the A-10 as a ground-attack aircraft capable of providing close air support and has announced plans to finally retire all its remaining A-10s.

It should be noted, however, that the version of the JSF ordered by the air force is a supersonic fighter. This alone suggests that it is probably not really intended for a ground-attack role but is actually intended to replace the F-16 fighter. Indeed, the air force has admitted as much, declaring that the JSF "will be measured by the high standards set by the F-16."[82] Unfortunately, from the perspective of the optimal provision of close air support, the standards set by the F-16 are a bit too high. In the realm of close air support, said Colonel Hans Rudel, a German World War II Stuka pilot credited with destroying more than 500 Soviet tanks and a pioneer in the techniques of ground attack, "speed is poison."[83] An aircraft capable of providing close air support should be designed for low-speed performance rather than high-speed maneuvers. It would appear that the air force is simply using the JSF to rid itself of the A-10s.

Thus, the development of the A-10 represented a strategy of deception rather than a military innovation. The air force hoped to blunt army plans to expand attack helicopter capabilities and, with great fanfare, announced that it would develop and deploy an attack plane far deadlier than the army's Apaches. When this ploy failed and the army continued its helicopter deployment, the air force worked to rid itself of an aircraft that was now useless from its perspective. Viewing close air support as a mission that involved subordination to the army, and viewing the A-10 as a threat to its "fighter mafia," the air force was unwilling to actually give in to pressure to innovate in the realm of weapons and tactics for this purpose. Instead, it resorted to the bureaucratic tactic of deceptive deployment—a move hardly likely to further the nation's military interests.

Organizational Interests and Public Interests

The story of the A-10 may seem an extreme case, but organizational biases of this sort are common and can produce quite expensive and damaging political and social consequences. Take, for example, the "war on drugs" that the U.S. government has been waging, in different forms, for the past several decades. Since the enactment of the 1914 Harrison Narcotics Act, effectively outlawing the sale of opiates and cocaine, and the 1937 Marijuana Act, prohibiting the sale and possession of cannabis, federal and state law enforcement officials have waged an enormously expensive and fruitless effort to prevent the distribution and use of these drugs. Efforts to prevent the production of the drugs, to interdict their importation into the United States, to interfere with their distribution, and to block their possession and use have all proven to be expensive failures. For every ton of drugs destroyed or seized by law enforcement officials, a hundred other tons are distributed and sold. For every drug dealer arrested, a hundred others are ready to risk punishment in the hope of turning a profit. Targeting one drug, such as cocaine, has prompted producers to develop new drugs, such as methamphetamines. The major effect of unrelenting federal law enforcement activities has been the imprisonment of tens of thousands of petty drug criminals at great expense; endemic corruption problems within government and law enforcement agencies; and, even worse, the creation of a black market dominated by violent regional, national, and even international drug gangs that pose an ever-growing threat to public order and safety.[84]

Of course, the same lessons were learned during the 1920s when the United States sought to ban the sale and consumption of alcoholic beverages. Prohibition was an enormously expensive failure, which corrupted law enforcement agencies and helped fuel the rise of violent criminal gangs that plagued American society for decades. Eventually, prohibition was repealed and the consumption of alcoholic beverages subjected to taxation and regulation. Although this meant that alcohol consumption and abuse would become permanent features of American life, it was generally recognized that the attempted cure had only increased the virulence of the disease. The same is clearly true for drugs. Like alcohol abuse, drug abuse is a scourge that can be somewhat mitigated by education and regulation but is only made worse by efforts at prohibition.

Why have the rather obvious lessons derived from alcohol prohibition not been applied to the case of drugs? One reason is organizational bias. To fight the war on drugs, the United States established or expanded a set of agencies that currently spend $12.5 billion annually in their fruitless and hapless efforts to eliminate drug use. These include the Drug Enforcement Administration (DEA), with an annual budget of more than $2 billion; the National Institute on Drug Abuse, with an annual budget of about $1 billion; the Substance Abuse Administration, with a $2.4 billion budget; and the Office of National Drug Control Policy (ONDCP), headed by the presidentially appointed "drug czar," charged with developing and coordinating all U.S. drug-control programs.

These and other drug-control agencies have an obvious and enormous stake in the war on drugs and, over the years, have engaged in a campaign of lobbying, public information, and even intimidation to promote continuation or expansion of current antidrug efforts and to discredit proponents of alternative approaches. Thus, for example, the ONDCP has used federal tax dollars to fight state ballot measures aimed at legalizing the medical use of marijuana.[85] In a similar vein, drug-control officials have sought to prevent the collection of data that might undermine their programs by supporting congressional legislation that would have prohibited all federal agencies from conducting or financing any research involving the legalization of drugs, including research on the possible medical use of marijuana.[86] And the ONDCP has attempted to discredit critics of the drug war by accusing them of seeking to put dangerous drugs in the hands of America's children. According to former drug czar Barry R. McCaffrey, those who advocate alternative approaches to drug abuse "want drugs made widely available, in chewing gum and sodas, over the Internet and at the corner store, even though this would be tantamount to putting drugs in the hands of children."[87] Few politicians, legislators, public officials, or even academic specialists want to be accused of allowing children to acquire addictive drugs. As a result, criticism of America's foolish drug policies has been muted, and an organizational bias has continued to dominate this important policy arena.

Private Capture

A third common policy pathology is associated with the government's growing reliance upon private entities to administer public programs. Privatization is one way of putting the market to work for the government. It introduces competitive bidding into public programs and thereby avoids the supposed inefficiencies of the government's monopoly on public services. But privatization is not just a way to get the most for the taxpayer's dollar. It is also an instrument for achieving privileged access to power, and once achieved, that power is sometimes exercised to impose additional costs on American taxpayers.

In the United States, privatization rarely means the outright sale of public assets to private purchasers. There have been exceptions—for instance, the sale of public lands to settlers and their transfer as a subsidy to railroads and, more recently, the sale of the government's interest in Conrail. In most cases, however, privatization refers to the use of nongovernmental organizations to run government programs.[88] Today, almost every federal agency relies heavily on private contractors. Although the federal government directly employs fewer than two million civilian workers, one recent study estimates that more than twelve million Americans are employed by a "shadow government" of private corporations, universities, research laboratories, foundations, and state and municipal governments that hold government contracts, receive federal grants, or are required to carry out federal mandates.[89] Many federal agencies have responded to presidential and congressional efforts to "downsize" their workforces by replacing civil service workers with contract employees. Between 1984 and 1996, for example, the Department of Education, in response to presidential directives, reduced its civil service workforce by 6 percent. During the same period, however, the agency's contract workforce increased by 129 percent.[90] In this case, downsizing actually meant growth.

A number of federal agencies could barely function without the support of this shadow government. The Department of Energy (DOE), for example, employs fewer than 17,000 actual civil servants while relying upon an army of 150,000 contract employees who work for private sector and not-for-profit entities with DOE contracts.[91] Increasingly, however, even the monitoring of contractors is being contracted out to private auditing and accounting firms.

The government's use of nongovernmental organizations to administer its programs is intended to promote a number of public interests. Private sector firms radiate a capitalist halo of competitive spirit, efficiency, flexibility, and discipline.[92] Voluntary and not-for-profit agencies, on the other hand, are supposed to bring a sense of mission to their missions.[93] Both are viewed as antidotes to the tired, bureaucratic inertia of "big government."[94]

When the private organizations performing public services are profit-seeking companies, an overriding preoccupation with the bottom line may divert them from the public purposes of the benefits that they sell. They do not see themselves as providing citizens with assistance to which they are entitled by virtue of their membership in the American political community. They are simply selling a product to customers to whom they have no obligation beyond the exchange of a fee for a service. These customers need feel no connection with one another. They are "buying alone," to paraphrase Robert Putnam. Detaching them from their government also separates them from their political community and may reduce their sense of commitment to public authority itself. As customers of a private service provider, after all, they have only an indirect business relationship with government.

Not-for-profit organizations generally have a high level of commitment to the programs they administer and are less likely than for-profit firms to place revenue considerations ahead of service provision. But nonprofit organizations have their own social and political goals. A mandate from the government often allows such groups to use public power and resources to achieve what are essentially private aims. When nongovernmental organizations, whether for profit or nonprofit, are used as vehicles for government programs, the danger is that they will displace the public agenda with one of their own.

Finally, whether privatization devolves government functions to profit-seeking or nonprofit organizations, its effect may be the political demobilization of would-be activists. A government contract can bring influence over public policy that might otherwise have been generated by rousing a public constituency. For nonprofit groups, in fact, a contract can make the mobilization of support unnecessary. The organization now has a source of income that does not come from grassroots adherents, and its agenda of responsibilities now includes tasks other than agitation. As a social service provider, moreover, the nonprofit may also call for a new kind of activism from its members. Instead of assembling them for rallies, marches, protests, and letter-writing campaigns, it now recruits them as community service volunteers who turn away from the frustrating mission of trying to influence the government to the more immediate gratification of personal democracy—doing good directly. The new voluntarism, as David Wagner pointed out, represents "the encapsulation of oppositional groups within the landscape of social service and therapeutic endeavors."[95]

Government-Sponsored Enterprises

Among the most important but least understood private vehicles of public policy are government-sponsored enterprises (GSEs). As we saw in Chapter 2, the GSEs are privately owned, profit-making corporations created by the government to make credit available to borrowers and markets designated by Congress. Though federally chartered for specific purposes, the GSEs have boards of directors, sell shares on the open market, compete with other private firms, and try to reward their shareholders with dividends. Because a GSE was created by the government with a mission defined by Congress, it represents one of the most "public" vehicles of privatization. Its history demonstrates that even when private organizations are so closely tied to government purposes, they can use their public powers to pursue private purposes of their own.

The best-known of the GSEs are the Federal National Mortgage Corporation (Fannie Mae) and the Federal Home Loan Mortgage Corporation (Freddie Mac). The others are the Student Loan Marketing Association (Sallie Mae), the Farm Credit System (FCS), the Federal Home Loan Bank (FHLB) System, and the Federal Agricultural Credit Corporation (Farmer Mac). The GSEs are among the nation's largest banking institutions, collectively controlling assets of nearly $3 trillion. Fannie Mae alone is currently the nation's twenty-sixth-largest business enterprise in terms of revenues and ranks third in total assets. Each of these six GSEs was originally established to overcome perceived flaws in credit markets.[96] The FCS, for example, was organized in 1916 to enhance the availability of credit in rural areas, which were then isolated from the nation's financial centers.[97] Fannie Mae was chartered in 1938 as part of an effort to create a secondary market for residential mortgages, thus encouraging financially weak, Depression-era banks to make loans available to home purchasers. Fannie Mae was a wholly owned government corporation until 1968, when it was converted into a GSE. Sallie Mae was established in 1972 to increase the supply of tuition loans to college students, a market that many commercial banks had avoided. Today, rather than compensating for perceived market failures, the GSEs operate to provide off-budget subsidies to specific groups favored by Congress.[98]

Though there are individual variations, the GSEs operate in similar ways. To begin with, GSEs raise money in the credit markets by issuing bonds and mortgage-backed securities. In principle, GSE bonds and securities, unlike U.S. Treasury and other government bonds, are not backed by the formal promise of the U.S. government to repay investors. Because of the GSEs' quasi-governmental standing, however, investors treat their securities as though they were backed by the full faith and credit of the U.S. government. This perception allows the GSEs to borrow money at a rate only slightly higher than that paid by the U.S. Treasury itself and substantially below the rate paid by commercial institutions. GSEs also benefit from exemption from state and local taxes and from a variety of other valuable privileges normally enjoyed by federal agencies. According to Federal Reserve Board Chairman Alan Greenspan, lower borrowing costs and tax exemptions are worth $6 billion per year to Fannie Mae and Freddie Mac alone.[99]

The GSEs use the funds that they borrow to make loans to private lending institutions that issue mortgages to home buyers, credit to farmers, and tuition loans to college students. These institutions borrow from the GSEs at a rate higher than the GSEs' cost of funds, and the profit generated by this difference has provided a comfortable return for the GSEs and their investors. Fannie Mae, for example, produced a 25 percent return on equity in 1998, and Freddie Mac earned nearly 23 percent.[100] The GSEs also provide primary lenders with a secondary market for their loan portfolios, further encouraging them to extend credit to borrowers. By the end of 1999, Fannie Mae and Freddie Mac together owned single-family mortgage loans worth nearly $550 billion and representing 47 percent of all conventional single-family mortgages in the United States.[101]

Generally speaking, the GSEs have successfully carried out their primary missions of enhancing the availability of credit to defined classes of borrowers. But public purposes often get sidelined in private corporations, even those sponsored by government. To begin with, the GSEs are primarily responsible to their shareholders, not the government, and they regard the president, Congress, and regulatory agencies as interlopers in their affairs.[102] The president appoints a minority block of directors to each GSE's board—five of eighteen directors in the case of Fannie Mae. But the duties of these presidentially appointed directors are unclear. Though they may seem to represent the public's interests, their fiduciary responsibility is actually to the shareholders rather than to the public at large.[103] Where public directors have sought to question a government corporation's practices, they have often been frozen out of decision-making processes and, in some instances, not even notified of board and committee meetings.[104] GSEs are less accountable to the Congress than almost any other government-sponsored organizations. In general, the most effective instrument of congressional control is the power of the purse. But the GSEs have purses of their own. They finance their own activities through the profits they earn on their operations.[105] Government regulations are no more effective. Federal regulatory agencies have limited statutory power over the GSEs and often find themselves politically unable to exercise the few powers they possess.[106]

Limited public accountability means that Congress and the president have scarcely any leverage to induce GSEs to carry out missions inconsistent with their central goal of financial profitability. For example, despite congressional legislation and pressure from the Department of Housing and Urban Development (HUD), both Fannie Mae and Freddie Mac have been slow to amend their lending standards in ways that might increase the availability of conventional mortgages to minority and working-class borrowers.[107] Instead, according to critics, both GSEs have sought to push such borrowers into the so-called subprime market, where they are charged substantially higher mortgage rates. Since Fannie and Freddie lend money to subprime lenders, they may actually profit from the discrimination against subprime borrowers.[108] In addition, despite recurrent criticism from Congress, federal regulatory agencies, and consumer advocates, the GSEs have refused to pass along to consumers the borrowing, tax, and regulatory advantages that go with their quasi-governmental status. According to a study by the Congressional Budget Office, Fannie Mae and Freddie Mac retain for their shareholders approximately one-third of the subsidies they receive from the federal government.[109] Sallie Mae, according to analysts, retains its entire subsidy as profit.[110] And GSE executives are sometimes lavishly compensated. Between 1998 and 2003, Fannie Mae's chief executive, Franklin Raines, earned a total of more than $90 million in salary, options, and earnings-related compensation. Chief Financial Officer Timothy Howard earned $30 million; and during the same period, Vice Chairman Jaime Gorelick pocketed more than $26 million.[111] In 2006, federal investigators discovered that Fannie's accounting methods seemed to be designed expressly to inflate the performance-related incomes of top executives. Fannie paid a $400 million fine to settle the matter.

The absence of accountability has also allowed the GSEs to shift their operations from less to more profitable markets, notwithstanding their public missions. Critics call this "mission creep."[112] All the GSEs have interpreted their charters expansively, arguing that they contain "implied powers" allowing them to tailor their activities to changing economic conditions and to respond to circumstances that may not have been anticipated when they were chartered.[113] On these grounds, Fannie Mae and Freddie Mac have recently diverted funds from the mortgage market to potentially more profitable investment activities, including financial arbitrage; home-equity lending; mortgage, life, and disability insurance; and the sale of repossessed property.[114] Fannie and Freddie, chartered to operate in the secondary market, have gradually been invading primary loan markets as well. The FHLBs offer an even more telling example of mission shifting. Many of the savings and loan associations that were to have been their principal clients were forced into bankruptcy during the 1980s. Though their original public purpose has evaporated, the FHLBs borrow more than a trillion dollars each year at the discounted rate their quasi-governmental status makes possible. They use the money to engage in complex financial arbitrage activities designed to produce a handsome—and taxpayer-subsidized—profit.[115]

Sallie Mae has virtually completed the vertical integration and monopolization of the student loan business. In 1997, Sallie Mae shareholders ousted the company's management and replaced it with an executive team that pledged to maximize profits. They used its taxpayer-subsidized profits to buy out the competition. In 1999, Sallie acquired the assets of two regional rivals for $440 million, and in 2000 it purchased its largest competitor, the USA Group, for $770 million, leaving Sallie a commanding market position. Ironically, Sallie's only serious competitor is the U.S. government's direct student loan program. Sally, in other words, receives a federal subsidy to compete against the federal government.

When criticized for losing sight of their public missions, as we saw in Chapter 2, the GSEs typically respond with furious lobbying and public relations campaigns. Since they are private corporations, GSEs are permitted to lobby, make political contributions, and engage in other political and public relations activities that are forbidden to government agencies.[116] Although the GSEs claim to be public entities when it comes to borrowing money, they are decidedly private when it comes to using the political process to protect their privileges. All the GSEs, and Fannie Mae in particular, spend enormous amounts of money on lobbying, public relations, and political campaigns, donating hundreds of thousands of dollars each year to political candidates.[117] In 1998, moreover, Fannie Mae and Freddie Mac together spent nearly $8 million on Capitol Hill lobbying efforts and in 1999 increased their combined spending to $11 million. In 2000, Fannie Mae spent more than $8 million on one advertising campaign alone.[118]

Through vigorous lobbying, Fannie and Freddie were able to resist HUD efforts to force them to change their lending standards to the advantage of minority borrowers, and to defeat the Clinton administration's recent efforts to force them to pay the customary SEC registration fees on the securities they issue. Fannie and Freddie save tens of millions of dollars each year by claiming exemption from these fees. Fannie and Freddie have recently stepped up their lobbying efforts to block congressional threats to consolidate regulatory oversight of the GSEs and to strip them of their line of credit from the U.S. Treasury—a move that might weaken Wall Street's confidence that GSE securities are backed by the government. Sallie Mae is also lobbying heavily to improve its competitive position with respect to the government's direct student lending efforts.[119]

Fannie Mae and Freddie Mac employ advertising agencies to burnish their corporate images while countering any charges made against them. In summer 2000, Fannie and Freddie launched an $8 million campaign designed to influence "opinion leaders." In a series of ads in publications such as the *Washington Post, Wall Street Journal,* and *New York Times,* the two corporations portrayed their critics as a so-called coalition for higher mortgage costs—a cabal of anonymous bankers and bureaucrats furtively plotting to drive up interest rates for home owners.[120]

In addition to conventional corporate advertising and public relations efforts, Fannie Mae has sought to use financial assistance to co-opt potential opponents. In 1996, Fannie created the FNMA Foundation, beginning with a gift of $350 million in stock. The foundation has awarded grants totaling $50 to $70 million a year, usually to community organizations active in the cause of affordable housing. Critics point out that a substantial percentage of the grants seems to be awarded to groups based in districts or states represented by members of Congress who happen to serve on committees of particular importance to Fannie, such as the Senate and House Banking Committees. Still other grants have gone to groups willing to publicly endorse Fannie's lending practices.[121] In 1996, Fannie donated a total of $1.3 million to forty-one organizations in its home base, the District of Columbia. Fannie worked closely with city schools and was the leading supporter of housing and community development projects in the city. This largesse may have helped local political activists forget that Fannie's tax-exempt status cost Washington, D.C., as much as $300 million in annual tax revenues.[122] Fannie Mae representatives denied that the foundation's efforts were motivated by political concerns. One referred to the organization's critics as "paranoid."[123] Paranoid or sane, they are frustrated in their attempts to mobilize the public against Fannie Mae because Fannie's philanthropy is designed to keep the most likely activists sitting on their hands. Fannie has also made it a practice to fill its executive suite with politically well-connected individuals, such as former Deputy Attorney General Jaime Gorelick and David Jeffers, former chief of staff to Rep. Richard Baker (R-LA), who has major oversight responsibilities for the GSEs.[124]

Though created by government to serve public purposes, the GSEs' main goal is profitability. Though their profits depend on substantial public subsidies and government-bestowed privileges, they face scarcely any public accountability. Groups and public officials who threaten to change these generous ground rules are quietly bought off. The GSEs need not appeal for public support themselves because they can finance their survival with private revenues—generated by secure public privileges.

Public Power and Private Purpose

The case of the GSEs is a particularly egregious example of private entities using public power for their own purposes, but it is hardly unique. Private prison contractors operate their facilities on the basis of a business model rather than in a manner linked to traditional penal models of deterrence and rehabilitation. One study showed that private prisons denied inmates "good time," that is, credit for an earlier release based upon good conduct, at a rate eight times as high as the rate for inmates at private institutions.[125] Why? The earlier the release, the less the revenue generated by the inmate for the corporate jailer. Similarly, private military contractors frequently ignore or circumvent legislative controls and restrictions on military action in order to maximize their profits.[126] And even not-for-profits use government contract dollars to advance their political or religious agendas while they provide—or rather don't provide—the public service they have undertaken to supply. As Harold Seidman and others have observed, this particular pathology has grown as the government has come to rely heavily upon private entities to provide more and more public services. Of course, public employees nominally supervise all contracts and contractors. In many instances, however, federal agencies such as the EPA routinely contract out for managerial and supervisory services. In other words, contractors are watched by other contractors, who, perhaps, are watched by other contractors. Where, then, might the public purpose be found?

PATHOLOGIES OF GOVERNMENT

As their critics are fond of noting, private markets can produce inequities, inefficiencies, and harmful externalities. Unfortunately, however, government intervention is no panacea. Public policies also produce inefficiencies and inequities, and, as to harmful externalities, the power and reach of international drug cartels is a tribute to the damage that can be done by misguided public policies.

If the problems caused by public policy were simply the result of errors, misunderstandings, and misinformation, they might easily be corrected. The problem, though, is that the policy pathologies we have examined are inherent to the governmental process. Organized and mobilized groups will generally prevail over broader public interests. Bureaucratic agencies will generally act on the basis of their own external and internal preoccupations rather than some diffuse concern with the public good. And, given an opportunity, private interests will gladly use public power for their own purposes. Perhaps government can resolve one set of problems, but not without introducing many others.

5

Popular Influence
and State Power

Critics of the American political process seldom hesitate to propose remedies for the nation's supposed political ills. Proponents of new campaign finance rules, lobbying regulations, voting reforms, and the like all seem confident that their nostrums will promote civic virtue and enhance popular influence. Few reformers, however, are sufficiently radical to confront the fundamental problem of citizen influence in political life. To put the matter succinctly, popular influence is inversely related to the state's power. Weak governments are vulnerable to popular pressure. The more powerful the government and the greater the scope of its activities, the less the chance that it will concern itself with citizens' views.

In the absence of electoral and representative institutions, this inverse relationship is quite clear. Dictators tend to be most concerned with their subjects' wishes when their own power to govern is weakest or most insecure and least interested in citizens' preferences when they are confident that their military and police forces are strong enough to quell expressions of popular discontent. The monarchs of early modern Europe, for example, were generally most solicitous of their subjects' opinions when they lacked the power to collect taxes by force. Monarchs with sufficient military strength to brush aside taxpayer resistance had considerably less interest in their subjects' preferences than those whose income might depend upon the goodwill of the citizenry.[1] General awareness of the essentially adversarial character of the relationship between the citizen and the state was expressed in popular aphorisms such as those usually attributed to Tom Paine, referring to government as, at best, "a necessary evil" and averring that the best government was the one that "governed least."

With the advent of electoral and representative institutions in the eighteenth and nineteenth centuries, the fundamentally adversarial character of the relationship between the citizen and the state was partly hidden from public view. The availability of elections and representative institutions suggested that popular influence no longer would be dependent upon the state's weakness. Not even the most powerful elected official, after all, is immune to reprisal at the polls. This apparent possibility for coexistence between popular influence and governmental power promised to transform the relationship between the citizen and the state. Democratic elections and representative institutions seemed to mean that citizens could use the state's capabilities for their own benefit, rather than simply benefiting from rulers' inability to construct a governmental apparatus sufficiently powerful to compel their obedience. Indeed, citizens would now be better off with a powerful state than with a weak one. If the government had become a servant, then the more powerful it became, the greater would be its capacity to serve.

The public's belief in its ability to control the state's actions is among the primary reasons that Americans have lost their traditional fear of government. Citizens no longer think that the best government governs least. Instead, survey after survey suggests that most Americans want the government to govern more.[2] Even modern-day conservatives have lost their fear of Big Brother. Of course, contemporary liberals and conservatives engage in a kind of ritual sparring over the virtues and vices of government. But this debate is less about the need for a powerful government than it is a form of haggling over what, exactly, the government should do. Liberals promote a social and regulatory agenda, whereas conservatives advocate a moral, international, and economic agenda. Both see big government as a necessary instrument for carrying out their plans. And, in a sense, both sides get what they want. Today's federal government undertakes a myriad of social, regulatory, moral, international, and economic policies. This is the turn-of-the-century liberal-conservative detente. The two sides have reached a compromise in which the federal government does everything.

Indeed, the standard-bearer of the conservative revolution, the late President Ronald Reagan, said in his 1981 inaugural address, "It is not my intention to do away with government. It is, rather, to make it work."[3] Reagan's views were praised by another conservative, columnist George Will, who found them "agreeably free of the feckless antigovernment spirit" that once characterized conservatism.[4] Certainly, America's most recent conservative president, George W. Bush, hardly hesitated to use and expand the power of the state for what he saw as necessary purposes. These ranged from homeland security and the "war on terror" to prescription-drug benefits for seniors. Bush is often described correctly as an exemplar of the new "big government" conservatism.[5]

Ironically, it was a recent liberal president, Democrat Bill Clinton, who, in his 1996 State of the Union message, famously proclaimed, "The era of big government is over." Clinton's assertion was said to represent a liberal surrender to the conservative agenda of laissez-faire economics, deregulation, privatization, and devolution that some thought was designed to diminish the size and power of the national government at the turn of the century.[6] Of course, Clinton's proclamation was premature. The federal government is larger and more active than ever. Although the nominal size of the federal civilian workforce has shrunk over the past ten years, it is only because tens of thousands of civil servants have been replaced by an even larger number of contract employees. These are not counted as official government workers even though all their work is undertaken on behalf of the government.[7] And, of course, after proclaiming the end of big government, Clinton fought to expand the government's health care, social, and environmental programs.

Early-twentieth-century political theorist Karl Mannheim, a proponent of the notion that democratic processes fundamentally changed the relationship between the citizen and the state, wrote, "In a democratic state, sovereignty can be boundlessly strengthened by plenary powers without renouncing democratic control."[8] If Mannheim was correct, citizens could use the power of the state to improve their lives while fearing no harm from it. This would, indeed, be a felicitous state of affairs.

Unfortunately, however, the problem of popular influence and state power is not so easily resolved. The problem is that in the United States and the other democracies, the institutions through which popular influence is exerted most govern least, while those that actually govern most are least subject to popular control. To the extent that it exists, popular influence is exerted mainly through representative legislatures such as the Congress of the United States. But such institutions are not well-equipped to engage in the actual tasks of governance. Unless they are rigidly organized by political parties, legislatures are individualistic and slow to act. They find it difficult to reach agreement on details. More fundamentally, the U.S. Congress, like most other legislatures, has little capacity of its own for action. Congress cannot collect the taxes; command the troops; enforce the law; secure the homeland; protect the environment; issue Social Security checks; or undertake any of the administrative, extractive, or coercive activities that, taken together, constitute the governance of the United States. Congress may formulate policies and make laws, but it does not actually govern. Congress delegates this task to the president and to the bureaucracy.

Who Governs?

The president, of course, is a more-or-less democratically elected official. But only Congress governs in anything approaching a democratic and pluralistic manner. Despite its numerous flaws and imperfections, at its core, the congressional policy-making process revolves around open hearings, public debate, and vigorous contestation among a host of disparate groups. Presidential decision-making, on the other hand, generally takes place in private and is often shrouded in secrecy. The agencies of the executive branch, as we shall see, are required by law to engage in an extensive process of consultation with interested parties when they make decisions. Presidents, however, have no such obligation.

Not only are the deliberations leading up to presidential decisions often removed from the public domain, even the decisions themselves are sometimes not revealed to the public or even to Congress. Many so-called national security directives issued by presidents in recent years, such as President Bush's controversial 2002 orders to the NSA launching a domestic eavesdropping program, have been used to initiate secret missions by intelligence and defense agencies.[9] For many years, too, presidents signed secret executive agreements with other governments obligating the United States to various forms of action without congressional knowledge, much less approval. In 1972, Congress enacted the Case-Zablocki Act, which requires the president to annually provide it with a list of all international agreements entered into during the previous year. Presidents have never fully complied with the terms of this act, claiming that it did not cover national security directives and other sensitive matters. Even when presidential actions are not veiled in secrecy or protected from scrutiny by claims of executive privilege, presidential decision-making tends to lack transparency and to offer access to only a narrow range of interests, groups, and competing political forces.[10] Thus, although presidents may be able to claim to be democratically elected, they certainly do not govern democratically. And bureaucratic agencies, for their part, have no direct responsibility to the citizenry.

Congress seems to have considerable power over the executive branch. Under the Constitution, in addition to its primary legislative powers,

Congress exercises war powers, treaty powers, appointment and removal powers, and the power to override presidential vetoes of its legislative enactments. Thus, at least in principle, presidents cannot pursue domestic priorities, conduct the nation's foreign and military affairs, or appoint important officials without congressional support. In principle, too, Congress can remove the president from office through the impeachment process. The executive agencies, of course, were created by Congress via statute and are subject to congressional scrutiny through the oversight process. Congressional committees and subcommittees hold frequent hearings to examine the behavior of the executive agencies. As a result of these hearings, Congress may enact new legislation to change agency conduct; may use its budgetary powers to punish agency misconduct; and may, again via statute, rescind agency rules and regulations of which it does not approve. Thus, in principle, executive agencies must bow before the authority of Congress.

The reality, though, is that Congress's capacity to obstruct the president's plans or to control the bureaucracy is limited and, ironically, tends to diminish as the complexity and scope of executive action increase. First, consider congressional control of bureaucratic agencies. In the nineteenth century, the nation's bureaucratic establishment was small and its tasks routine and straightforward. Congressional committees had little difficulty exercising supervision over agency programs and expenditures. According to America's foremost administrative historian, the late Leonard White, in the nineteenth century, Congress "absolutely controlled the civil establishment in number, in pay and in allocation of personnel to the respective agencies and their subdivisions."[11] When it came to agency budgets, said White, "Congress knew for what the taxpayers' money was being spent; the spending agencies were put in the position of having to justify in particular each small object of expenditure; variation was made difficult; audit was made easy and exacting; and the sense of congressional power was magnified."[12] Thus, the 1870 congressional budget for the Department of Agriculture specified that the agency would be allowed $1,500 for the keep of horses, $250 for subscriptions to periodicals, $250 for equipment, and $100 for the collection of minerals.[13] No agency deviation from this budget would be considered.

DELEGATION OF POWER

Congressional control of the bureaucracy was a simple matter when the government's tasks were limited and uncomplicated. As the size and role of the federal government increased, however, congressional enactments required executive agencies to make decisions and determinations about a variety of complex matters over long periods of time. Beginning in the 1930s, under the auspices of Franklin D. Roosevelt's New Deal, the federal government began to take responsibility for management of the economy, provision of social services, protection of the public's health, maintenance of employment opportunities, promotion of social equality, protection of the environment, and a host of other tasks. As the government's responsibilities and ambitions grew, Congress assigned more and more complex tasks to the agencies of the executive branch. It was no longer a matter of feeding horses and collecting minerals. Rather, executive agencies came to be tasked with the responsibility for analyzing and acting upon economic data; assessing the environmental impact of programs and projects; responding to fluctuations in the labor market; safeguarding the food supply; regulating the stock market; supervising telecommunications and air, sea, and land transport; and, in recent years, protecting the nation from terrorist plots. When Congress writes legislation addressing these and a host of other complex issues, legislators cannot anticipate every issue and problem that might arise under the law over the coming decades. Congress cannot establish detailed air-quality standards or draw up rules for drug testing or legislate the ballistic properties of artillery rounds for a new army tank. Inevitably, as its goals become more ambitious, more complex, and broader in scope, Congress must delegate considerable discretionary authority to the agencies charged with giving effect to the law. Just the sheer number of programs it has created in recent decades forces Congress to delegate authority. Congress can hardly administer the thousands of programs it has enacted and must delegate power to the president and to the bureaucracy to achieve its purposes. To be sure, if Congress delegates broad and discretionary authority to the executive, it risks seeing its goals subordinated to and subverted by those of the executive branch.[14] On the other hand, if Congress attempts to limit executive discretion by enacting very precise rules and standards to govern the conduct of the president and the executive branch, it risks writing laws that do not conform to real-world conditions and that are too rigid to be adapted to changing circumstances.[15] As the Supreme Court said in a 1989 case, "In our increasingly complex society, replete with ever changing and more technical problems, Congress simply cannot do its job absent an ability to delegate power under broad general directives."[16]

The increased scope and complexity of governmental activities promotes congressional delegation of power to the bureaucracy in another way as well. When Congress addresses broad and complex issues, it has far less difficulty reaching agreement on broad principles than on details. For example, every member of Congress might agree that enhancing air quality is a desirable goal. However, when it comes to the particular approach to be taken to achieve this noble goal, many differences of opinion are certain to manifest themselves. Members from automobile-producing states are likely to resist stiffer auto-emissions standards and to insist that the real problem lies with coal-fired utilities. Members from districts that contain coal-fired utilities might argue that auto emissions are the problem. Members from districts that are economically dependent upon heavy industry would demand exemptions for their constituents. Agreement on the principle of clean air would quickly dissipate as members struggled to achieve agreement on the all-important details. Delegation of power to an executive agency, on the other hand, allows members to enact complex legislation without having to reach detailed agreement. Congress can respond to pressure from constituents and the media to "do something" about a perceived problem while leaving the difficult details to administrators to hammer out.[17]

As a result of these factors, when Congress enacts major pieces of legislation, legislators inevitably delegate considerable authority to administrators to write rules and regulations designed to articulate and implement the legislative will. Of course, in some instances, Congress attempts to set standards and guidelines designed to govern administrative conduct. For example, the 1970 Clean Air Act specified the pollutants that the Environmental Protection Agency (EPA) would be charged with eliminating from the atmosphere as well as a number of the procedures that the EPA was obligated to undertake.[18] The act, however, left many other matters—including enforcement procedures, who should bear the burden of cleaning the air, and even how clean the air should ultimately be—to EPA administrators.

Many other statutes give administrators virtually unfettered discretion to decide how to achieve goals that are only vaguely articulated by Congress. For example, the statute establishing the Federal Trade Commission outlaws, without expressly defining, "unfair methods of competition." Precisely what these methods might be is largely left to the agency to determine. Similarly, the statute creating the Occupational Health and Safety Administration (OSHA) calls upon the agency "to protect health to the extent feasible." What that extent might be is for the agency to determine. In its enabling act, the EPA is told to protect human health and the environment "to an adequate degree of safety."[19] As Congress continued to enact statutes setting out general objectives without specifying how the government was supposed to achieve them, the federal bureaucracy was left to fill in the blanks.

In some instances, to be sure, Congress does write detailed standards into the law only to see them rewritten by administrators. For example, in

2006, the Securities and Exchange Commission (SEC) announced that it was issuing new rules that would significantly change key provisions of the 2002 Sarbanes-Oxley accounting reform and investor protection act. The act had been passed in the wake of the Enron scandal to reform corporate governance and prevent fraud. As enacted by Congress, Sarbanes-Oxley contained very specific standards. However, in response to industry lobbying, the SEC announced that it would issue new standards to ease corporate obligations under Section 404 of the act, which covers the financial statements issued by public corporations.[20] The agency determined that the law, as written by Congress, had forced corporations to engage in "overly conservative" practices.

Simply comparing the total volume of congressional output with the gross bureaucratic product provides a rough indication of where lawmaking now occurs in the federal government. The 106th Congress (1999–2000) was among the most active in recent years. It passed 580 pieces of legislation, 200 more than the 105th Congress and nearly twice as many as the 104th. Some, such as campaign finance reform, were significant, and many others were not. But the legislative legacy of this congressional session was judged by most observers to be relatively slight. Partisan and ideological divisions as well as ineffective leadership prevented most major items, such as needed revisions of federal budget rules, from even coming to the floor.[21]

During the same two years, executive agencies produced 157,173 pages of new rules and regulations in the official *Federal Register*.[22] OSHA, for example, introduced new regulations affecting millions of workers and thousands of businesses; the EPA drafted new air-quality standards; and the SEC and Commodities Futures Trading Commission announced significant revisions of futures-trading rules affecting billions of dollars in transactions. In principle, agency rules and regulations are designed merely to implement the will of Congress as expressed in statutes. In fact, agencies often draft regulations based upon broad statutory authority granted years or even decades earlier by congresses whose actual intent has become a matter of political interpretation.

The issue of delegation of power has led to a number of court decisions over the past two centuries, generally revolving around the question of the scope of the delegation. As a legal principle, the power delegated to Congress by the people through the Constitution cannot be redelegated by the Congress. This "nondelegation doctrine" implies that directives from Congress to the executive should be narrowly defined and should give the latter little or no discretionary power. A broad delegation of congressional authority to the executive branch could be construed as an impermissible

redelegation of constitutional power. A second and related question sometimes brought before the courts is whether the rules and regulations adopted
by administrators are consistent with Congress's express or implied intent.
This question is closely related to the first because the broader the delegation
to the executive, the more difficult it is to determine whether the actions of
the executive comport with the intent of Congress.

With the exception of three New Deal–era cases, the Court has consis-
tently refused to enforce the nondelegation doctrine.[23] In the nineteenth
century, for the most part, Congress itself enforced the principle of nondelegation by writing laws that contained fairly clear standards to guide
executive implementation.[24] Congressional delegation tended to be either
contingent or interstitial.[25] Contingent delegation meant that Congress had
established a principle defining alternative courses of action. The executive
was merely authorized to determine which of the contingencies defined
by Congress applied to the circumstances at hand and to act accordingly.
For example, the Tariff Act of 1890 authorized the president to suspend
favorable tariff treatment for countries that imposed unreasonable duties on
American products. In *Field v. Clark,* the Court held that this delegation
was permissible because it limited the president's authority to ascertaining
the facts of a situation. Congress had not delegated its law-making authority
to him.[26] The Court also accepted what might be called interstitial rule-
making by the executive. This meant filling in the details of legislation where
Congress had established the major principles. In the 1825 case of *Wayman v. Southard,* Chief Justice John Marshall said Congress might lawfully
"give power to those who are to act under such general provisions to fill
up the details."[27] In 1928, the Court articulated a standard that, in effect,
incorporated both of these doctrines. In the case of *J. W. Hampton & Co. v.
U.S.,* the Court developed the "intelligible principles" standard. A delegation of power was permissible "if Congress shall lay down by legislative act
an intelligible principle to which [the executive] is directed to conform."[28]
As Congress and the president worked together to expand governmental
power during the New Deal era, Congress enacted legislation, often at the
president's behest, that gave the executive virtually unfettered authority to
address a particular concern. For example, the Emergency Price Control Act
of 1942 authorized the executive to set "fair and equitable" prices without
offering any indication of what these terms might mean.[29] The Court's initial
encounters with these new forms of delegation led to three major decisions
in which the justices applied the "intelligible principles" standard to strike
down delegations of power to the executive. In the 1935 Panama case, the
Court held that Congress had failed to define the standards governing the

authority it had granted the president to exclude oil from interstate commerce. In the Schechter case, also decided in 1935, the Court found that the Congress had failed to define the "fair competition" that the president was to promote under the National Industrial Recovery Act (NIRA). Justice Benjamin Cardozo called the NIRA an example of "delegation running riot."[30] In a third case, *Carter v. Carter Coal Co.*, decided in 1936, the Court concluded that a delegation to the coal industry itself to establish a code of regulations was impermissibly vague.[31]

These decisions were seen as a judicial assault on the New Deal and helped spark President Roosevelt's "court-packing" plan. The Court retreated from its confrontation with the president, and, perhaps as a result, no congressional delegation of power to the president has been struck down as impermissibly broad in the more than six decades since *Carter*. Over the ensuing years, though, the nondelegation doctrine gradually fell into disuse as federal judges came to accept the notion that professional administrators in the agencies were more competent than politicians in the Congress to identify solutions to the nation's problems. Congress might, via statute, identify broad policy directions, and federal courts increasingly found that it was perfectly appropriate to leave the search for solutions in the hands of administrators. Thus, so long as the statute offered some vague indication of Congress's general intent, it was likely to pass muster. Indeed, the Supreme Court has said that a delegation can be valid if it "sufficiently marks the field within which the administrator is to act."[32]

Take, for example, the case of *Mistretta v. U.S.*[33] This case concerned the federal sentencing guidelines promulgated by the U.S. Sentencing Commission established by Congress in 1984 in response to concern that some judges were too lenient when meting out sentences to convicted criminals. The commission was charged with the task of developing a set of mandatory "guidelines" that would remove judicial discretion in this realm. In creating the commission, Congress offered few guidelines of its own. The language of the statute was vague, mandating that the commission should develop sentencing rules that would guarantee such things as "certainty and fairness" in sentencing. On this basis, the commission promulgated hundreds of pages of rules and regulations specifying how sentences were to be calculated given the severity of the crime and the criminal history of the defendant. In *Mistretta*, the Supreme Court found that the statute's vague standards were entirely sufficient to guide the commission's work and upheld the congressional delegation of power to the agency. In 2005, to be sure, the Supreme Court decided that the use of mandatory sentencing guidelines was prohibited by the Sixth Amendment but did not readdress the issue of delegation.[34]

Also signaling the Court's acceptance of expanded administrative exercise of legislative power is the so-called Chevron standard. This standard emerged from a 1984 case called *Chevron v. Natural Resources Defense Council*.[35] An environmental group had challenged an EPA regulation as contrary to the intent of the statute it was nominally written to implement. A federal district court sided with the environmentalists against the agency, but the lower court's decision was reversed by the Supreme Court. In its decision, the Supreme Court declared that so long as the executive developed rules and regulations "based upon a permissible construction" or "reasonable interpretation" of the statute, the judiciary would accept the views of the executive branch. This standard implies that considerable judicial deference should be given to the executive rather than to Congress. Indeed, the courts now look to the agencies to develop clear standards for statutory implementation rather than to Congress to develop standards for the executive branch to follow.[36] In the 2001 case of *U.S. v. Mead Corp.*, the Court partially qualified the Chevron holding by ruling that agencies were entitled to Chevron deference only where they were making rules carrying the force of law and not when they were merely issuing opinion letters or undertaking other informal actions.[37] Despite this qualification, Chevron still applies to the most important category of administrative activity.

Congressional Oversight of the Bureaucracy

Congress, of course, does not have to depend upon the courts to ensure that agencies will adhere to their statutory mandates. Congress possesses substantial oversight power of its own vis-à-vis the bureaucracy. Congress can hold hearings; enact new legislation; and, if it so desires, slash agency budgets. Under the Congressional Review Act (CRA), moreover, agencies are required to submit proposals for significant new rules and regulations to Congress sixty days before their adoption. The act prescribes an expedited procedure through which Congress may disallow agency proposals. Bureaucratic agencies obviously cannot completely ignore Congress. In recent years, oversight hearings into such topics as failures on the part of the Federal Emergency Management Agency (FEMA) in the wake of Hurricane Katrina and the DoD's handling of the Abu Ghraib prison scandal in Iraq ended the careers of agency officials and forced both agencies to adopt new procedures.

In practice, Congress is better able to respond to heavily publicized abuses and crises than to engage in day-to-day supervision of the bureaucracy. This has been called the "fire alarm" form of oversight.[38] Routine oversight is often conducted by a committee that is inclined to be friendly to the agency in question or to the interest groups that support that agency.[39] Members of Congress, moreover, seldom see much political advantage to be gained from devoting time, energy, and effort to oversight, particularly if their own party is in power. As one Republican member said during the Bush administration, "Our party controls the levers of government. We're not about to go out and look beneath a bunch of rocks to cause heartburn."[40] Even during the 1990s, a period of divided party government, the number of oversight hearings in both the House and Senate declined sharply as members decided that there was little political payoff to be derived from routine supervision of executive agencies.[41]

Congress's chief instruments of bureaucratic control—statutory and budgetary sanctions—require the approval of majorities in both houses and the signature of the president. In today's fragmented Congress, there are days on which it would be difficult to assemble a majority in favor of the proposition that the marigold is a pretty flower, and because the president is often the agent pushing the bureaucracy in directions Congress finds problematic, the chance of securing presidential approval for the use of congressional sanctions against an errant agency is usually not very good. Precisely because congressional action requires presidential assent, the much-vaunted CRA has been used only once, and that was in 2001 to invalidate ergonomics standards adopted by OSHA in the last weeks of the Clinton administration. Newly elected President Bush opposed the standards. Had Clinton still occupied the White House, Congress would not have been able to muster the two-thirds majority needed to override what would have been a certain presidential veto of its actions.

During the 1960s and '70s, Congress tried to police the bureaucracy's exercise of discretion by providing for a legislative veto that would enable the legislature to invalidate administrative regulations issued under statutes that delegated congressional authority to the executive branch. Though it appended such provisions to more than two hundred pieces of legislation that granted rule-making authority to administrative agencies, it actually exercised its veto in only a handful of cases. The record prompted one senator to declare that the idea of controlling administrative discretion through the legislative veto was "hogwash."[42] At least one version of the legislative veto was eventually struck down by the U.S. Supreme Court as an unconstitutional violation of the separation of powers.[43]

Bureaucratic Power

In principle, as Lowi, Schoenbrod, and others have suggested, Congress could write narrowly drawn statutes that limited bureaucratic discretion. In principle, the courts could reinstitute the nondelegation doctrine and stop deferring to administrative interpretations of statutory mandates. In principle, Congress might invest more time and energy in oversight of the administrative agencies. But the reality is that the more ambitious the programs and policies that Congress develops, the more power it must delegate to the bureaucracy. And the more power it delegates to the bureaucracy, the less able legislators will be to oversee their creations.

Once power is delegated to them, executive agencies inevitably have substantial control over its use, and in most instances, neither Congress nor the judiciary is able or willing to second-guess their actions. The result is that federal agencies typically write the law according to their own lights rather than those of the Congress. Indeed, whatever policy goals Congress may have had, often all that remains of a statute after many years and many congresses have passed is its delegation of power to the executive branch. As policy analyst Jerry L. Nashaw has observed, "Most public law is legislative in origin but administrative in content."[44]

Take, for example, the Family and Medical Leave Act (FMLA) of 1993.[45] The act requires employers to allow employees to take up to twelve weeks of unpaid leave each year to deal with childbirth, health problems, family emergencies, and other serious matters that might render employees temporarily unable to perform their duties.[46] In its report on the proposed legislation, the Senate Committee on Labor and Human Resources indicated that problems justifying leave under the law would include such matters as heart attacks, strokes, spinal injuries, recovery from childbirth, and other serious conditions that clearly justified an extended period of absence from work. Congress delegated authority to the Department of Labor to develop appropriate rules and regulations to implement the act. The record of legislative hearings attendant to the act, though, makes it clear that Congress intended the legislation to cover only serious problems, not short-term conditions or minor illnesses. The Labor Department, however, had other ideas.

Each year that the department developed new rules, it expanded the scope of the act's coverage and even the number of weeks of leave to which employees were entitled. For example, under rules adopted by the department, a case of flu was considered a medical condition covered by the act. This expansion of the FMLA was upheld by a federal court, which, citing the Chevron doctrine, deferred to the agency's interpretation of the statute.[47] Subsequently, the Labor Department ruled that medical leave granted by employers under their own plans would be in addition to rather than concurrent with the leave required under the FMLA.[48] This rule meant that some employees might be entitled to considerably more than the twelve weeks mandated by Congress. Perhaps the Labor Department should not be faulted for its generosity. No doubt ill employees are more deserving of sympathy than giant corporations. Nevertheless, in this as in so many other instances, a bureaucratic agency ignored congressional intent and wrote its own laws. When Congress delegated power, it gave up control.

Presidential Power

In many instances, when Congress delegates power, authority is granted directly to the president rather than to an administrative agency. For example, in drafting the Uniform Code of Military Procedure, Congress gave the president, in his constitutional capacity as commander-in-chief, the authority to set sentencing standards.[49] Thus, if an enemy combatant were to be sentenced to death by a military tribunal, it could very well be on the basis of rules promulgated by the chief executive rather than by Congress or the courts. Presidents, however, typically do not wait for power to be delegated to them; they grab it whenever possible. And the expansion of governmental power through the creation of an enormous federal administrative apparatus has provided presidents with the means to enhance their own power. Presidents seize and make use of the power of the bureaucracy through the mechanism of the executive order.

An executive order is a directive from the president to a government agency to undertake a specified task. The president's authority to issue such orders derives from Article II, Section 3 of the Constitution, which requires the president to "take care that the laws be faithfully executed." In the case of *Myers v. U.S.*, the Supreme Court said that this language created a presidential obligation to "supervise and guide executive officers in their construction of the statutes under which they act."[50] This case is frequently cited by presidents as providing justification for what might appear to be unilateral action by the White House.

Presidents have, of course, issued directives on their own authority since George Washington's neutrality proclamation and Thomas Jefferson's Louisiana Purchase. But these, along with Lincoln's orders during the Civil War, were extraordinary actions. In recent decades, though, what was once extraordinary has become routine. Expansion of the size and scope of the government's administrative presence allows presidents to use "guidance to executive officers" as an instrument of unilateral governance, often bypassing or ignoring Congress. In this way, the expansion of government has opened the door to an expansion of the unilateral power of the presidency.

The modern era of executive orders began with President Franklin D. Roosevelt. Between 1940 and 1945, FDR issued 286 executive orders related to military preparedness and the prosecution of World War II.[51] Many had sweeping implications for the lives of civilians. They created such agencies as the National War Labor Board, the Office of Price Administration, the Office of Civilian Defense, the Office of Censorship, the War Food Administration, and the Office of War Mobilization.[52] Other orders empowered government to seize private businesses engaged in defense production.[53] As in the Civil War, Congress had no choice but to unite behind the president in the face of national emergency. Congress, in fact, authorized such seizures under the War Labor Disputes Act of 1943, which allowed the president to take over privately owned factories and mines needed to supply military needs. After a brief decline following the defeat of the Axis powers, the volume of executive orders spiked once again during the Korean War.

In peacetime, executive orders became less numerous, but mere numbers can be misleading. Recent presidents have issued directives that are not called executive orders but have the same legal force—presidential memoranda, executive agreements, national security directives, signing statements, and presidential determinations. Numbers also tell us nothing about substance. A mere enumeration of executive orders does not reveal how consequential their content may be.[54] Recent presidents have developed a variety of new mechanisms to transform themselves into lawgivers, and their unilateral decisions cover the entire range of governmental concerns. Direct presidential policy-making—once reserved for times of war or national emergency—has now become a routine affair, even in routine times. Under the permanent state of war precipitated by the attacks of September 11, presidential government has emerged as a state within the state.

In foreign policy, unilateral presidential actions in the form of executive agreements have virtually replaced treaties as the nation's chief foreign policy instruments.[55] In domestic policy, executive orders have frequently served as vehicles for national antidiscrimination and affirmative action programs. FDR used an executive order to create the Fair Employment Practices Commission. Truman decreed the desegregation of the armed forces. Kennedy prohibited banks from engaging in discriminatory lending practices. Johnson's order 11246 mandated minority hiring by government contractors. In his Philadelphia Plan, Richard Nixon went a step further by requiring federal contractors to establish specific goals for hiring minority workers on projects financed by the federal government.[56]

It is true that the president's power to carry out executive orders must be grounded in authority granted by the Constitution or federal statute, and the orders usually specify the statutory or constitutional foundation on which they rest. The courts have struck down executive orders judged to exceed the statutory powers of the president. In 1952, for example, the Supreme Court ruled against President Truman in *Youngstown Co. v. Sawyer* and held that he had no constitutional or statutory power to seize the nation's steel mills during the Korean War, even though a threatened steel strike would disrupt production of essential military materiel.[57] In 1995, President Clinton issued an executive order prohibiting federal agencies from contracting with firms that replaced striking employees with new workers. A bill designed to achieve the same result had failed to pass the Senate in 1994. The District of Columbia Circuit Court struck down the president's order, ruling that it violated the National Labor Relations Act, which gave employers the right to replace striking workers.[58]

The limits imposed by law still leave considerable latitude for presidential decrees. The courts have held that the statutory authority for executive orders need not be specifically granted but simply implied by statute. President Nixon, for example, instituted wage and price controls in 1971 on the basis of the Trading with the Enemy Act.[59] The courts have also held that Congress might approve presidential action after the fact or, in effect, ratify presidential action through "acquiescence"—simply keeping quiet—or by continuing to vote appropriations for programs established by executive orders. Federal judges have upheld presidential orders even when they lie in what Supreme Court Justice Robert Jackson called the "zone of twilight," where Congress and the president might hold concurrent authority and no statute prohibits presidential action.[60] The Supreme Court invoked the twilight zone to uphold orders issued by Presidents Carter and Reagan prohibiting certain types of claims by American businesses against Iranian assets in the United States that had been frozen during the Iranian hostage crisis of 1979–1980.[61] The courts have also designated some areas, notably military policy, as inherently presidential and allow presidents wide latitude to use executive decrees there.

In theory, Congress could overturn an executive order simply by enacting a statute to negate it. Of course, the bill would have to command a majority sufficient to override a presidential veto. Congress would also have to be alert to the potential for presidential aggrandizement that lies beneath the legal language of executive orders. When Louis Brownlow drafted the order creating the executive office of the president in 1939, his intentional obfuscation concealed the powers inherent in a new executive unit that the order left unnamed. It would later emerge as the Office of Emergency Management, and it gave FDR the power to create on his own authority the armada of agencies that would run the country during World War II. Brownlow likened his handiwork to "a rabbit stowed in a hat," and "the little rabbit ... was so disguised in small print, with no capital letters that it occasioned" scarcely any comment.[62] The task of finding out what powers lurk within an executive order is especially difficult because the issuance of orders is not covered by the Administrative Procedure Act that governs the rule-making process for all the other agencies of the executive branch. In other words, the president is not required to give advance notice of an order or to hold public hearings about its substance. The procedures for issuing executive orders are specified only by executive orders.[63]

Presidents Bill Clinton and George W. Bush made frequent use of executive orders. Clinton faced a conservative Congress that refused to act on his administration's legislative agenda in matters of environmental protections, support for organized labor, expansions of affirmative action programs, and government regulation. The legislators were also skeptical about Clinton's effort to shift the country's foreign policy toward a multilateralism that envisioned cooperation with international organizations such as the United Nations and collegial relations with allies. According to conservative legal scholar Todd Gaziano, Clinton tried to enact his administration's legislative program by executive order, thereby avoiding the inconvenience of having to consult a hostile Congress.[64] Clinton himself seemed to acknowledge the shift toward unilateral action. In an interview given shortly after the Republicans took control of Congress, Clinton observed, "I had overemphasized in my first two years ... the importance of legislative battles as opposed to the other things that the president might be doing. And I think now we have a better balance of both using the Presidency as a bully pulpit and the President's power of the Presidency to *do* things, actually accomplish things, and ... not permitting the Presidency to be defined only by relations with Congress."[65]

Clinton would issue more than thirty executive orders relating to the environment and natural resources alone. Executive Order 13061 established the American Heritage Rivers Initiative, designed to protect several major river systems from commercial and industrial development but also overriding the land-use powers of state and local governments. When Congress failed to approve the administration's Children's Environmental Protection Act, Clinton incorporated a number of its provisions into an executive order he issued on Earth Day.[66] Another Clinton order, Environmental Justice for Minority Populations, required all federal agencies to show that their plans and projects took into account implications for environmental justice. An accompanying presidential memorandum held that existing civil rights legislation empowered federal agencies to revoke grants to state and local projects whose adverse environmental consequences disproportionately affected members of minority groups.[67] During his last days in the White House, President Clinton issued orders closing off millions of acres in ten Western states to residential and commercial development. The orders declared that the lands were protected national monuments under the 1906 Antiquities Act.

During the 2000 presidential campaign, George W. Bush denounced Clinton's high-handed seizure of Western lands. But in 2003, when Western conservatives challenged Clinton's executive order before the Supreme Court, President Bush sent his solicitor general, Theodore Olson, to defend the authority of presidents to issue such orders. Olson suggested, in fact, that the Court had no legal basis to question the orders issued by Clinton.[68] Clinton had demonstrated that an activist president with an ambitious policy agenda could achieve a substantial measure of success without a congressional majority. George W. Bush, elected by the thinnest of margins, did not want to surrender the presidential capacity to do the same.

President Bush issued more than forty executive orders during his first year in office. One of his first prohibited the use of federal funds to support any international family planning organizations that provided abortion counseling services. It also imposed limits on the use of embryonic stem cells in federally funded research. But the terrorist attacks eight months after Bush's inauguration gave his administration an intense new focus fired by anger, grief, and fear. By executive order, the president created the Office of Homeland Security, and not long afterward, he issued another order authorizing the creation of military tribunals to try noncitizens accused of participating in terrorist acts against the United States. The directive also prohibits defendants from appealing their treatment to any federal or state court. Other orders froze the American assets of those associated with terrorism; provided expedited citizenship for foreign nationals serving in the U.S. military; and ordered the CIA to use all means possible to oust President Saddam Hussein of Iraq, who stood accused of plotting terrorist strikes.

Some of President Bush's orders were issued and carried out in secret. Soon after the 9/11 terrorist attacks, the president issued national security directives authorizing the NSA to eavesdrop on Americans and others inside the United States who communicated via telephone or e-mail with persons outside the United States.[69] The NSA was authorized to engage in what is sometimes called "data mining," a process of sifting through millions of calls and e-mails searching for words and phrases that might signal terrorist involvement. Under the terms of the relevant statute, the Foreign Intelligence Surveillance Act, the government is required to obtain warrants from a special court, the Foreign Intelligence Surveillance Court, which holds secret sessions at the Justice Department. Normally such a warrant would be sought by the FBI, not the NSA, which is statutorily authorized to engage only in operations outside the United States. President Bush, however, decided to bypass statutory restrictions in order to make use of the NSA's superior electronic information-gathering capabilities. Encountering a firestorm of protest when the existence of the secret orders was leaked to the press in 2005, President Bush and his advisers asserted that the president had acted properly.

The president said he based his actions on Article II of the Constitution and Congress's 2001 resolution giving the president the authority to use "all necessary and appropriate force against those nations, organizations or persons he determines planned, authorized, committed or aided" the September 11 attacks against the United States. A 2006 Justice Department memorandum asserted that the president's constitutional position was supported by the *Federalist Papers,* numerous court cases, the writings of Republican and Democratic presidents, and many scholarly papers.[70] Critics, however, contended that the president's logic seemed to suggest that there were really no restrictions upon presidential power. Georgetown law professor Jonathon Turley said, "There's no limiting principle to that theory."[71] Although the president denied that he was claiming unilateral powers, his own advisers painted a different picture. Presidential legal adviser John Yoo said in a 2001 memorandum that no statute enacted by Congress "can place any limits on the president's determinations as to any terrorist threat, the amount of military force to be used in response, or the method, timing and nature of the response."[72] Yoo is widely believed to have written the legal justification cited by the president for his secret domestic eavesdropping orders.

Terrorism did not eliminate the administration's initiatives in domestic policy. Unable to overcome congressional opposition to stepping up domestic energy exploration, the president signed an executive order, closely following a recommendation from the American Petroleum Institute, that freed energy companies from a number of federal regulations. Another executive order created a task force charged with expediting the issuance of permits for energy-related projects. Still another presidential directive effectively prohibited federal agencies from requiring union-only work crews on federally funded projects. Enforcement of the order was enjoined by the U.S. District Court, but the Court of Appeals held that Bush had the authority to issue the order.[73]

Regulatory Review

Another unilateral presidential instrument making use of the power of the bureaucracy is the process of regulatory review. The invention of this process during the Nixon administration, and its subsequent expansion, has given presidents a mechanism to engage in rule-making without significant participation by the lawmakers in Congress. The immediate occasion for this expansion of presidential power was the creation of the Environmental Protection Agency in 1970. The new agency's regulations represented alarming increases in costs for American industry. Nixon responded to business concerns by establishing a "quality of life" review process within the newly renamed Office of Management and Budget (OMB). Nixon required the EPA to submit proposed regulations for month-long review prior to their publication in the *Federal Register*. The OMB, in turn, circulated the proposals to other agencies for comment, mainly to allow the measures' adversaries more time to mobilize the opposition. In 1974, President Ford issued an executive order formalizing this review process. Ford required that the OMB subject proposed regulations to an "inflationary impact analysis" before their publication in the *Register*. President Carter issued a new executive order replacing this procedure with a requirement that the OMB analyze the cost of major proposed regulations, evaluate plausible alternatives, and approve the least cumbersome form of regulation.[74]

The Nixon, Ford, and Carter efforts fell short of full-blown presidential control of the rule-making process. Though agencies might follow the procedures mandated by the president, in the end they were not obligated to change their proposed regulations to comply with the president's policy goals. Congress paid little heed to the procedures for regulatory review because they seemed to be mere symbolic gestures to placate important constituency groups. But these initial presidential regulatory initiatives established precedents and prototypes for more determined efforts in the Reagan administration and its successors to bring federal regulation under presidential control. Congress itself unwittingly contributed to the expansion of presidential power in 1979 by enacting the Paperwork Reduction Act, which created the Office of Information and Regulatory Affairs (OIRA) within the OMB. Congress was responding to complaints that business-people were spending too much time and money on the forms and records required by government regulations. Through the OIRA, the OMB was authorized to monitor and limit the impositions of regulatory agencies on the businesses and industries that they regulated.[75]

A month after taking office in 1981, Reagan issued Executive Order 12291, establishing a process for centralized presidential oversight of agency rule-making. The order required that regulatory agencies use cost-benefit analysis to justify proposed regulations. Rules were not to be adopted unless the potential benefits to society outweighed the potential costs. To prove that they had complied with this mandate, agencies were now required to prepare a formal regulatory impact analysis (RIA), which was to include an assessment of the costs and benefits of any proposed rule as well as an evaluation of alternative regulations that might impose lower costs. The OIRA was responsible for evaluating these RIAs. Agencies were prohibited from publishing proposed rules without OIRA clearance, and they were required to incorporate OIRA revisions into the rules that they eventually published. The OIRA could block the publication and implementation of any rule that it disapproved.

In effect, the Reagan administration used the statutory cover of the Paperwork Reduction Act to achieve a unilateral extension of White House power. The intention was not simply to reduce red tape for regulated business firms. The OIRA became the instrument through which the White House seized control of the rule-making process so that it could block or amend rules at will. Since rule-making is essential to the implementation of virtually every statute, the presidential establishment had not only asserted its control of the rule-making process but also enlarged on its constitutional role in the legislative process by dictating the way in which laws would be implemented. The administration quickly used the regulatory review process to curtail the impact of federal environmental and health and safety legislation. It blocked the promulgation of new rules by the EPA and OSHA.[76]

During the eight years of the Reagan administration, an average of eighty-five proposed rules were returned to agencies each year for reconsideration or withdrawal.[77] Although this figure represents only a small fraction of the rules proposed by federal agencies, the rejected rules naturally tended to be controversial and therefore politically important. Reagan's opponents in Congress denounced the president's intervention in the rule-making process but were able to wrest only minor concessions from the White House.[78]

Administrators in the regulatory agencies raised few obstacles to the new regime in rule-making. Under the Civil Service Reform Act of 1978, presidents gained greater control over the assignment of senior bureaucrats to the top positions in federal agencies, and the Reaganites had taken full advantage of this opportunity to fill strategic positions with administrators sympathetic to the president's objectives.[79] The clarity of those objectives left little room for bureaucratic improvisation, especially since agency compliance was regularly monitored.[80] Given presidential control over budgets, staffing, and the general quality of agency life, most career bureaucrats find cooperation more sensible than struggling with the White House.

In 1985, President Reagan further expanded presidential control over rule-making. By executive order, he required every regulatory agency to report its objectives for the coming year annually to the OIRA. The OIRA would assess each agency's regulatory agenda for consistency with the president's program and notify agencies of modifications needed to bring their plans into alignment with the views of the president. This new order went beyond Reagan's initial regulatory review program. Executive Order 12291 had authorized the White House to review rules after they were proposed. Its sequel enabled the White House to intervene before rules were drafted.[81] Reagan's order forced agencies to take account of presidential goals and not just congressional intent when formulating the rules that carried legislation into effect. With the stroke of a pen, Reagan had expanded the White House role in rule-making and enhanced its power to determine what the will of Congress would mean in practice.

President George H. W. Bush continued Reagan's practices but shifted much of the responsibility for regulatory review from the OIRA to the Council on Competitiveness, headed by Vice President Dan Quayle. Shifting responsibility from a statutory agency to a purely presidential office further reduced the ability of congressional opponents to interfere with presidential control of the review process.[82] President Bill Clinton abolished the Council on Competitiveness shortly after taking office in 1993, but instead of retreating from White House regulatory review, Clinton extended presidential control of regulatory agencies by directing the OIRA to issue "regulatory prompts"—orders instructing agencies to adopt particular regulations. Although Reagan had used regulatory review to prevent the imposition of rules to which he objected, Clinton took the further step of requiring agencies to formulate rules that he wanted.[83] Elena Kagan, a law professor and official in the Clinton White House, explained that Clinton felt hemmed in by congressional opposition during most of his presidential tenure. Determined to make his mark in domestic policy, Clinton used the bureaucratic rule-making process to accomplish unilaterally what he was unable to achieve through Congress.[84]

In 1993, Clinton issued Executive Order 12866 to replace Reagan's two orders regarding regulatory review. Clinton preserved the essential components of Reagan's regulatory oversight system: He required agencies to submit major regulations to the OIRA for review, and he extended the use of cost-benefit analysis for the evaluation of proposed rules. He also continued an annual regulatory planning process like the one created by Reagan. But Clinton added two new elements to the regulatory review process. First, he extended regulatory review to independent agencies such as the Social Security Administration.[85] President Clinton did not require the independent agencies to submit proposed rules for review, but he did order them to submit their annual regulatory agendas to the OIRA, which reviewed them for their consistency with the president's priorities. Though Congress had placed the independent agencies outside the orbit of presidential power, Clinton was trying to bring them under presidential control.

Second, and more important in the short run, Clinton's new order asserted that the president had full authority to direct the rule-making activities of executive agencies, not just to block rules to which he objected but to order the adoption of rules that advanced the administration's policy objectives. Clinton's order said only that conflicts between agencies and the OIRA over proposed rules would be resolved by presidential decision, but soon after issuing the order, Clinton began issuing formal orders directing executive agencies to propose for public comment rules that the president had conceived. On 107 occasions, Clinton ordered regulatory agencies to publish in the *Federal Register* rules that had originated in the White House. Presidential rule-making covered a wide variety of topics. Clinton ordered the Food and Drug Administration (FDA) to issue rules designed to restrict the marketing of tobacco products to children. The White House and the FDA then collaborated for several months on nearly 1,000 pages of new regulations affecting tobacco manufacturers and vendors.[86] In other cases, the president devised rules for the Departments of Labor, Agriculture, Health and Human Services, Interior, and Treasury governing water pollution, the inspection of imported foods, patients' rights, and assault pistols. In principle, agencies might have objected to these presidential directives and appealed to Congress for support, but Clinton did not mandate any rules that he expected the agencies to reject.[87]

Clinton thus avoided agency resistance and recourse to Congress. In the process, however, he was building a body of precedent that would empower the president to take full control of the regulatory process. After the

Republicans captured Congress in 1994, Clinton turned more frequently to administrative directives to achieve his legislative objectives. Administrative rule-making allowed him to legislate on matters of health care, parental leave, gun control, and environmental protection without the inconvenience of consulting a hostile Congress. Republicans denounced Clinton's actions as a usurpation of congressional power.[88] But after winning the White House in 2000, President George W. Bush went right on exercising the powers that Clinton had seized. In fact, Bush's OIRA administrator, John D. Graham, issued a memorandum announcing that the president's chief of staff expected federal agencies to "implement vigorously" the principles and procedures outlined in former president Clinton's Executive Order 12866.[89]

During the first seven months of Bush's presidency, the OIRA returned twenty major rules to agencies for further analysis.[90] One was a rule drafted by the National Highway Traffic Safety Administration (NHTSA) to implement legislation enacted by Congress requiring tire-pressure-monitoring devices on new cars. The auto industry objected to the cost of implementing the NHTSA's proposal. The OIRA, responding to the industry complaints, told the NHTSA to study alternative rules and thereby blocked the will of Congress. At the same time, Bush continued Clinton's use of presidential "prompt letters" instructing agencies to issue new regulations. Five such letters went out during Bush's first year in office.[91] One "prompt" encouraged OSHA to require large employers to use automated external defibrillators to prevent heart-attack deaths. Another told HHS to require that food labels disclose trans-fatty acid content.[92] Since both agencies were eager to adopt the presidentially mandated regulations, it appeared that Bush was following the Clinton example of ordering agencies to undertake actions they favored in order to establish precedents that would legitimate the power of the presidential prompt. OIRA Chief Graham may have been hinting at broader use of the president's regulatory powers when he announced that the administration would welcome suggestions from citizens and groups concerning the abolition of existing rules as well as proposals for new rules. The scope of the OIRA's influence became evident in 2003 when several members of Congress, concerned with the expansion of presidential control of agency rule-making, asked the General Accounting Office (GAO) to prepare an assessment of the OIRA's role. The GAO examined eighty-five important rules adopted by federal agencies during the prior year. The study found that the OIRA had exercised significant influence on the rules adopted by federal agencies in twenty-five of these eighty-five cases.[93] In several instances, representatives of interest groups affected by proposed rules had met directly with OMB and OIRA officials to press their cases, thereby circumventing the agencies and Congress. The lobbying community, ever sensitive to Washington's shifting political currents, had apparently detected a new configuration of bureaucratic power. In February 2007, President Bush issued executive orders that expanded regulatory review once again. The president ordered federal agencies to obtain White House approval for "guidance letters." These letters explain to affected parties how agencies plan to enforce or interpret laws and regulations. Guidance letters are important instruments, and their control by the White House strengthens presidential power yet again.

Through the process of regulatory review, successive presidents have built up a significant capacity to reshape legislation and even to achieve significant policy goals without any congressional action at all. They have achieved this success with surprisingly little media scrutiny or public awareness. Few Americans have heard of the OIRA, and the media pay little attention to the agency. But the obscure office buried in the OMB has added substantially to the power of the president.

Signing Statements

Executive orders and regulatory review are presidential orders to the bureaucracy to take some form of action. Contemporary presidents have also developed an instrument designed to signal to the bureaucracy that it should refrain from carrying out an act of Congress. This instrument is the signing statement. Presidents have issued signing statements from time to time ever since George Washington, though many of these statements were unrecorded and never became part of the legislative record. Others were innocuous benedictions issued in anticipation of a law's benefits for the nation and its citizens. Occasionally, however, presidents have used the signing statement to call attention to provisions of a bill that they regarded as improper or unconstitutional even though they were willing to approve the statute in general.[94] President Truman, for example, issued a signing statement when he approved the 1946 Hobbs Anti-Racketeering Act. It outlined his interpretation of ambiguous sections of the statute and indicated how the federal government would implement the new law.[95]

Ronald Reagan's attorney general, Edwin Meese, along with Samuel Alito, then a Justice Department lawyer and now, of course a Supreme Court justice, receive the credit for converting the signing statement into a systematic mechanism of presidential direct action that frequently overrides the intent of Congress. Meese argued that carefully drafted signing statements would provide a warrant for executive agencies to act on the basis of the president's interpretation of a statute rather than guessing at congressional intent. Perhaps even more important, the statement would become part of the statute's legislative history when the occasion arose for the courts to rule on its meaning. To establish the place of presidential signing statements in the official legislative record, Meese and Alito reached an agreement with the West Publishing Company to have them included in its authoritative texts on federal law.[96]

President Reagan began to issue detailed and carefully drawn signing statements—prepared by the Department of Justice—to reinterpret the bills that reached his desk from Congress. When signing the Safe Drinking Water Amendments of 1986, for example, Reagan interpreted sections of the act that appeared to require mandatory enforcement so that they would allow discretionary enforcement.[97] In other cases, Reagan's signing statements simply nullified portions of statutes enacted by Congress. In approving the 1988 Veterans Benefits Act, he declared that sections of the bill would violate the integrity of the executive branch and would not be enforced.[98] In the same year, Reagan signed a bill prohibiting construction on two pristine Idaho waterways but declared that one portion of the bill was unconstitutional and would not be enforced.[99]

The signing-statement stratagem did not always succeed. When signing the Competition in Contracting Act in 1984, Reagan declared that portions of the law were unconstitutional and directed executive branch officials not to comply with them. But U.S. District Court Judge Harold Ackerman upheld the act and ruled that the president did not have the power to declare acts of Congress unconstitutional.[100] The Ninth Circuit Court of Appeals later reached a similar conclusion when it decided that the president did not have the authority to "excise or sever provisions of a bill with which he disagrees."[101]

Unfavorable judicial rulings posed no obstacle to the continued use of presidential signing statements to reshape the bills enacted by Congress. When George H. W. Bush signed the 1991 Civil Rights Act, he asserted in a signing statement that one of its provisions might be unfairly applied to businesses. In effect, he intervened in the act's legislative history to give direction to administrators charged with carrying out the law. During the same year, Bush signed a bill requiring that contractors building the Superconducting Supercollider in Texas would have to pursue affirmative action in their hiring practices. The president's signing statement asserted that there was no valid basis for affirmative action in this case—even though the courts at the time had held otherwise—and directed the secretary of energy to ignore the affirmative action requirements.[102] Bush had opposed the passage of the bill. Now he nullified it, but without giving Congress the opportunity to override a presidential veto.

Presidents Reagan and Bush used signing statements for mostly conservative ends—to limit the scope of affirmative action programs, to block business regulation, to reduce the impact of environmental programs, and to thwart new labor laws. President Clinton demonstrated that signing statements could just as easily serve progressive causes. Faced with Republican-controlled congresses for six of his eight years in office, Clinton used his signing statements to neutralize the conservative crusade proclaimed in the 1994 Contract with America. In 1996, for example, Congress enacted a Defense Appropriations Bill with a provision that required the discharge of any member of the military who was HIV-positive. President Clinton signed the appropriations bill but asserted that this provision was unconstitutional. He ordered the Justice Department not to defend the HIV ban in court if it were challenged, which, in effect, represented an announcement that the provision would not be enforced. For Democratic and Republican presidents alike, the signing statement has served as a weapon for frustrating congressional initiatives. The courts have added the weight of judicial opinion to presidential signing statements by referring to them when interpreting the meaning of statutes.[103]

Presidential use of signing statements to challenge legislative provisions has grown sharply during the Bush years. President Reagan used signing statements to attack 71 legislative provisions, and President Clinton used signing statements to question 105 provisions. By the end of 2005, with three years still remaining of his second term, President Bush had already challenged 500 legislative provisions with his signing statements.[104] Ed Meese's contrivance has become a full-blown instrument of presidential power.

THE CITIZEN AND THE STATE

Thus, the expansion of government has empowered the bureaucracy and the president while reducing the ability of Congress to control the executive branch. Mannheim was wrong. Sovereignty cannot be "boundlessly strengthened" without any cost to the citizen. Expansion of the state's role and authority means an increase in its executive power and administrative capabilities. Inevitably, this increase gradually subjects citizens to governmental power that acts according to its own lights and is, at best, marginally responsible to them. The state, in other words, has acquired a measure of autonomy from civil society.[105]

One important, if not often noticed, indication of this contemporary shift in the relationship between the citizen and the state is the ongoing transformation of the criminal law. Most individuals do not view themselves as criminals and so do not think the criminal law applies to them except, perhaps, to protect them from theft and violence. Yet the criminal law is about more than deterring thuggish conduct. As it evolved, beginning with the centuries of struggle between Crown and Parliament over the rights of Englishmen and the prerogatives of the king, the criminal law was filled with numerous safeguards designed to protect the liberty of *all* citizens by creating obstacles to the arrest, conviction, and punishment of those whose conduct evoked the Crown's displeasure.[106] These safeguards include such principles as the presumption of innocence, proof beyond a reasonable doubt, attorney-client privilege, protection from compulsory self–incrimination, and the *mens rea* requirement limiting the state to punishing those who can be shown to have acted intentionally.

These and a host of other legal safeguards are critically important. Left to themselves, rulers and bureaucrats will be inclined to deal arbitrarily and harshly with those whom they view as posing even small challenges to their powers, prerogatives, and missions. Kings sent important enemies of the state to the Tower for indefinite periods of time, but contemporary government agencies seem to prefer "renditions" to secret locations. During the seventeenth century, the king's officials could and did mete out harsh summary punishments to even minor offenders. In its own way, the U.S. Sentencing Commission sought to do the same thing when it promulgated mandatory sentencing guidelines that often added years of extra time to prison sentences, based upon information that was never presented or proven to the trial jury.[107]

As the power of the national government, hence the power of the executive, increases, the safeguards protecting the citizen from the state are gradually being undone. In recent years, thousands of new federal criminal statutes have been written. There are currently some 4,000 federal criminal laws on the books, nearly half enacted since 1970.[108] Most of these statutes deal with environmental protection, securities regulation, corporate governance, product and workplace safety, terrorism, and the myriad of other matters related to the expansion of the national government's authority and responsibility. Not surprisingly, given the growing number of federal laws that it is now possible to violate, the number of federal prosecutions has increased as well—by nearly 150 percent since 1980.[109]

Accompanying this expansion of federal criminal law has been a determined effort by the executive branch to circumvent the limitations that traditional procedural safeguards impose upon the ability of the government to incarcerate those it deems blameworthy. Under pressure from the Justice Department and afraid of appearing soft on crime, Congress has enacted statutes that federal prosecutors have been able to use to remove one after another impediment to the prosecution and conviction of the targets of their investigations. For example, a number of federal criminal statutes, such as the Clean Water Act, weaken the traditional *mens rea* requirement, allowing criminal prosecution of individuals who were, at most, negligent. In one recent case, a construction supervisor was sentenced to six months in prison and a $5,000 fine for Clean Water Act violations when a backhoe operator on his crew accidentally pierced an oil pipeline, discharging oil into a nearby river.[110] The Supreme Court has said that overlooking questions of intent may be necessary to protect complex regulatory arrangements.[111]

In a similar vein, Congress has enacted statutes that have been used by the Justice Department to criminalize efforts by individuals to defend themselves or even to assert their innocence. For example, in a well-known recent case, Martha Stewart was prosecuted for violating the federal fraud statute as well as the statute that prohibits making false statements to federal investigators in her response to the government's allegations that she engaged in insider trading. The government was never able to muster the evidence needed actually to charge Stewart with insider trading. This inconvenient fact did not stop Justice Department prosecutors from charging that she made false statements to federal investigators and committed securities fraud by frequently and publicly asserting her innocence. The government claimed that Stewart's assertions of innocence were actually efforts to halt the slide in value of her company's stock and thus constituted a form of fraud.[112]

In addition, acting without a clear statutory mandate, the Justice Department has worked to develop new techniques to circumvent limits on prosecutorial discretion. One of many important prosecutorial strategies that has evolved in recent years is the tactic of discouraging white-collar—especially corporate—defendants from fully availing themselves of the legal advice to which their resources would normally give them access. At least since 1999, the Justice Department has told defendants that they would be more likely to face criminal charges if they "lawyered up." This policy was formalized in the often-cited "Thompson Memorandum," drafted in 2003 by then Deputy Attorney General Larry Thompson.[113] The Thompson memorandum states that in deciding whether to charge a corporation with a crime, federal prosecutors should consider "the corporation's timely and voluntary disclosure of wrongdoing and its willingness to cooperate in the investigation of its agents, including, if necessary, the waiver of corporate attorney-client and work product protection." The memorandum goes on to say that the prosecutor should consider "whether the corporation appears to be protecting its culpable employees and agents" and may consider "the advancing of attorneys' fees" and sharing of information pursuant to a joint defense agreement. In other words, corporate officers are to be discouraged from retaining counsel, refusing to disclose privileged information, or developing complex defense strategies by the threat that the government will treat these as indications of likely guilt. Some of these policies were modified but not ended by the Justice Department in 2006.[114]

Lest it be thought that the erosion of legal safeguards affects only greedy corporate chieftains or dangerous terrorists, it is worth taking note of some contemporary federal cases. In recent years, a Michigan landowner was convicted of a criminal violation of the Clean Water Act for moving sand onto his property without a federal permit. A minor union leader was convicted of making false statements for replying "no" to federal investigators who asked if he had accepted a bribe. A college teacher was convicted of mail fraud for granting degrees to students whose work had been plagiarized.[115] Perhaps these cases remain the exceptions rather than the norm, but they illustrate the possibilities. As sovereignty is boundlessly strengthened, not only the influence but the security of the citizenry is reduced, and the chance that ordinary citizens will be subjected to arbitrary treatment is increased.

Of course, all this is sugarcoated by government agencies that claim to be acting only for the benefit of the public. Security services need to spy on millions of Americans to protect us from foreign terrorists. NASA needs to spend billions to launch elderly politicians into orbit to promote the public's interest in preparing senior citizens for the rigors of space travel. The Justice Department needs to protect the public against maniacal sand-hauling landowners. And if the public does not wish to be served in these ways? One leading public administration text counsels bureaucrats to remember that "when you deal with the general public you should expect its members to have a limited understanding of the complexity of most issues.... While it is to your advantage to have the public on your side, this may not always be possible. Your organization may have a mission that is in conflict with ... community groups.... Your job is to uphold your organization's mission.... Be prepared to suffer through public outcries, insults and demonstrations while supporting your program goals."[116]

Of course, administrators are prepared to suffer only so much. If their agony becomes too intense, surely one of those 4,000 federal criminal statutes can be employed to alleviate it.

6

Conclusion: Why
Participate in Politics?

Americans are continually exhorted to participate; to make their views known; to vote for the best person; and, in a variety of other ways, to play an active role in political life. But for most people, most of the time, politics is not ennobling, particularly efficacious, or even interesting. Clausewitz was correct to equate politics with war. Each in its own way is an unrewarding, albeit sometimes necessary, activity for most participants. Common soldiers seldom find war an edifying experience, even when it can be said that the reasons to fight were valid and legitimate. In political combat, most participants are foot soldiers in battles fought for the benefit of others, for goals that are seldom fully revealed to the public at large.

According to democratic mythology, popular participation somehow drives the political process, but, as we have seen, this is a dubious proposition. Ordinary people, to be sure, can enter the political arena spontaneously, in "moments of madness."[1] Sustained popular participation, though, is usually associated with efforts by political elites to mobilize popular support for their own struggles against their political antagonists. As astute a practitioner of politics as V. I. Lenin knew that to participate in political life, the working class needed the leadership of a "vanguard" drawn from the bourgeois intelligentsia.[2] Elites, whether they view themselves as a revolutionary vanguard or defenders of property and the status quo, do not recruit ordinary folks into the political arena for altruistic reasons. Political elites battle for power, for status, and for wealth. If it serves their interests to do so, they will endeavor to recruit armies of supporters just as rival

189

feudal lords once recruited battalions of armed retainers to do battle on their behalf. Of course, these retainers usually expected some small reward for their service, and no doubt received bits of bunting and heroic speeches along with their pittances. But warring magnates and rival political elites, alike, retain the lion's share of the booty for themselves. They understand the purpose of political struggle even if their multitude of hapless followers does not. Much of the time, those Americans who heed the call to get involved, make their opinions known, and so forth get little for their trouble except, perhaps, temporary psychic gratification.[3] How exactly did the millions of working-class Americans who voted for President Bush in 2000 and 2004 benefit from their political participation? They were rewarded with tax policies that helped their wealthier neighbors and a foreign policy that put their children in harm's way. They would have done better to stay home on election day.

The Myth of Political Leadership

Many Americans look to their nation's leaders for guidance and inspiration. They believe that even if the current crop of officials is wanting in character or judgment, somewhere out there, better ones are to be found. This view is strongly encouraged by biographers and historians who depict the leaders of the past as giants. Political biographers function as the cleanup crew of American history. Presidents and other politicians who were known to be inept, foolish, duplicitous, or just plain scoundrels when they lived can, with a bit of scholarly touch-up, be presented as wise, albeit misunderstood, statesmen. Thus, in the hands of the cleanup crew, the somnolent Calvin Coolidge became a man who believed that a national leader should not try to "go ahead of the majestic army of human thought and aspiration, blazing new and strange paths."[4] In the hands of the cleanup crew, the third-rate politician Harry S. Truman, considered by his political colleagues in Kansas City to be a nice fellow but "too light" for the Senate, became a tribune of the people.[5] John F. Kennedy, a man with ample style but hardly any substance, in the efficient hands of the cleanup crew has become an individual every bit as courageous as those profiled in Kennedy's own ghostwritten work—for which the future president dishonestly accepted a Pulitzer Prize.[6] Lyndon Johnson, a rather bizarre and troubled person who nearly wrecked the country, has been recast as somewhat flawed but, nevertheless, a great man.[7]

Of course, the images of these relatively recent politicians will receive more polishing over the years to come. Have not the political hacks of the nineteenth century already joined the pantheon of the demigods? No doubt, if American history is still being written two centuries or so from now, the somewhat stained reputations of some of our current leaders will enjoy a renaissance. Perhaps it will be discovered that Richard Nixon was actually a kind man who secretly harbored a deep and abiding love for his fellow citizens. Bill Clinton, perhaps, will turn out to have been a quiet but staunch advocate of training in Kantian ethics for the nation's youth. And, as to George W. Bush, it may well be discovered by the cleanup crew that it was the seemingly hapless Dubya's long-standing interest in theoretical physics and computer science—not Al Gore's—that inspired the creation of the Internet.

Despite the ongoing efforts of the cleanup crew, it seems rather obvious that politics generally attracts mediocre individuals. During the 2004 presidential campaign, much was made of George W. Bush's abysmal grades at Yale, a school that almost certainly admitted him only because of his family connections. Yet, as we saw earlier, his Democratic opponent, John Kerry, was hardly a scholar, earning even worse marks than Bush at Yale. It is true that intellectual prowess and practical intelligence are not one and the same. Franklin D. Roosevelt was no intellectual but possessed enormous practical intelligence. Justice Oliver Wendell Holmes, indeed, famously characterized FDR as a man with a second-class intellect but a first-class temperament. Yet this combination is not easy to find among contemporary politicians. Many seem to be driven by petty ambitions and appear to be coarsened as they rise through the political ranks. Alexander Hamilton feared that political life would appeal to individuals who possessed no more than "talents for low intrigue and the little arts of popularity."[8] Hamilton might have been describing nearly every candidate for middle school and high school class office. These are often eager but untalented students whose parents worry that they will not be accepted by the best colleges on the basis of intellect, serious achievements, or even family connections. Politics is an alternative path to success for these individuals that requires only the base aptitudes indicated by Hamilton.

Some of these smarmy mediocrities gradually acquire a taste for political intrigue and authority as they take part in a succession of cockamamy student councils and model congresses where they can flatter themselves that they are important personages. Perhaps, as one psychologist has suggested, politics appeals particularly to those who already possess narcissistic tendencies and who, as a result, are readily seduced by the opportunity to exercise even the tiniest snippet of power.[9] At any rate, some former student council officers can be found, years later, prowling the halls of the Capitol, the

White House's West Wing, the state legislatures, and the various municipal governing bodies, still practicing and perfecting their little arts. The most cunning and cutthroat of these individuals might have a chance to rise to positions of real power. The White House, which stands at the pinnacle of American power, is typically occupied by ruthless and ambitious individuals for whom *Machtkampf* has become an obsession.

Perhaps this is more true today than during earlier periods in American history.[10] Changes in the methods for choosing presidents over the life of the republic have changed the kinds of people who can qualify for election. With a few notable and obvious exceptions, the politicians that the major parties chose to elevate to the White House during the nineteenth century held views and ambitions that posed little threat to party dominance or solidarity. The parties did not send their foremost leaders to the White House. Instead, they usually nominated "dark horses," little-known and innocuous individuals who were deemed to pose no threat to the factional balance of power within the party. Near the start of the twentieth century, however, as political parties began to decline in strength, presidential aspirants began to run for office on their own account instead of waiting to be called by their parties. A different sort of person came to occupy the White House. To make oneself president required a powerful, driving ambition rarely found in the politicians who waited for their parties to make them presidents. Self-made presidents have generally wanted something more than the title and the office. They have tried to use the office to make history. The decline of political parties and the emergence of today's candidate-centered campaigns tend to favor presidential aspirants who are driven, aggressive, tenacious, and perhaps even ruthless. Conventional political wisdom holds that those who lack the requisite "fire in the belly" should not even apply for the job.

The making of a modern president can take years. Raising millions, building a campaign organization, courting supporters, maintaining a positive presence in the public consciousness—all of this demands not only time but a candidate with an obsessive drive approaching Captain Ahab's. Indeed, would it be an overstatement to assert that, at least since Franklin D. Roosevelt, many American presidents have been monsters? Who but the most aggressive, supremely ambitious individual would be willing to devote years and even decades to campaigning for the presidency? What normal individual would be willing to tolerate the public airing of every last utterance and event and private moment of his or her life? In some cases, the drive and ambition have been obvious and have been amply discussed. Bill Clinton, Jack Kennedy, Lyndon Johnson, and Richard Nixon, albeit for different reasons, were determined to seek office and preferment and made little effort to hide their overweening ambition. Nixon, according to his biographers, was driven to campaign even, perhaps especially, when the odds seemed hopeless. Thus, after his defeat in the 1960 presidential race, Nixon decided to make a run for the California state house, though the likelihood of success was small. "It was the only campaign available to him … and Nixon was hooked on campaigning."[11]

Other recent presidents—Truman, Eisenhower, Reagan, perhaps George W. Bush—have been able to present themselves as ordinary Americans reluctantly accepting the burden of office. But, of course, nothing could be further from the truth. Truman, according to his biographer, was a man who all his life "sought to channel as much authority to himself as possible."[12] Reagan launched his political career in the 1940s and spent decades cultivating supporters and practicing the arts of politics, steadily seeking, as his biographer says, "new stages" on which to star.[13] George W. Bush, caricatured by the press as the hapless "Dubya," is known by his staff to be extremely disciplined, guarded, and given to cold, "fierce anger" toward his opponents.[14] As for the apparently genial "Uncle Ike," though presenting himself as a man lacking political ambition but willing to do his duty, Eisenhower began planning his campaign to capture Washington not long after his army occupied Berlin.[15] Despite his famous grin, Ike was known to his intimates as a supremely ruthless man. "He's cold, terribly cold," Richard Nixon once said of his patron.[16] The contemporary presidential selection process favors the election of these driven, aggressive, and ambitious individuals—Type A personalities, to use the contemporary parlance.

PUBLIC LIES AND PRIVATE PURPOSES

In their campaigns and once in office, many of these individuals habitually stretch the truth as it serves their political purposes. As we saw in Chapter 1, politicians construct a variety of imaginative fibs to present self-serving conduct as actually serving broader public purposes, to build or demolish political coalitions or to mobilize and energize their supporters. Perhaps some of these fibs could be seen as the "little white lies" of the political process. Elimination of the marriage tax penalty, for example, probably would not shake the foundations of the republic. Some political lies, however, are more significant and, potentially, more dangerous. One of these is, of course, the use of patriotic claims to mobilize supporters or shut off potential dissent. Why is a piece of legislation designed to expand law enforcement powers and diminish civil liberties called the "U.S.A. Patriot

Act"? Presumably, the purpose is to discourage opponents from raising objections to the policy. Who, after all wants to be opposed to a piece of legislation dubbed a patriot act?

A second and even more malicious political lie is the use of religious appeals and themes to mask political interests. The Bush administration, for example, frequently affirms its commitment to strong religious and moral values. This interest in religion, however, seems to peak in the months prior to national elections. Thus, prior to the 2004 presidential election, the administration made much of its opposition to same-sex marriage, and in the months preceding the 2006 national contests, the president loudly proclaimed his support for a constitutional amendment defining marriage as a union of a man and a woman. In both instances, the president hoped to energize religious conservatives with a ringing affirmation of their beliefs. One of my favorite teachers, Theodore J. Lowi of Cornell, often remarked in class that when a politician invokes the name of God, he or she is really saying, "Follow me," or, better yet, "God wants you to follow me." Unfortunately, as we have seen in recent years, the politicians around the world who most frequently invoke God's name seem to be the ones most likely to engage in ungodly activities.

STATE SECRETS

Of course, lies and deceptions are not just the work of unscrupulous politicians. As we saw in Chapter 2, duplicity and mendacity have become routine features of the modern governmental process. In the nineteenth century, governments feared public opinion but had little ability to influence it. In fact, rulers could hardly assess or analyze shifts in the popular mood. As public opinion scholar W. Phillips Davison observed, "Rulers looked upon public opinion with something akin to terror." Eighteenth- and nineteenth-century political elites often would have only the vaguest understanding of popular attitudes before "the government, the church hierarchy and the aristocracy suddenly saw the roof blown off."[17] During this premodern era, the two most important tools used by governments to manage opinion were secrecy and censorship. By blocking access to information, governments sought to inhibit the development of hostile ideas. In the United States, secrecy became part of official policy as early as 1792 when President George Washington attempted to block a congressional inquiry into a disastrous military expedition led by General Arthur St. Clair. Washington claimed what later would be named "executive privilege." Subsequently, citing the importance of secrecy, Washington declined to provide Congress with information concerning his negotiations with Great Britain.

All contemporary governments, of course, continue to employ censorship and secrecy to guard against real or imagined dangers and antagonisms. But during the twentieth century, national policies toward public opinion began to undergo an important change. Using polling, the mass media, and public relations techniques, modern governments began to manipulate and manage popular opinion. In the modern era, the censor was joined by the public relations officer in dealing with public opinion.

In the United States, management of popular opinion became a routine official function during World War I. During the war, the Wilson administration created a censorship board, enacted sedition and espionage legislation, and attempted to suppress groups such as the International Workers of the World that voiced opposition to the war effort. At the same time, however, World War I was the first modern "industrial" war requiring a total mobilization of popular effort on the home front for military production. This prodigious industrial effort required the government to convince the civilian population to bear the costs and make the sacrifices needed to achieve industrial and agricultural as well as battlefield success. The instrument developed by the government to build needed popular support was the Committee on Public Information (CPI), chaired by journalist and publicist George Creel. The CPI organized a massive public relations and news management program aimed at promoting popular enthusiasm for the war effort. This program included the dissemination of favorable news reports; the publication of patriotic pamphlets, films, photos, cartoons, bulletins, and periodicals; and the organization of "war expositions" and speakers' tours. Special labor programs were aimed at maintaining the loyalty and productivity of the work force. Much of the CPI's staff was drawn from the major advertising agencies. According to Creel, the work of the committee "was distinctly in the nature of an advertising campaign ... our object was to sell the war."[18]

The CPI was a temporary wartime agency, but its work was a harbinger of the permanent expansion of government opinion management that began with the New Deal and has persisted to the present. The enlargement of the scope of governmental activity that began during the Roosevelt era was accompanied by an explosion of official public relations efforts. Every new department, agency, bureau, office, or committee quickly established a public relations or public information arm to persuade the citizenry to cooperate with its efforts and support its objectives. The link between the expansion of government and the growth of opinion management was put into clear focus by Chester Bowles. Early in his long career in public life, Bowles served as director of the New Deal's Office of Price Administration (OPA). Under Bowles's leadership, the OPA developed an extensive public information program whose large budget drew congressional fire. Bowles's defense of the program is recalled in his memoirs:

> At one point, Congress threatened to cut our information budget. I testified that if they deprived us of the means of explaining our program to the people, our requirements for investigators and inspectors to enforce our regulations would be greatly increased. With a $5 million annual budget for information, I said I could keep the American people reasonably informed about our regulations and their own obligations and rights as citizens. But, if Congress cut this $5 million, I would have no alternative but to make a request for $15 million to hire law enforcement inspectors to prosecute the many people who, often through their own ignorance and lack of information, had acted illegally.[19]

In other words, manipulation is cheaper than coercion.

The government's interest in "explaining programs to the people" has, of course, increased substantially since the New Deal. Every federal agency now engages in opinion management efforts that dwarf the OPA's $5 million program. The federal government now spends hundreds of millions each year on advertising, public information, and related matters. As we saw in Chapter 2, Americans are now constantly exposed to efforts by the government to explain things to them.

PRACTICING DEFENSIVE POLITICS

Rather than become ensnared in this manipulative machinery, most people would be better off if they did not have to engage in political activity at all. They could more profitably spend the time with their families—or even singing; dancing; writing poetry; taking part in sports; or attending the theater, opera, or cinema. President Lyndon Johnson, who eventually became disillusioned with politics, told the young Doris Kearns, "I'd have been better off looking for immortality through my wife and children and their children in turn."[20] "Get married," said Johnson to Kearns. "Have children, spend time with them."[21] Many Americans show by their actions, if not their words, that they agree with LBJ. Quite a few demonstrate a healthy detestation of the world of government and politics. They disdain political discussion, seldom attend political meetings, almost never seek political office, and refuse to waste time listening to the tedious Sunday-morning pundits vie with one another to rehash and puff their vapid political lines. Of course, since they are taught that politics and citizen involvement are supposed to be important, most citizens are unwilling to admit that they really have no interest in watching the politicos preen for the camera. Yet the reality is that few can bring themselves to pay serious attention to the often repulsive political spectacle.

Americans are also taught to equate political participation with personal empowerment and individual freedom. Yet the relationship between politics and freedom is more complex than the civics teachers acknowledge or know. Whatever its other virtues, popular political participation functions as a source of state power. James Wilson, as we saw in Chapter 3, urged his fellow Constitutional Convention delegates to accept widespread popular participation as the price of raising the "federal pyramid" to a "considerable altitude."[22] But real freedom does not simply mean a formal opportunity to take part in organized political activity. Real political freedom must include a considerable measure of freedom from politics as well as the freedom to take part in politics. Freedom implies a measure of personal autonomy, a sphere within which individuals are not followers of movements, causes, candidates, or parties and are not subject to policies, initiatives, or programs. Nietzsche might have been gazing at Wilson's pyramid when he cried, "Break the windows and leap to freedom."[23]

Unfortunately, though, the government and the members of the meddlesome political class, more generally, are seldom content to leave their fellow citizens to their own devices. Officials and politicians not only want to explain things to their benighted fellows, but for better or worse—too often for worse—they seem to suffer from some compulsion to interfere in everyone's lives. When not merely engaged in their normal rent-seeking endeavors, a gaggle of officials wants to seize homes and turn them over to private developers. Other politicians and officials want to redistribute incomes for the benefit of their friends and supporters. Still others endeavor to impose their own moral values on everyone else. And, of course, there are those who insist upon sending other people's children to die on distant shores for reasons that are usually difficult to explain.

It is, alas, because the political class is relentlessly intrusive that ordinary citizens must leave their hearths and homes and gird themselves for political struggle despite their proper disdain for the activity. To be sure, neither the political class nor the state can ever truly be defeated. Occasionally one crowd of barnacles is replaced by another and one pyramid razed to make room for a new one. The new political class assures all who will listen that its slogans and mythologies are infinitely superior to the lies spun by its predecessors. Sometimes they might be, but often enough the differences are outweighed by the fundamental similarities of power and deceit. Nietzsche, after all, was not referring to any particular state when he had Zarathustra observe, "Whatever the state speaks is falsehood."[24]

But even if it cannot be defeated, the political class can and should continually be subjected to embarrassment, ridicule, and harassment. Not only does constant pressure keep the politicians and officials uncertain and off balance, but the exercise reminds the citizenry of the clay feet of their erstwhile idols. This, in turn, helps individuals maintain some critical distance from the state and its rulers and preserve at least a measure of inner freedom—a sphere within which each person may remain herself or himself.[25] This effort should be understood as *defensive politics,* an attempt to maintain individual autonomy and freedom from conventional politics.

The first rule of defensive politics is always to be cynically realistic. When any politician intones, "Ask not," assume he or she has something to hide. When a politician presents himself as an advocate for children, be careful about leaving him alone with your children. The political class hides information; it lies, schemes, and manipulates. Much of what officialdom keeps secret under such rubrics as national security and executive privilege is designed to protect politicians or the bureaucracy, not the nation or the public at large. Are we to suppose that Vice President Cheney was thinking of the public welfare when he claimed executive privilege and refused to reveal the details of his meetings with energy-company executives? Was FEMA concerned with the public interest when it sought to restrict press coverage of its operations in the wake of Hurricane Katrina?[26] This seems rather unlikely. Every year, more than 20 million pieces of information are declared secret by the government. Many of these would not help America's enemies, but they might hurt America's politicians and bureaucrats. And much of what is revealed turns out to be false. What did happen to those Iraqi weapons of mass destruction?

Despite frequent reminders that neither those in power nor those who aspire to power can be trusted, millions of Americans remain surprisingly credulous and hopeful. In the 1990s, Americans voted against congressional Democrats because the House banking and post office scandals proved to them that the Democratic leadership could not be trusted with power. Ten years later, many Americans voted against congressional Republicans because lobbying and moral scandals proved to them that the GOP's leadership could not be trusted with power. One lesson that might possibly be drawn from these events is that neither group of politicians can be trusted with power. Perhaps no group of politicians can be trusted with power. Politics generally does not attract good people and often brings out the worst in those it attracts. If Americans were less trusting and hopeful, they might be more difficult to deceive.

The second rule of defensive politics is to choose action over participation. Participation implies taking part in politics through the formal processes established for that purpose. In some instances, this may be a worthwhile undertaking. One or another candidate for public office may, indeed, be a trustworthy champion of ideas and positions that are worth supporting at the polls. Alternatively, a candidate may be sufficiently villainous to warrant engaging in a vigorous campaign against his or her election to public office. Of course, voters may have considerable difficulty disentangling the myths created by candidates' slogans and claims from the realities of their abilities, actions, and intentions. Millions of Americans voted for Woodrow Wilson in 1916 because, according to his campaign slogans, Wilson, "kept us out of war." Perhaps this slogan continued to inspire Americans as they marched to war. In 1976, Americans responded to Jimmy Carter's question, "Why not the best?" Today, some might say he was the better, but surely no one examining Carter's record would confuse him with the best. Politicians lie about their plans for the future and lie about their past behavior. They lie about their intellectual abilities, experience, character, and backgrounds. Sometimes the lies are revealed, but very frequently they are not.

Short of engaging in painstaking research, which the media claim to provide but seldom deliver, what is a voter to do? One simple rule of thumb might be captured in a slogan. If politicians can have their catchwords and shibboleths, voters are certainly entitled to their own political slogans. I would propose as the voters' motto, *"If in doubt, vote them out."* In the absence of solid information to the contrary, voters may safely assume that their elected officials are duplicitous, venal, and self-serving. Perhaps this characterization would not be true of some, but it is true of so many that voters would seldom be wrong if they simply resolved to vote against all incumbents unless they knew of some compelling reason to do otherwise. In most elections, more than 90 percent of congressional incumbents are returned to office. Given Congress's usually abysmal record, it seems unlikely that so many actually deserved to be reelected. In 2006, a number of prominent incumbents, including senators George Allen, Rick Santorum, and Conrad Burns, were defeated. This was certainly a good start.

Throwing the rascals out is a step in the right direction. But, as we saw in Chapter 3, electoral processes are not designed to maximize popular political influence. They are constructed, instead, to delimit popular involvement in political life and to protect the political class from popular interference. Moreover, voters often find themselves merely replacing one set of rascals with another. In 1994, Democratic congressional corruption led voters to give Republicans control of the Congress. In 2006, Republican congressional corruption persuaded voters to hand control of Congress back to the Democrats. Some of these Democrats, like Congressman John Murtha of Pennsylvania, were previously implicated in corrupt practices. It is safe to predict that in a few years, voters will be disgusted by Democratic corruption and turn again to the Republicans. Might the moral of the story be that, given a bit of power, both sides are easily corrupted? Just a thought.

The practice of defensive politics requires voters to learn to think outside the (ballot) box.[27] There are many simple and nonviolent forms of political action through which ordinary individuals can oblige the government to listen and, sometimes, to respond to them. These include protests, demonstrations, boycotts, embarrassing revelations, and so forth. College students are often assigned lengthy readings from the *Federalist Papers,* which, among other things, defend limited popular involvement in the political process. I have often thought that students should, instead, read Saul Alinsky's *Rules for Radicals.*[28] In Chapter 7, Alinsky discusses thirteen useful political tactics designed to achieve results outside the normal participatory framework. Generally speaking, Alinsky's tactics are designed to disrupt and irritate and to subject our more pompous officials and bureaucrats to public ridicule or even shame. Thinking outside the ballot box can be remarkably effective. In one instance recounted by Alinsky, he and his followers forced Chicago authorities to yield to the demands of a black neighborhood group by threatening to send hundreds of members to form long lines that would tie up all the lavatories at Chicago's O'Hare International airport for an entire day. The mere threat of humiliating media coverage for what Alinsky dubbed the nation's first "shit in" forced a hurried surrender by the usually arrogant Mayor Daley and his toadies.[29]

Many of the tactics developed by Alinsky and other shrewd dissidents are aimed at exploiting the gaps between the official rhetoric and the actual character of those in power. Sometimes this is called a strategy of provocation and reprisal or, in more poetic terms, a tactic designed to force the government to reveal the "mailed fist" beneath the "velvet glove" through which it pretends to rule.[30] As Alinsky put it, the authorities "publicly pose as the custodians of responsibility, morality, law and justice" but beneath the surface are usually neither moral nor just.[31] The most effective political tactics are those that use disruption and agitation to compel power-holders to choose between living up to their own rhetoric or revealing that their claims are false. This was essentially the strategy employed by Dr. Martin Luther King and other leaders of America's civil rights movement. While millions of Americans watched on their television screens, King and his followers mounted peaceful boycotts, sit-ins, demonstrations, and marches that forced Southern segregationist leaders to choose between surrendering to the movement's demands or revealing the brutal reality that lurked beneath the rhetoric of "separate but equal" and similarly vacuous political claims. Analogous tactics were employed against the British by America's founders. When Samuel Adams and his "sons of liberty" dumped British tea into Boston Harbor, they provoked the authorities into undertaking harsh reprisals against innocent residents of Boston. This revealed to thousands of colonists the gaps between British claims of justice and the Crown's actual conduct. Had they not first been successful practitioners of Alinsky-style tactics, the nation's founders would never have won the opportunity to later caution against the dangers of too democratic a politics in the *Federalist*.

Today, technology is opening new avenues for popular political action. The Internet has become a powerful tool for political organization. Weblogs, popularly known as "blogs," and other Internet forums allow the rapid dissemination of information, ideas, and opinions outside the control of the government or other institutions. To be sure, many of the ideas and opinions found in the various weblogs are utterly foolish. America's always active flying-saucer community, for example, is well-represented in the blogosphere. Moreover, corporations and politicians have learned to create and use blogs for their own purposes. Blogs, nevertheless, sharply lower the technological and financial barriers that previously prevented all but a few individuals and interests from reaching mass audiences and potentially increase the ability of ordinary people to engage in effective political action. In 2003, for example, bloggers took the lead in publicizing a story that cost Senate Majority Leader Trent Lott his job. Lott had praised the late Senator Strom Thurmond, a fervent segregationist, as a man who would have made a good president. Only after the blogs broke the story did the mainstream media seem to become aware of the significance of Lott's comments. In 2004, bloggers demonstrated that then-CBS anchor Dan Rather had presented unsubstantiated and possibly bogus information in a major story. Rather was forced into retirement. In 2006, bloggers publicized evidence of racist comments by Florida House candidate Tramm Hudson, derailing Hudson's candidacy. And that same year, bloggers helped to bring about Senator Joseph Lieberman's defeat in the Connecticut Democratic primary election.

Magnifying the power of the Internet is the universal availability of digital cameras. Particularly since cell phones are now equipped with cameras, millions of Americans have the capacity to photograph or film events that they may witness. At the same time, Internet sites such as YouTube permit users to upload photos and video clips that are then viewed by hundreds of thousands of subscribers and are sometimes picked up by the mainstream media for even wider dissemination. In 2006, a YouTube video showing Virginia Senator George Allen making a racist comment to one of his opponent's campaign workers caused an uproar. Allen, who had been positioning himself for a possible 2008 presidential race, was defeated for reelection to the Senate from Virginia when his victory had previously been seen as a sure thing. His presidential aspirations were dashed. With a bit of technology, citizens had ended the career of a once-powerful politician. This example illustrates the way in which technology can be a tool of popular political action. Because they are pervasive and intrusive, the new media technologies sometimes allow ordinary citizens to break into the private world of the political class and to observe the differences between the carefully cultivated appearance and the less-attractive reality of that world. Members of eighteenth-century mobs sometimes told astonishing tales of what they saw when they stormed the gates of the lord's castle. In a similar vein, modern-day electronic rioters sometimes astonish the nation with what their cameras are able to show millions of users of the Internet.

The final rule of defensive politics is never to trust the state. Whatever ideologies they may happen to profess, those who have power will always abuse it. On this point, Alinsky and the authors of the *Federalist* agree. Officials abuse power in petty ways—pardoning well-connected felons, for example, and they abuse power in big ways—such as creating phony pretexts for unnecessary wars. It is important to support restrictions on governmental power and to be wary of claims that we need more government. Occasionally, we do need the protection and services of the state, but often it is only the government that needs more government. In 2006, the U.S. government cut Homeland Security funds for the protection of the citizens of New York and Washington, the most likely targets of future terrorist attacks. At the same time, the government funded elaborate plans for the continuation and, if necessary, relocation of every last government agency—even the U.S. Patent Office—in the event of some catastrophe.[32] Clearly, the government views its primary mission as protection of the government. The citizenry, it seems is expendable.

Notes

NOTES TO CHAPTER 1

1. Mason L. Weems, *The Life of George Washington*, ed. by Marcus Cunliffe (Cambridge, MA: The Belknap Press of Harvard University, 1962).

2. Mary Ann Akers, "Heard on the Hill," *Roll Call*, January 4, 2007, p. 1.

3. David Kirkpatrick, "Congress Finds Ways of Avoiding Lobbyist Limits," *Washington Post*, February 11, 2007, p. 1.

4. Pew Center for the People and the Press, "The State of the News Media 2004."

5. Joseph Nye, Philip Zelikow, and David King, *Why People Don't Trust Government* (Cambridge, MA: Harvard University Press, 1997), p. 5.

6. Kevin Mattson and Richard C. Leone, *Engaging Youth: Combating the Apathy of Young Americans Toward Politics* (New York: Century Foundation Press, 2003).

7. Ilene Grossman, "To Combat Cynicism and Voter Apathy, States Turn to Civic Education." In The Midwestern Council of State Governments, *Firstline* 7, no. 5 (May 2000): p. 1.

8. Dale Turner, "Cynical Voices Can't Sing a Song of Peace," *Seattle Times*, March 29, 2003, p. B4.

9. For recent examples, see Frank Rich, *The Greatest Story Ever Sold* (New York: Penguin, 2006).

10. Quoted in Alexander Cockburn and Jeffrey St. Clair, eds., "Weapons of Mass Destruction: Who Said What When," *Counterpunch*, May 29, 2003, p. 1.

11. Ambrose Bierce, *The Unabridged Devil's Dictionary* (Athens: University of Georgia Press, 2001).

12. American National Election Studies, *Guide to Public Opinion and Electoral Behavior*, Center for Political Studies, University of Michigan, 1952–2004.

13. According to a 2002 Roper Poll, 70 percent of all Americans believe the government is hiding information about UFOs.

14. The phrase is associated with Fang Lejun, Liu Wei, and other artists working in the aftermath of the 1989 Tiananmen Square massacre.

15. Niccolo Machiavelli, *The Prince* (New York: Mentor, 1952), p. 50.

16. Ibid., p. 90.

17. Steven Pinker, *How the Mind Works* (New York: W. W. Norton, 1997), p. 495.

18. Vamik Volkan, "Narcissistic Personality Disorder and Reparative Leadership," *International Journal of Group Psychotherapy* 30 (1980): 131–152.

19. Angus Campbell, Philip E. Converse, Warren E. Miller, and Donald E. Stoker, *The American Voter* (New York: Wiley, 1960), ch. 6.

20. David Kuo, *Tempting Faith: An Inside Story of Political Seduction* (New York: The Free Press, 2006).

21. Donald Kagan, *The Peloponnesian War* (New York, Penguin, 2003), p. 212.

22. Henry A. Turner, *General Motors and the Nazis* (New Haven, CT: Yale University Press, 2005).

23. James Madison, *The Federalist*, no. 10, in Clinton Rossiter, ed., *The Federalist Papers* (New York: Mentor, 1961), p. 79.

24. Quoted in Paul Koistinen, *The Hammer and the Sword: Labor, the Military and Industrial Production, 1920–1945* (New York: Arno Press, 1979), p. 580.

25. Jill Barshay, "Insurers Risk Loss of Special Status," *Congressional Quarterly Weekly,* January 24, 2005, p. 156.

26. Frank Baumgartner and Beth Leech, *Basic Interests: The Importance of Groups in Politics and Political Science* (Princeton, NJ: Princeton University Press, 1998).

27. Thomas Hobbes, *Leviathan* (New York: Collier, 1962), p. 80.

28. John R. Wilke, "Seat in Congress Helps Mr. Taylor Help His Business," *Wall Street Journal,* October 11, 2006, p. 1.

29. Richard Shenkman, *Presidential Ambition: Gaining Power at Any Cost* (New York: Harper Perennial, 1999).

30. Matthew A. Crenson and Benjamin Ginsberg, *Presidential Power: Unchecked and Unbalanced* (New York: W. W. Norton, 2007).

31. James Madison, *The Federalist*, no. 51, in Clinton Rossiter, ed., *The Federalist Papers* (New York: Mentor, 1961), p. 322.

32. *Final Report of the National Commission on Terrorist Attacks upon the United States* (New York: W. W. Norton, 2004), ch. 11.

33. Louis Fisher, *Congressional Abdication on War and Spending* (College Station: Texas A&M Press, 2000).

34. Crenson and Ginsberg, *Presidential Power,* ch. 5.

35. See Hans J. Morgenthau, *Politics Among Nations,* 6th ed. (New York: Knopf, 1985); and John Mearsheimer, *The Tragedy of Great Power Politics* (New York: W. W. Norton, 2003).

36. J. H. Hertz, ed., *The Pentateuch and Haftorahs* (London: Soncino Press, 1992), p. 14.

37. William Shakespeare, *Julius Caesar,* Act I, Scene 2.

38. Pinker, *How the Mind Works,* p. 493.

39. Quoted in John O. McGinnis, "The Human Constitution and Constitutive Law," *Journal of Contemporary Legal Issues* (Spring 1997): 222.

40. Joseph J. Ellis, *His Excellency, George Washington* (New York: Knopf, 2004), p. 151.

41. Ibid., p. 171.

42. Joseph J. Ellis, *Founding Brothers: The Revolutionary Generation* (New York: Knopf, 2000), p. 167.

43. Ellis, *His Excellency,* p. 38.

44. Ron Chernow, *Alexander Hamilton* (New York: Penguin, 2004), p. 8.

45. Ibid., p. 33.

46. Robert Caro, *The Years of Lyndon Johnson: The Path to Power* (New York: Knopf, 1982), ch. 7.

47. Christopher Matthews, *Kennedy and Nixon: The Rivalry That Shaped Postwar America* (New York: Simon and Schuster, 1996), p. 126.

48. Donald A. Ritchie, *Reporting from Washington: The History of the Washington Press Corps* (New York: Oxford, 2005), p. 249.

49. Robert Trivers, "The Evolution of Reciprocal Altruism," *Quarterly Review of Biology* 46 (1971): 35–46.

50. *Babylonian Talmud,* Chagigah 5a.

51. Ibid., Bava Bathra 9b.

52. T. Harry Williams, *Huey Long* (New York: Knopf, 1969), p. 107.

53. David McCullough, *Truman* (New York: Simon and Schuster, 1992), p. 183.

54. Ibid., p. 585.

55. Quoted in ibid., p. 585.

56. Quoted in ibid., p. 585.

57. Robert Remini, *Henry Clay: Statesman for the Union* (New York: W. W. Norton, 1991), p. 186.

58. Ibid., p. 250.

59. Quoted in ibid., p. 410.

60. David Cowles, "Kerry Sour-Grapes Watch," *New Republic,* April 25, 2005, p. 8.

61. Eric Kandel, James Schwartz, and Thomas Jessell, *Essentials of Neural Science and Behavior* (Stamford, CT: Appleton & Lange, 1995), pp. 613–615.

62. Martin Seligman, "Phobias and Preparedness," *Behavior Therapy* 2 (1971): 307–320.

63. Joseph LeDoux, *The Emotional Brain* (New York: Simon and Schuster, 1996), p. 236.

64. Adam Cohen and Elizabeth Taylor, *American Pharaoh: Mayor Richard J. Daley—His Battle for Chicago and the Nation* (Boston: Little, Brown, 2000), p. 65.

65. Quoted in ibid., p. 145.

66. Ibid., p. 311.

67. Martin Shefter, *Political Parties and the State* (Princeton, NJ: Princeton University Press, 1994), p. 82.

68. Lois Romano and Mike Allen, "Secret Tapes Not Meant to Harm, Writer Says," *Washington Post,* February 21, 2005, p. A2.

69. David Kuo, *Tempting Faith: An Inside Story of Political Seduction* (New York: Free Press, 2006).

70. David Guarino, "Hill at Tufts: Use Bible to Guide Poverty Policy," *Boston Herald,* November 11, 2004, p. 23.

71. Senator Robert Byrd, *Losing America: Confronting a Reckless and Arrogant Presidency* (New York: W. W. Norton, 2004).

72. See, for example, D. Eisenstadt, M. R. Leippe, J. A. Rivers, and M. A. Stambush, "Counterattitudinal Advocacy on a Matter of Prejudice," *Journal of Applied Social Psychology* 33, no.10 (October 1, 2003): 2123–2152.

73. Philip Zimbardo and Richard Gerrig, *Psychology and Life,* 15th ed. (New York: Longman, 1999), p. 753.

74. David Garrow, *Protest at Selma: Martin Luther King, Jr., and the Voting Rights Act of 1965* (New Haven, CT: Yale University Press, 1978).

75. *Daily Variety,* November 3, 1987.

76. "A Special Report," *Chronicle of Higher Education* 50, no. 35 (May 7, 2004): A12–13.

77. Ibid.

78. Don Phillips and Richard Morin, "Amtrak Subsidy Support Strong, Survey Shows," *Washington Post,* August 5, 2002, p. 9.

79. Quoted in John Samples, "Making the World Safer for Incumbents," *Policy Analysis,* no. 393, March 14, 2001, p. 8

80. Paul R. Pescatello, *Westway: The Road from New Deal to New Politics,* unpublished Ph.D. dissertation, Department of Government, Cornell University, 1986.

81. *Sierra Club v. U.S. Army Corps of Engineers,* 772 F. 2d 1043, C.A. 2 (N.Y.), 1985.

82. *Near v. Minnesota,* 283 U.S. 697 (1931).

83. Timothy A. Byrnes, *Catholic Bishops in American Politics* (Princeton, NJ: Princeton University Press, 1991).

84. The notion that the marriage tax penalty is designed by demonic forces to destroy the family is a common theme in certain quarters of the religious right. A quick Internet search will reveal thousands of discussions of this topic among religious conservatives.

85. Benjamin Ginsberg and Martin Shefter, *Politics by Other Means,* 3rd ed. (New York: W. W. Norton, 2002), pp. 115–116.

86. Todd Gitlin, *The Sixties: Years of Hope, Days of Rage* (New York: Bantam, 1993).

87. Dallas A. Blanchard, *The Anti-Abortion Movement and the Rise of the Religious Right* (Boston: Twayne, 1994).

88. Eric Hoffer, *The True Believer: Thoughts on the Nature of Mass Movements* (New York: Perennial, 2002).

Notes to Chapter 2

1. James Bryce, *The American Commonwealth,* vol. 2 (New York: Macmillan, 1910), p. 259.

2. Poll by American National Election Studies, Center for Political Studies, University of Michigan.

3. Lawrence R. Jacobs and Robert Y. Shapiro, *Politicians Don't Pander: Political Manipulation and the Loss of Democratic Responsiveness* (Chicago: University of Chicago Press, 2000).

4. See Martin Shefter, "Party and Patronage: Germany, Italy and England," *Politics and Society* 7, no. 4 (1977): 409.

5. For an excellent review of the literature, see Carroll Glynn, Susan Herbst, Garret O'Keefe, Robert Shapiro, and Mark Lindeman, *Public Opinion,* 2nd ed. (Boulder, CO: Westview Press, 2004).

6. Theda Skocpol, *Boomerang: Health Care Reform and the Turn Against Government* (New York: W. W. Norton, 1997).

7. W. P. Davison, "The Third-Person Effect in Communication," *Public Opinion Quarterly* 47 (1983): 38–67.

8. Erika Falk, Erin Grizard, and Gordon McDonald, "Legislative Issue Advertising in the 108th Congress," Annenberg Public Policy Center, March 2005.

9. Ibid., p. 8.

10. Ibid., p. 11.

11. Burdett A. Loomis and Eric Sexton, "Choosing to Advertise: How Interests Decide," in Allan J. Cigler and Burdett A. Loomis, ed., *Interest Group Politics*, 3rd ed. (Washington, DC: CQ Press, 1993), pp. 203–210.

12. "Corporate Ads Help Improve Reputation," *Editor and Publisher*, October 12, 1977, p. 38.

13. Quoted in Michael Barbaro, "A New Weapon for Wal-Mart: A War Room," *New York Times*, November 1, 2005, p. C4.

14. *Congressional Quarterly Weekly*, May 30, 2005, back cover.

15. U.S. Public Interest Research Group, Clean up Southern Company, http://cta.policy.net/cusc.

16. *Congressional Quarterly Weekly*, October 31, 2005, back cover.

17. Kathleen Day, "Greenspan Urges Review of Fannie, Freddie Subsidies," *Washington Post*, May 24, 2000, p. E3.

18. Thomas Stanton, *Government Sponsored Enterprises: Mercantilist Corporations in the Modern World* (Washington, DC: American Enterprise Institute Press, 2001), p. 17.

19. Matthew Crenson and Benjamin Ginsberg, *Downsizing Democracy: How America Sidelined Its Citizens and Privatized Its Public* (Baltimore, MD: Johns Hopkins University Press, 2002), p. 209.

20. Patrick Barta, "Fannie Mae, Freddie Mac Counter Critics," *Wall Street Journal*, July 19, 2000, p. B6.

21. Jacqueline L. Salmon and Gilbert Gaul, "Red Cross Spent $500,000 in 3 Years to Raise Its Profile," *Washington Post*, February 27, 2006, p. A8.

22. *New Republic*, December 5, 2005, back cover.

23. Craig Unger, *House of Bush, House of Saud* (New York: Scribners, 2004).

24. Rachel Ehrenfeld, "The Saudi Connection," *National Review Online*, www.nationalreview.com, June 1, 2004.

25. Falk et al., "Legislative Issue Advertising," p. 3.

26. Ibid., p. 37.

27. Ibid., p. 40.

28. Ibid., p. 28.

29. Ibid., p. 19.

30. Kate Phillips, "The Senate Takes a Look at All Those Happy Pamphleteers," *New York Times*, March 12, 2006, p. 3.

31. Stanley Kurtz, "Climate of Fear," *National Review Online*, www.nationalreview.com, October 7, 2004.

32. Deborah Burlingame, "Gitmo's Guerrilla Lawyers," *Wall Street Journal*, March 8, 2007, p. A17.

33. Peter Applebome, "The Man Behind Rosa Parks," *New York Times*, December 7, 2005, p. 1.

34. David Garrow, *Bearing the Cross: Martin Luther King, Jr., and the Southern Christian Leadership Conference* (New York: Random House, 1986).

35. Hugh Davis Graham, *The Civil Rights Era: Origins and Development of National Policy, 1960–1972* (New York: Oxford, 1990).

36. David Garrow, *Protest at Selma: Martin Luther King, Jr., and the Voting Rights Act of 1965* (New Haven, CT: Yale University Press, 1978).

37. Stephen Lawson, *Black Ballots: Voting Rights in the South, 1944–1969* (New York: Columbia University Press, 1976).

38. Howell Raines, *My Soul Is Rested: Movement Days in the Deep South Remembered* (New York: Putnam's, 1977).

39. Quoted in Crenson and Ginsberg, *Downsizing Democracy*, pp. 168–169.

40. *New Republic*, December 26, 2005, pp. 13–21.

41. Mark Blyth, *Great Transformations: Economic Ideas and Institutional Change in the Twentieth Century* (New York: Cambridge University Press, 2002), pp. 156–161.

42. Stanley Rothman, S. Robert Lichter, and Neil Nevitte, "Politics and Professional Advancement Among College Faculty," *Forum* 3, no. 1 (2005): article 2.

43. Robin Wilson, "We Don't Need That Kind of Attitude," *Chronicle of Higher Education*, December 16, 2005, p. A8.

44. *New York Times v. U.S.*, 403 U.S. 713 (1971).

45. Michael Massing, "The Press: The Enemy Within," *New York Review of Books*, December 15, 2005, p. 36.

46. Michael Lascelles, "Press Release Journalism," Pharma Watch, http://pharmawatch. blogspot.com/2005_10_01_pharmawatch_archive.html, October 25, 2005.

47. Brian Montopoli, "Press Release Journalism," *Columbia Journalism Review Daily*, April 18, 2005, www.cjrdaily.org/behind_the_news/press_release_journalism.php.

48. Anne Lineham, "Another Example of Press Release Journalism?" BlogHouston.net, April 18, 2005, www.bloghouston.net/archive/1/2005-04.

49. "LA Times: County Homeless Population Tops Two Kazillion, No Further Reporting Required," Independent Sources, http://independentsources.com/2005/06/16/la-times-county-homeless-population-tops-two-kazillion-no-further-reporting-required, January 4, 2006.

50. Dennis L. Wilcox and Glen T. Cameron, *Public Relations: Strategy and Tactics*, 8th ed. (Boston: Pearson, 2006), p. 357.

51. See, for example, Davis Merritt, *Knightfall: Knight Ridder and How the Erosion of Newspaper Journalism Is Putting Democracy at Risk* (New York: Amacom, 2005).

52. Wilcox and Cameron, *Public Relations*, p. 357.

53. Ben Fritz, Bryan Keefer, and Brendan Nyhan, *All the President's Spin: George W. Bush, the Media, and the Truth* (New York: Touchstone, 2004), pp. 252–253.

54. Ibid., p. 357.

55. Jeff Gerth, "Military's Information War Is Vast and Often Secretive," *New York Times*, December 11, 2005, p. 1.

56. Ibid., p. 18.

57. Ibid., p. 18.

58. Howard Kurtz, "Administration Paid Commentator," *Washington Post*, January 8, 2005, p. 1.

59. Anne Kornblut and Philip Shenon, "Columnist Resigns His Post Admitting Lobbyist Paid Him," *New York Times*, December 17, 2005, p. A15.

60. Eamon Javers, "This Opinion Brought to You By … ," *BusinessWeek*, January 20, 2006, p. 35.

61. Ibid., p. 36.

62. Anna Wilde Matthews, "At Medical Journals, Writers Paid by Industry Play Big Role," *Wall Street Journal*, December 13, 2005, p. 1.

63. Jon Fine, "Polluting the Blogosphere," *BusinessWeek*, July 10, 2006, p. 20.

64. Amy Cowles, "Wanted: A Few Good Advisers," *Gazette*, February 24, 2003, p. 7.

65. "Half-Naked and Wet, All for the Joy of Alma Mater," *Baltimore Sun*, October 19, 2005.

66. Paul Starr, *The Creation of the Media: Political Origins of Modern Communications* (New York: Basic Books, 2004), p. 78.

67. Jeffrey L. Pasley, *The Tyranny of Printers: Newspaper Politics in the Early American Republic* (Charlottesville: University Press of Virginia, 2003).

68. See, for example, Rowan Scarborough, "Leftist Press? Reporters Working in Washington Acknowledge Liberal Leanings in Poll," *Washington Times*, April 16, 1996, p. 1. A 2004 Pew poll found that only 7 percent of America's journalists consider themselves conservatives. By contrast, 33 percent of the general public calls itself conservative.

69. See, for example, Bernard Goldberg, *Bias: A CBS Insider Exposes How the Media Distort the News* (New York: Harper, 2002).

70. Michael Massing, "The End of News?" *New York Review of Books*, November 15, 2005, pp. 23–27.

71. Ibid., p. 25.

72. Lawrence H. Suid, *Guts and Glory: The Making of the American Military Image in Film* (Louisville: University Press of Kentucky, 2002).

73. Robert Lindsey, "Top Gun: Ingenious Dogfights," *New York Times*, May 27, 1986, p. C15.

74. Katherine Q. Seelye, "When Hollywood's Big Guns Come Right from the Source," *New York Times*, June 9, 2002, p. 1.

75. Ibid.

76. For examples, see Tom Fenton, *Bad News: The Decline of Reporting, the Business of News, and the Danger to Us All* (New York: HarperCollins, 2005), ch. 4.

77. Anne Marie Squeo and John D. McKinnon, "Cheney Role Risks Political Fallout," *Wall Street Journal*, February 11, 2006, p. A4.

78. Frank Rich, *The Greatest Story Ever Sold: The Decline and Fall of Truth from 9/11 to Katrina* (New York: Penguin, 2006).

79. Karlyn Bowman, "AEI Studies in Public Opinion," June 28, 2005, www.aei.org/doclib/20050630_Patriotism0630.pdf.

80. Paul Rutherford, *Weapons of Mass Persuasion: Marketing the War Against Iraq* (Toronto: University of Toronto Press, 2004), ch. 2.

81. George Gallup and Saul Rae, *The Pulse of Democracy: The Public Opinion Poll and How It Works* (New York: Simon and Schuster, 1940), p. 14.

82. Scott Althaus, *Collective Preferences in Democratic Politics* (New York: Cambridge University Press, 2003); Benjamin Ginsberg, *The Captive Public: How Mass Opinion Promotes State Power* (New York: Basic Books, 1986); and Susan Herbst, *Numbered Voices: How Opinion Polling Has Shaped American Politics* (Chicago: University of Chicago Press, 1993).

83. Chester Barnard, *Public Opinion in a Democracy*, pamphlet (Princeton, NJ: Herbert Baker Foundation, Princeton University, 1939), p. 13.

84. See Eugene Webb, Donald T. Campbell, Richard D. Schwartz, and Lee Sechrest, *Unobtrusive Measures: Normative Research in the Social Sciences* (Chicago: Rand McNally, 1966).

85. For an excellent discussion of information effects on survey outcomes, see Althaus, *Collective Preferences*, chs. 4 and 5.

86. This discussion is based upon Ginsberg, *The Captive Public*. For a critique, see Philip

E. Converse, "The Advent of Polling and Political Research," *PS* 29 (December 1996): 653–654.

87. Hadley Cantril, "The Intensity of an Attitude," *Journal of Abnormal and Social Psychology* 41 (1946): 129–135.

88. See Aage Clausen, Philip Converse, and Warren Miller, "Electoral Myth and Reality: The 1964 Election," *American Political Science Review* 59 (June 1968): 321–332.

89. The literature on this topic is discussed by George F. Bishop, *The Illusion of Public Opinion: Fact and Artifact in American Public Opinion Polls* (Lanham, MD: Rowman and Littlefield, 2005), ch. 2.

90. See Althaus, *Collective Preferences*, ch. 2.

91. Converse, "The Advent of Polling."

92. Charles W. Roll and Albert H. Cantril, *Polls: Their Use and Misuse in Politics* (Cabin John, MD: Seven Locks Press, 1972), p. 153.

93. See Richard Jensen, "American Election Analysis," in Seymour Martin Lipset, ed., *Politics and the Social Sciences* (New York: Oxford University Press, 1969), p. 229.

94. Bishop, *The Illusion of Public Opinion*, pp. 42–44.

95. Ibid., pp. 164–166.

96. See Justin Lewis, *Constructing Public Opinion: How Political Elites Do What They Like and Why We Seem to Go Along with It* (New York: Columbia University Press, 2001), ch.4.

97. Althaus, *Collective Preferences*, p. 255.

98. Ibid., p. 255.

99. John Mueller, *Policy and Opinion and the Gulf War* (Chicago: University of Chicago Press, 1994), pp. 117–118.

100. "Victory in Iraq or Victory in the Polls?" *Editor and Publisher,* December 3, 2005, p. 1.

101. Jacobs and Shapiro, *Politicians Don't Pander*, p. xv.

102. Alan Monroe, "Consistency Between Public Preferences and National Policy Decisions," *American Politics Quarterly* 7 (1979): 3–18. See also Alan D. Monroe, "Public Opinion and Public Policy, 1980–1993," *Public Opinion Quarterly* 62, no. 1 (1998): 6–18.

103. Benjamin Page and Robert Y. Shapiro, "Effects of Public Opinion on Policy," *American Political Science Review* 77 (1983): 175–190. See also Jeff Manza, Fay Lomax Cook, and Benjamin I. Page, eds., *Navigating Public Opinion: Polls, Policy, and the Future of American Democracy* (New York: Oxford University Press, 2002), part 1.

104. Glynn et al., *Public Opinion*, p. 293.

105. Bishop, *The Illusion of Public Opinion*, p. 35.

106. Ibid., pp. 34–35.

107. For a number of examples, see ibid., chs. 2 and 7.

108. See for example, Jacob S. Hacker and Paul Pierson, *Off Center: The Republican Revolution and the Erosion of American Democracy* (New Haven, CT: Yale University Press, 2005), p. 67.

109. Some scholars, to be sure, have argued that although many individuals may lack information or coherent policy preferences, public opinion in the aggregate may still be reasonable and sensible. Benjamin I. Page and Robert Y. Shapiro, in *The Rational Public: Fifty Years of Trends in Americans' Policy Preferences* (Chicago: University of Chicago Press, 1992), for example, assert that "public opinion as a collective phenomenon is … meaningful. And indeed rational … it is organized in coherent patterns; it is reasonable … and it is adaptive to new information" (p. 14). As Althaus, however, has demonstrated in ch. 2 of *Collective Preferences*, this argument rests upon very shaky statistical foundations. Moreover,

the notion that aggregate opinion may be reasonable despite the ignorance of individuals assumes that individuals do not communicate with or influence one another. This condition is usually violated in the case of political opinion, where the ignorant influence one another and are influenced by politicians and the media. Anyone who doubts this should listen to talk radio. See James Surowiecki, *The Wisdom of Crowds: Why the Many Are Smarter Than the Few and How Collective Wisdom Shapes Business, Economies, Societies and Nations* (New York: Doubleday, 2004).

110. Jacobs and Shapiro, *Politicians Don't Pander*, p. xv.

111. Dick Morris, *Behind the Oval Office: Getting Reelected Against All Odds* (Los Angeles: Renaissance, 1999); quoted in Jacobs and Shapiro, *Politicians Don't Pander*, p. xv.

112. Michael Graetz and Ian Shapiro, *Death by a Thousand Cuts: The Fight over Taxing Inherited Wealth* (Princeton, NJ: Princeton University Press, 2005).

113. Hacker and Pierson, *Off Center*, ch. 2.

114. Joseph A. Schumpeter, *Capitalism, Socialism and Democracy*, 3rd ed. (New York: Harper, 1970), p. 263.

NOTES TO CHAPTER 3

1. Data from American National Election Studies, Center for Political Studies, University of Michigan.

2. The University of the State of New York, The State Education Department, Bureau of Elementary Curriculum Development, Social Studies—Grade 1: A Teaching System (Albany, NY, 1971), p. 32. These guidelines are still in use today.

3. Thomas Frank, *What's the Matter with Kansas? How Conservatives Won the Heart of America* (New York: Metropolitan Books, 2004).

4. James Madison, *The Federalist*, no. 57, in Clinton Rossiter, ed., *The Federalist Papers* (New York: Mentor, 1961), p. 352.

5. See, for example, E. J. Hobsbawm, *Primitive Rebels: Studies in Archaic Forms of Social Movement in the 19th and 20th Centuries* (New York: W. W. Norton, 1959). See also George Rudé, *The Crowd in the French Revolution* (New York: Oxford University Press, 1959).

6. See, for example, Jon Agnone, "Effectiveness of Environmental Protest," paper presented at the Annual Meeting of the American Sociological Association, San Francisco, CA, August 17, 2004.

7. Walter Lippman, *The Essential Lippman*, ed. by Clinton Rossiter and James Lare (New York: Random House, Vintage Books, 1965), p. 12.

8. U.S. Senate, Committee on the Judiciary, Hearings before the Subcommittee on Constitutional Amendments on S.J. Res. 8, S.J. Res. 14, and S.J. Res. 78, relating to lowering the voting age to eighteen, May 14, 15, and 16, 1968 (Washington, DC: U.S. Government Printing Office, 1968), p. 12.

9. Ibid., p. 3.

10. Frances Fox Piven and Richard A. Cloward, *Poor People's Movements: Why They Succeed, How They Fail* (New York: Random House, 1979), pp. 231–235.

11. Ibid., p. 233.

12. Steven Schier, *You Call This an Election? America's Peculiar Democracy* (Washington, DC: Georgetown University Press, 2003), pp. 110–112.

13. "Cost of 2004 Elections," *USA Today* online, www.usatoday.com, November 2, 2004.

14. Philip E. Converse, "Attitudes and Non-attitudes: Continuation of a Dialogue," in Edward R. Tufte, ed., *The Quantitative Analysis of Social Problems* (Boston: Addison-Wesley, 1970), pp. 168–189.

15. Andrew Higgins, "Careful Planning Pays off for French Protestors," *Wall Street Journal,* March 17, 2006, p. A6.

16. Alexander Hamilton, *The Federalist,* no. 71, in Clinton Rossiter, ed., *The Federalist Papers* (New York: Mentor, 1961), p. 432.

17. For example, see Martin Malia, *Alexander Herzen and the Birth of Russian Socialism* (Cambridge, MA: Harvard University Press, 1961).

18. Benjamin Ginsberg and Robert Weissberg, "Elections as Legitimizing Institutions," *American Journal of Political Science* 22, 1 (February 1978): 31–55.

19. Sar Levitan and Diane Werneke, *Productivity: Problems, Prospects and Policies* (Baltimore, MD: Johns Hopkins University Press, 1984), ch. 3.

20. Max Farrand, ed., *The Records of the Federal Convention of 1787,* vol. 1 (New Haven, CT: Yale University Press, 1966), p. 49.

21. Ibid., p. 132.

22. Matthew A. Crenson and Benjamin Ginsberg, *Downsizing Democracy: How America Sidelined Its Citizens and Privatized Its Public* (Baltimore, MD: Johns Hopkins University Press, 2002), pp. 38–40.

23. Goran Therborn, "The Rule of Capitalism and the Rise of Democracy," *New Left Review* 103 (May 1977): 3–41.

24. Edward Cody, "One Riot Breaks Ground in China," *Washington Post,* June 28, 2006.

25. Reuters, November 8, 2005, "French Riots Undermine Confidence in Euro."

26. For a review of the campaign literature, see Carroll J. Glynn, Susan Herbst, Garret O'Keefe, Robert Shapiro, and Mark Lindeman, *Public Opinion,* 2nd ed. (Boulder, CO: Westview Press, 2004), ch. 10.

27. See Diana C. Mutz, Richard A. Brody, and Paul M. Sniderman, eds., *Political Persuasion and Attitude Change* (Ann Arbor: University of Michigan Press, 1996).

28. Dennis Johnson, *No Place for Amateurs: How Political Consultants Are Reshaping American Democracy* (New York: Routledge, 2001).

29. Barbara G. Salmore and Stephen A. Salmore, *Candidates, Parties and Campaigns: Electoral Politics in America,* 2nd ed. (Washington, DC: CQ Press, 1989), pp. 2–3.

30. Christopher Matthews, *Kennedy and Nixon: The Rivalry That Shaped Postwar America* (New York: Simon and Schuster, 1996), p. 105.

31. Ibid., p. 117.

32. Ibid., p.115

33. Ibid., p.115.

34. Ibid., pp. 115–116.

35. David Maraniss, *First in His Class: A Biography of Bill Clinton* (New York: Simon and Schuster, 1995), pp. 331–332.

36. David T. Canon, *Actors, Athletes and Astronauts: Political Amateurs in the U.S. Congress* (Chicago: University of Chicago Press, 1990).

37. Stephen E. Ambrose, *Eisenhower: Soldier and President* (New York: Simon and Schuster, 1990), pp. 245–246.

38. Juliet Carlisle and Thomas Knecht, "The Rise of the Millionaire Candidate: Self Funding in House and Senate Elections, 1984–2000," paper presented to the Midwest Political Science Association Annual Meeting, Chicago, IL, April 3–6, 2003.

39. Joan Didion, "Cheney: The Fatal Touch," *New York Review of Books,* October 5, 2006, pp. 51–56.

40. Jon Gertner, "The Very, Very Personal Is the Political," *New York Times,* February 15, 2004, p. 1.

41. Johnson, *No Place for Amateurs,* p. 176.

42. Gertner, "The Very, Very Personal."

43. Adam Nagourney, "Internet Injects Sweeping Change into U.S. Politics," *New York Times,* April 2, 2006, p. 1.

44. V. O. Key Jr., *The Responsible Electorate: Rationality in Presidential Voting, 1936-1960* (Cambridge, MA: Harvard University Press, 1966), p. 2.

45. The classic study is Angus Campbell, Phillip Converse, Warren Miller, and Donald Stokes, *The American Voter* (New York: Wiley, 1964).

46. Walter Dean Burnham, *Critical Elections and the Mainsprings of American Electoral Politics* (New York: W. W. Norton, 1970).

47. Kevin Phillips, *American Theocracy: The Peril and Politics of Radical Religion, Oil, and Borrowed Money in the 21st Century* (New York: Viking, 2006).

48. Peter Baker, "Democracy in Iraq Not a Priority in U.S. Budget," *Washington Post,* April 5, 2006, p. 1.

49. Angus Campbell, Philip E. Converse, Warren E. Miller, and Donald E. Stokes, *Elections and the Political Order* (New York: Wiley, 1967).

50. Richard Clarke, *Against All Enemies: Inside America's War on Terrorism* (New York: The Free Press, 2004).

51. Jim Rutenberg, "9/11 Panel Comments Freely," *New York Times,* April 15, 2004, p. 1.

52. Steven Ansolabehere and Shanto Iyengar, *Going Negative: How Attack Ads Shrink and Polarize the Electorate* (New York: Free Press, 1995).

53. Paul Greenberg, "The Invisible Ethnic Group," *Jewish World Review* online, http://jewishworldreview.com, October 29, 2004.

54. Susan Schmidt and James Grimaldi, "Nonprofit Groups Funneled Money for Abramoff," *Washington Post,* June 25, 2006, p. 1.

55. Johnson, *No Place for Amateurs,* p. 175.

56. Ibid., p. 176.

57. Institute for Politics, Democracy and the Internet, "Small Donors and Online Giving: A Study of Donors to the 2004 Presidential Campaigns," George Washington University Graduate School of Political Management, March 2006.

58. Ibid., p. 5.

59. David Johnston and Neil A. Lewis, "How the Religious Right Pushed for Ashcroft's Nomination," *San Francisco Chronicle,* January 7, 2001, p. 1.

60. Richard Dunham and Eamon Javers, "Shakedown on K Street," *BusinessWeek,* February 20, 2006, pp. 34–36.

61. Jeffrey H. Birnbaum, *The Money Men: The Real Story of Political Power in the USA* (New York: Crown, 2000), p. 75.

62. Ibid., p. 75.

63. Eliza Carney, "Cleaning House," *National Journal,* January 28, 2006, p. 36.

64. Brody Mullins, "Growing Role for Lobbyists: Raising Funds for Lawmakers," *Wall Street Journal,* January 27, 2006, p. 1.

65. Jonathan Weisman and Charles H. Babcock, "K Street's New Ways Spawn More Pork," *Washington Post,* January 27, 2006, p. 1.

66. Frank Clemente and Craig Holman, "Fallout from Abramoff: Congress for Sale? Religious Right for Sale?" Institute for Public Accuracy, www.accuracy.org/newsrelease. php?articleId=1196&type=&searchterms=congress%20for%20sale? January 4, 2006.

67. Darrell M. West, *Checkbook Democracy: How Money Corrupts Political Campaigns* (Boston: Northeastern University Press, 2000), p. 117.

68. David Mayhew, *Congress: The Electoral Connection* (New Haven, CT: Yale University Press, 1974), p. 40.

69. Ibid., pp. 116–119.

70. Birnbaum, *The Money Men,* p. 164.

71. Jeffrey Birnbaum, "'Client' Rewards Keep K Street Lobbyists Thriving," *Washington Post,* February 14, 2006, p. A1.

72. Mary Williams Walsh, "Major Changes Raise Concerns on Pension Bill," *New York Times,* March 10, 2006, p. 1.

73. See Jonathan Weisman, "Closed-Door Deal Makes $22 Billion Difference," *Washington Post,* January 24, 2006, p. 1.

74. Michael D. Shear, "Va. Growth Bolstered by Well-Funded Voting Bloc," *Washington Post,* January 30, 2006, p. B1.

75. John Wagner and Ann E. Marimow, "Largess Preceded Vote on Wal-Mart," *Washington Post,* February 10, 2006, p. B1.

76. Thomas Ferguson, *Golden Rule: The Investment Theory of Party Competition and the Logic of Money-Driven Political Systems* (Chicago: University of Chicago Press, 1995).

Notes to Chapter 4

1. Matthew A. Crenson and Benjamin Ginsberg, *Downsizing Democracy: How America Sidelined Its Citizens and Privatized Its Public* (Baltimore, MD: Johns Hopkins University Press, 2002), chs. 7 and 9.

2. Lester Salamon, "Economic Regulation," in Lester Salamon, ed., *The Tools of Government: A Guide to the New Governance* (New York: Oxford, 2002), p. 146.

3. Mancur Olson, *The Logic of Collective Action* (Cambridge, MA: Harvard University Press, 1965), p. 2.

4. Rebecca Adams, "Gas Prices Rise Along with Ethanol Use," *Congressional Quarterly Weekly,* April 24, 2006, p. 1070.

5. Robert Bryce, "Corn Dog: The Ethanol Subsidy Is Worse Than You Can Imagine," *Slate,* www.slate.com/id/2122961, July 19, 2005.

6. David Pimentel, "Limits of Biomass Utilization," *Encyclopedia of Physical Sciences and Technology,* September 2001, pp. 159–171.

7. University of California–Berkeley, "Study: Ethanol Production Consumes Six Units of Energy to Produce Just One," ScienceDaily, www.sciencedaily.com/ releases/2005/03/050329132436.htm, April 1, 2005.

8. Adams, "Gas Prices Rise," p. 1070.

9. Ibid., p. 1071.

10. Ibid., p. 1070.

11. Ibid., p. 1071.

12. Peter Slevin, "Thousands of Iowa's Corn Farmers See the Future in Fuel," *Washington Post*, May 21, 2006, p. A3.

13. Ibid.

14. Roger Lowenstein, "Who Needs the Mortgage-Interest Tax Deduction?" *New York Times*, www.nytimes.com, March 5, 2006.

15. Ibid., March 5, 2006.

16. Daniel Gross, "Location, Location—Deduction," *Slate*, www.slate.com/id/2116731, April 14, 2005.

17. Jason Furman, "End the Mortgage Interest Deduction!" *Slate*, www.slate.com/id/2130017, November 10, 2005.

18. Adam Carasso, Eugene Steuerle, and Elizabeth Bell, "Making Tax Incentives for Home Owners More Equitable and Efficient," Tax Policy Center Discussion Paper No. 21, The Urban Institute, Washington, DC, 2005.

19. Froma Harrop, "Reform the Mortgage-Interest Tax Deduction," Real Clear Politics, www.realclearpolitics.com, October 14, 2005.

20. Furman, "End the Mortgage Interest Deduction!"

21. Daniel Mitchell, "A Flat Tax with No Mortgage Deduction Would Probably Help Homeowners," *American Enterprise Online*, www.taemag.com/issues/articleID.16360/article_detail.asp, May–June 1996.

22. Elana Schor, "K Street Scrambles to Protect Mortgage Interest Tax Break," *The Hill*, thehill.com/thehill/export/TheHill/Business/101905_tax.html, October 19, 2005.

23. Ibid.

24. Inman News, www.inman.com, December 22, 2005.

25. Schor, "K Street Scrambles."

26. Ibid.

27. William A. Niskanen, *Bureaucracy and Representative Government* (Chicago: Aldine, 1971).

28. Rhodri Jeffreys-Jones, *The CIA and American Democracy*, 2nd ed. (New Haven, CT: Yale University Press, 1998).

29. Stephen Peter Rosen, *Winning the Next War: Innovation and the Modern Military* (Ithaca, NY: Cornell University Press, 1991).

30. Harold Seidman, *Politics, Position and Power: The Dynamics of Federal Organization*, 5th ed. (New York: Oxford University Press, 1998), ch. 8.

31. James Q. Wilson, *Bureaucracy: What Government Agencies Do and Why They Do It* (New York: Basic Books, 1989), p. 91.

32. Thomas E. Ricks, *Making the Corps* (New York: Touchstone, 1997), p. 138.

33. Herbert Kaufman, *The Forest Ranger: A Study in Administrative Behavior* (Baltimore, MD: Johns Hopkins University Press, 1960).

34. See Anita Huslin, "Grizzly Proposition Aims to Return Bears to Idaho," *Washington Post*, July 3, 2000, p. A3.

35. Seidman, *Politics, Position and Power*, p. 138.

36. Ibid., p. 118.

37. Thomas Stanton, *Government Sponsored Enterprises: Mercantilist Corporations in the Modern World* (Washington, DC: American Enterprise Institute Press, 2000).

38. See Richard Posner, *An Affair of State: The Investigation, Impeachment, and Trial of President Clinton* (Cambridge, MA: Harvard University Press, 1999), ch.3.

39. David C. Jones, "What's Wrong with Our Defense Establishment?" *New York Times Magazine,* November 7, 1982.

40. James R. Schlesinger, "Defense Planning and Budgeting: The Issue of Centralized Control," prepared for the Industrial College of the Armed Forces and quoted in Richard A. Stubbing, *The Defense Game: An Insider Explores the Astonishing Realities of America's Defense Establishment* (New York: Harper and Row, 1986), p. 110.

41. Nick Katz, "Where Have All the Warriors Gone?" *Washingtonian,* July 1984, p. 82.

42. For a skeptical view, see Michael O'Hanlon, *Technological Change and the Future of Warfare* (Washington, DC: Brookings Institution, 2000).

43. Stubbing, *The Defense Game,* p. 109.

44. D. Robert Worley, *Shaping U.S. Military Forces: Revolution or Relevance in a Post–Cold War World* (New York: Praeger, 2006), ch.4.

45. Thomas R. Ricks, "Target Approval Delays Cost Air Force Key Hits," *Washington Post,* November 18, 2001, p. 1.

46. Bob Woodward, "Secret CIA Units Playing a Central Combat Role," *Washington Post,* November 18, 2001, p. 1.

47. Quoted in Ricks, "Target Approval."

48. Giulio Douhet, *The Command of the Air* (New York: Coward McCann, 1942), p. 28.

49. Russell F. Weigley, *The American Way of War* (Bloomington: Indiana University Press, 1973), pp. 240–241.

50. Alexander de Seversky, *Victory Through Air Power* (New York: Simon and Schuster, 1942), p. 26.

51. Ibid., p. 255.

52. Perry M. Smith, *The Air Force Plans for Peace* (Baltimore, MD: Johns Hopkins University Press, 1970), p. 15.

53. Carl Builder, *The Masks of War: American Military Styles in Strategy and Analysis* (Baltimore, MD: Johns Hopkins University Press, 1989), p. 138.

54. Stubbing, *The Defense Game,* pp. 77–78.

55. Williamson Murray, "The U.S. Air Force: Past as Prologue," in Michael Mandelbaum, ed., *America's Defense* (New York: Holmes and Meier, 1989), pp. 231–278.

56. Thomas E. Ricks, "Bull's-Eye War: Pinpoint Bombing Shifts Role of GI Joe," *Washington Post,* December 2, 2001, p. 1; and John Keegan, "The Changing Face of War," *Wall Street Journal,* November 27, 2001, p. A22.

57. See Jonathan M. House, *Combined Arms Warfare in the Twentieth Century* (Lawrence: University Press of Kansas, 2001).

58. Ibid., p. 3.

59. Ibid., p. 116.

60. Michael Carver, "Conventional Warfare in the Nuclear Age," in Peter Paret, ed., *Makers of Modern Strategy: From Machiavelli to the Nuclear Age* (Princeton, NJ: Princeton University Press, 1986), p. 797.

61. David MacIsaac, "Voices from the Central Blue: The Air Power Theorists," in Paret, ed., *Makers of Modern Strategy,* pp. 624–647.

62. Franklin C. Spinney, "Notes on Close Air Support," in Donald Vandergriff, ed., *Spirit,*

Blood and Treasure: The American Cost of Battle in the 21st Century (Novato, CA: Presidio Press, 2001), pp. 199–213.

63. House, *Combined Arms Warfare*, p. 169.

64. Ibid., p. 171.

65. Ian Gooderson, *Air Power at the Battlefront: Allied Close Air Support in Europe, 1943–45* (London: Frank Cass, 1998), pp. 85–94.

66. Spinney, "Notes on Close Air Support," p. 206.

67. Ibid.

68. House, *Combined Arms Warfare*, p. 203.

69. Allan R. Millett, *Semper Fidelis: The History of the United States Marine Corps*, rev. ed. (New York: Free Press, 1991), p. 586.

70. Ibid., pp. 586–588.

71. Ibid., p. 589.

72. Spinney, "Notes on Close Air Support," p. 207.

73. Gregg Easterbrook, "All Aboard Air Oblivion," in Dina Rasor, ed., *More Bucks, Less Bang: How the Pentagon Buys Ineffective Weapons* (Washington, DC: Fund for Constitutional Government, 1983), pp. 50–66.

74. Stubbing, *The Defense Game*, p. 141.

75. Matthew Allen, *Military Helicopter Doctrines of the Major Powers* (Westport, CT: Greenwood Press, 1993), pp. 16–29.

76. Stubbing, *The Defense Game*, p. 142.

77. See Michael Gordon and General Bernard Trainor, *The Generals' War: The Inside Story of the Conflict in the Gulf* (Boston: Little. Brown, 1995).

78. Easterbrook, "All Aboard Air Oblivion," p. 52.

79. Morton Mintz, "The Maverick Missile: If at First You Don't Succeed," in Rasor, ed., *More Bucks, Less Bang*, pp. 135–185.

80. James G. Burton, *The Pentagon Wars: Reformers Challenge the Old Guard* (Annapolis: Naval Institute Press, 1993).

81. John E. Peters, *The U.S. Military: Ready for the New World Order?* (Westport, CT: Greenwood Press, 1993), pp. 76–77.

82. FAS Military Analysis Network, "DoD 101," www.fas.org/man/dod-101/sys/ac/jsf.htm. See also the U.S. Air Force Joint Strike Fighter home page, www.jast.mil/IEFrames.htm.

83. Quoted in Spinney, "Notes on Close Air Support," p. 200.

84. Robert MacCoun and Peter Reuter, *Drug War Heresies: Learning from Other Vices, Times, and Places* (New York: Cambridge University Press, 2001), ch. 5.

85. James P. Gray, *Why Our Drug Laws Have Failed and What We Can Do About It: A Judicial Indictment of the War on Drugs* (Philadelphia: Temple University Press, 2001), p. 145.

86. Ibid., p. 147.

87. Associated Press, "Drug Czar Takes Hard Line on Legalization Measures," June 17, 1999, quoted in Gray, *Why Our Drug Laws Have Failed*, p. 145.

88. The contemporary history of privatization is discussed in Daniel Guttman, "Public Purpose and Private Service: The Twentieth Century Culture of Contracting Out and the Evolving Law of Diffused Sovereignty," *Administrative Law Review* 52, 3 (Summer 2000).

89. Paul C. Light, *The True Size of Government* (Washington, DC: Brookings Institution, 1999).

90. Ibid., p. 25.

91. Seidman, *Politics, Position and Power,* ch.6.

92. Michael Froomkin, "Reinventing the Government Corporation," *University of Illinois Law Review* (1995): 543.

93. Lester Salamon, *Partners in Public Service: Government Nonprofit Relations in the Modern Welfare State* (Baltimore, MD: Johns Hopkins University Press, 1995), Part 3.

94. See, for example, Al Gore, *From Red Tape to Results: Creating a Government That Works Better and Costs Less,* Report of the National Performance Review (Washington, DC: U.S. Government Printing Office, 1993); and David Osborne and Ted Gaebler, *Reinventing Government: How the Entrepreneurial Spirit Is Transforming the Public Sector* (Reading, MA: Addison-Wesley, 1992).

95. David Wagner, *What's Love Got to Do with It? A Critical Look at American Charity* (New York: The New Press, 2000), p. 148.

96. Stanton, *Government Sponsored Enterprises.*

97. Ibid., p. 16.

98. Froomkin, "Reinventing," p. 18.

99. Kathleen Day, "Greenspan Urges Review of Fannie, Freddie Subsidies," *Washington Post,* May 24, 2000, p. E3.

100. Stanton, *Government Sponsored Enterprises,* p. 12.

101. Ibid.

102. Ibid., p. 44.

103. Froomkin, "Reinventing," pp. 34, 51.

104. Herman Schwartz, "Governmentally Appointed Directors in a Private Corporation," *Harvard Law Review* 79, 350 (1965). See also Ronald Gilson and Reinier Kraakman, "Reinventing the Outside Director," *Stanford Law Review* 43, 863 (1991).

105. Stanton, *Government Sponsored Enterprises,* p. 37.

106. Ibid., pp. 45, 48, 61.

107. Urban Institute, "A Study of the GSEs' Single Family Underwriting Guidelines: Final Report," prepared for the U.S. Department of Housing and Urban Development, April 1999. See also Michele Derus, "Mortgage Finance Giants Fail Those Who Earn Less, Critics Say," *Milwaukee Journal Sentinel,* May 14, 2000, p. 1F; and H. Jane Lehman, "Loan Goals Fall Short in Central Cities," *Washington Post,* April 23, 1994, p. E1.

108. See Mary Kane, "Critics Say Home-Buying Push Puts Some Consumers at Risk," *Minneapolis Star Tribune,* April 15, 2000, p. 7H.

109. Congressional Budget Office, *Assessing the Public Costs and Benefits of Fannie Mae and Freddie Mac* (Washington, DC: U.S. Government Printing Office, May 1996), p. xii.

110. Froomkin, "Reinventing," p. 63.

111. Terence O'Hara, "Regulator Says Mudd Knew of Misdeeds," *Washington Post,* May 24, 2006, p. D4.

112. Jerry Knight, "Fannie, Freddie in the Political Spotlight," *Washington Post,* July 31, 2000, Business section, p. 7.

113. Stanton, *Government Sponsored Enterprises,* p. 55.

114. Ibid., p. 17; Knight, "Fannie, Freddie in the Political Spotlight."

115. David Ignatius, "A U.S. Government Hedge Fund?" *Washington Post,* May 10, 1999, p. A23.

116. Froomkin, "Reinventing," p. 60.

117. Bloomberg News, "Freddie, Fannie Increase Giving to Campaigns," *Milwaukee Journal Sentinel,* April 30, 2000, p. 5F.

118. Patrick Barta, "Fannie Mae, Freddie Mac Counter Critics," *Wall Street Journal,* July 19, 2000, p. B6.

119. Stephen Burd, "Should Borrowers Fear a Student-Loan Behemoth?" *Chronicle of Higher Education,* August 11, 2000, p. A24.

120. Barta, "Fannie Mae, Freddie Mac Counter Critics."

121. Mary Jacoby, "Critics Question Fannie Mae's Influence," *St. Petersburg Times,* July 17, 2000, p. 1A.

122. Albert Crenshaw, "This Foundation Director Says Charity Begins at Home," *Washington Post,* May 6, 1996, p. F9.

123. Jacoby, "Critics Question Fannie Mae's Influence."

124. Annys Shin, "How a Former Chief Helped Shape the Company's Political Culture," *Washington Post,* May 24, 2006, p. D1.

125. Eric Bates, "Private Prisons," *The Nation,* January 5, 1998, pp. 11–18.

126. P. W. Singer, *Corporate Warriors: The Rise of the Privatized Military Industry* (Ithaca, NY: Cornell University Press, 2003), ch. 13.

NOTES TO CHAPTER 5

1. See, for example, Gabriel Ardant, "Financial Policy and Economic Infrastructure of Modern States and Nations," in Charles Tilly, ed., *The Formation of National States in Western Europe* (Princeton, NJ: Princeton University Press, 1975).

2. For examples, see the December 2005 Harris Poll, which shows strong popular support for a host of government services, www.harrisinteractive.com/harris_poll/index.asp?PID=620.

3. "President Reagan's Inaugural Address," *New York Times,* January 21, 1981, p. 1.

4. George Will, "The Odds Against Carter," *Newsweek,* August 18, 1980, p. 88.

5. Fred Barnes, "Big Government Conservatism," *Wall Street Journal,* August 15, 2003, p. 12.

6. Milton J. Esman, *Government Works: Why Americans Need the Feds* (Ithaca, NY: Cornell University Press, 2000), ch.1.

7. Paul C. Light, *The True Size of Government* (Washington, DC: Brookings Institution, 1999).

8. Karl Mannheim, *Man and Society in an Age of Reconstruction* (London: Kegan Paul, Trench, Trubner and Co., 1940), p. 341.

9. Christopher Simpson, *National Security Directives of the Reagan and Bush Administrations* (Boulder, CO: Westview Press, 1995).

10. Matthew A. Crenson and Benjamin Ginsberg, *Presidential Power: Unchecked and Unbalanced* (New York: W. W. Norton, 2007), ch. 9.

11. Leonard D. White, *The Republican Era: A Study in Administrative History, 1869–1901* (New York: The Free Press, 1958), p. 55.

12. Ibid., p. 56.

13. Ibid.

14. See Theodore J. Lowi, *The End of Liberalism,* 2nd ed. (New York: W. W. Norton,

1979); and David Schoenbrod, *Power Without Responsibility: How Congress Abuses the People Through Delegation* (New Haven, CT: Yale University Press, 1993).

15. Kenneth Culp Davis, *Discretionary Justice: A Preliminary Inquiry* (Baton Rouge: Louisiana State University Press, 1969), pp. 15–21.

16. *Mistretta v. U.S.*, 488 U.S. 361, 372 (1989).

17. Schoenbrod, *Power Without Responsibility*, ch.2.

18. Ibid., p. 61.

19. William F. Fox, *Understanding Administrative Law*, 4th ed. (New York: Lexis Publishing, 2000), pp. 36–37.

20. Kara Scannell and Deborah Soloman, "Business Wins Its Battle to Ease a Costly Sarbanes-Oxley Rule," *Wall Street Journal*, November 10, 2006, p. 1.

21. Andrew Taylor, "The Plan: Go Home, Limp Back After Voters Set the Agenda," *Congressional Quarterly Weekly*, November 4, 2000, p. 2587.

22. Harold W. Stanley and Richard G. Niemi, *Vital Statistics on American Politics* (Washington, DC: Congressional Quarterly Press, 2001), p. 262.

23. David M. O'Brien, *Constitutional Law and Politics*, 4th ed., vol. 1 (New York: W. W. Norton, 2000), p. 368.

24. Lowi, *The End of Liberalism*, pp. 94–97.

25. Jeffrey A. Wertkin, "Reintroducing Compromise to the Nondelegation Doctrine," *Georgetown Law Journal* 98, 1055 (April 2002): 1012–1013.

26. *Field v. Clark*, 143 U.S. 649 (1892).

27. *Wayman v. Southard*, 23 U.S. 1 (1825).

28. *J. W. Hampton & Co. v. U.S.*, 276 U.S. 394 (1928).

29. Emergency Price Control Act of 1942, 56 Stat. 23 (January 30, 1942).

30. *A.L.A. Schechter Poultry Corp. v. United States*, 295 U.S. 495 (1935) at 553.

31. *Carter v. Carter Coal Co.*, 298 U.S. 238 (1936).

32. *Yakus v. U.S.*, 321 U.S. 414, 425 (1944).

33. *Mistretta v. U.S.*, 488 U.S. 361 (1989).

34. *U.S. v. Booker*, 125 S. Ct. 738 (2005).

35. *Chevron v. Natural Resources Defense Council*, 467 U.S. 837 (1984).

36. See *Whitman v. American Trucking Associations*, 531 U.S. 457 (2001); and *AT&T Corp. v. Iowa Utilities Board*, 525 U.S. 366 (1999).

37. *U.S. v. Mead Corp.*, 533 U.S. 218 (2001).

38. Matthew D. McCubbins and Thomas Schwartz, "Congressional Oversight Overlooked: Police Patrols Versus Fire Alarms," *American Journal of Political Science* 28 (1984): 165–179.

39. Elena Kagan, "Presidential Administration," *Harvard Law Review* 114 (2001): 2347.

40. Quoted in Henry A. Waxman, "Free Pass from Congress," *Washington Post*, July 6, 2004, p. A19.

41. Shailagh Murray, "Storms Show a System out of Balance," *Washington Post*, October 5, 2005, p. A21.

42. Quoted in Jessica Korn, *The Power of Separation: American Constitutionalism and the Myth of the Legislative Veto* (Princeton, NJ: Princeton University Press, 1996), p. 43.

43. *Immigration and Naturalization Service v. Chadha*, 459 U.S. 1097 (1983).

44. Jerry L. Nashaw, *Greed, Chaos and Governance: Using Public Choice to Improve Public Law* (New Haven, CT: Yale University Press, 1997), p. 106.

45. Family and Medical Leave Act, 29 U.S.C. 2601.

46. Caitlyn M. Campbell, "Overstepping One's Bounds: The Department of Labor and the Family and Medical Leave Act," *Boston University Law Review* 84 (October 2004): 1077.

47. *Miller v. AT&T Corp.*, 250 F. 3d 820 (2001).

48. Campbell, "Overstepping One's Bounds," p. 1088.

49. See *Loving v. U.S.*, 116 S. Ct. 1737 (1996).

50. *Myers v. U.S.*, 272 U.S. 52, 135 (1935).

51. Kenneth R. Mayer, *With the Stroke of a Pen: Executive Orders and Presidential Power* (Princeton, NJ: Princeton University Press, 2001), p. 71.

52. Ibid., pp. 72–73.

53. Louis Fisher, *Constitutional Conflicts Between Congress and the President*, 4th ed. (Lawrence: University Press of Kansas, 1998), p. 110.

54. Philip J. Cooper, *By Order of the President: The Use and Abuse of Presidential Direct Action* (Lawrence: University Press of Kansas, 2002), pp. 13–14, 86.

55. Terry M. Moe and William G. Howell, "The Presidential Power of Unilateral Action," *Journal of Law, Economics and Organization* 15, 1 (January 1999): 164.

56. Mayer, *With the Stroke of a Pen*, ch. 6.

57. *Youngstown Co. v. Sawyer*, 346 U.S. 579 (1952).

58. *Chamber of Commerce v. Reich*, 74 F. 3d 1322 (D.C. Cir. 1996).

59. Cooper, *By Order of the President*, p. 22.

60. Quoted in ibid., p. 24.

61. *Dames & Moore v. Regan*, 453 U.S. 654 (1981).

62. Quoted in Kenneth R. Mayer and Thomas J. Weko, "The Institutionalization of Power," in Robert Y. Shapiro, Martha Joynt Kumar, and Lawrence R. Jacobs, eds., *Presidential Power: Forging the Presidency for the Twenty-first Century* (New York: Columbia University Press, 2000), p. 181.

63. Cooper, *By Order of the President*, p. 17.

64. Todd F. Gaziano, "The Use and Abuse of Executive Orders and Other Presidential Directives," *Texas Review of Law and Politics* 5 (Spring 2001): 283.

65. Quoted in Andrew Rudalevige, *Managing the President's Program: Presidential Leadership and Legislative Policy Formation* (Princeton, NJ: Princeton University Press, 2002), p. 159.

66. Tara L. Branum, "President or King? The Use and Abuse of Executive Orders in Modern-Day America," *Journal of Legislation* 28, no. 1 (April 2002): 1–59.

67. Cooper, *By Order of the President*, pp. 108–109.

68. Frank J. Murray, "Justice Fights to Keep Clinton Monument Edicts Intact," *Washington Times*, July 28, 2003, p. A3.

69. James Reisen and Eric Lichtblau, "Bush Lets U.S. Spy on Callers Without Courts: Secret Order to Widen Domestic Monitoring," *New York Times*, December 16, 2005, p. 1.

70. Eric Lichtblau and James Risen, "Legal Rationale by Justice Department on Spying Effort," *New York Times*, January 20, 2006, p. 1.

71. Joseph Curl, "Legal Scholars Split on Wiretaps," *Washington Times*, January 18, 2006, p. A4.

72. Scott Shane, "Behind Power, One Principle," *New York Times*, December 17, 2005, p. 1. Yoo's views are more fully spelled out in his 2005 book, *The Powers of War and Peace: The Constitution and Foreign Affairs After 9/11* (Chicago: University of Chicago Press, 2005).

73. *Building Construction Trades Department v. Allbaugh*, 295 F. 3d 28 (2002).

74. Mayer and Weko, "The Institutionalization of Power," p. 199.

75. James F. Blumstein, "Regulatory Review by the Executive Office of the President: An Overview and Policy Analysis of Current Issues," *Duke Law Journal* 51 (December 2001): 856.

76. Terry M. Moe, "The President and the Bureaucracy," in Michael Nelson, ed., *The Presidency and the Political System*, 4th ed. (Washington, DC: CQ Press, 1995), p. 432.

77. Elena Kagan, "Presidential Administration," *Harvard Law Review* 114 (June 2001): 2262.

78. Moe, "The President and the Bureaucracy," pp. 430–431.

79. Joel D. Aberbach and Bert A. Rockman, *In the Web of Politics: Three Decades of the U.S. Federal Executive* (Washington, DC: Brookings Institution, 2000), p. 169.

80. Marissa Martino Golden, *What Motivates Bureaucrats? Politics and Administration During the Reagan Years* (New York: Columbia University Press, 2000).

81. Blumstein, "Regulatory Review by the Executive Office," p. 859.

82. Bradley H. Patterson Jr., *The White House Staff: Inside the West Wing and Beyond* (Washington, DC: Brookings Institution, 2000), pp. 302, 92; and Moe, "The President and the Bureaucracy," p. 432.

83. Richard H. Pildes and Cass Sunstein, "Reinventing the Regulatory State," *University of Chicago Law Review* 62 (1995): 1.

84. Kagan, "Presidential Administration," p. 2247.

85. Ibid., p. 2267.

86. Ibid., p. 2265.

87. Blumstein, "Regulatory Review by the Executive Office," p. 860.

88. See, for example, Douglas W. Kmiec, "Expanding Executive Power," in Roger Pilon, ed., *The Rule of Law in the Wake of Clinton* (Washington, DC: Cato Institute Press, 2000), pp. 47–68.

89. Blumstein, "Regulatory Review by the Executive Office," p. 854.

90. Stephen Power and Jacob M. Schlesinger, "Bush's Rules Czar Brings Long Knife to New Regulations," *Wall Street Journal*, June 12, 2002, p. 1.

91. Ellen Nakashima, "Chief Plans Overhaul of Regulatory Process," *Washington Post*, March 20, 2002, p. A31.

92. Robert Percival, "Presidential Management of the Administrative State," *Duke Law Journal* 51 (December 2001): 1015.

93. John D. McKinnon and Stephen Power, "How U.S. Rules Are Made Is Still a Murky Process," *Wall Street Journal*, October 22, 2003, p. A6.

94. Mark Killenback, "A Matter of Mere Approval: The Role of the President in the Creation of Legislative History," *University of Arkansas Law Review* 48 (1995): 239; and Cooper, *By Order of the President*, p. 201.

95. Edward S. Corwin, *The President: Office and Powers*, 4th rev. ed. (New York: New York University Press, 1957), p. 283.

96. Cooper, *By Order of the President*, pp. 201, 203.

97. Ibid., p. 216.

98. Ronald Reagan, Statement on Signing a Veterans' Benefit Bill, November 18, 1988, Public Papers of the President, 1988–1989, Book 2 (Washington, DC: U.S. Government Printing Office, 1990), p. 1558.

99. Ronald Reagan, Statement on Signing the Bill Prohibiting the Licensing or

Construction of Facilities on the Salmon and Snake Rivers in Idaho, November 17, 1988, Public Papers of the President, 1988–1989, Book 2 (Washington, DC: U.S. Government Printing Office, 1990), p. 1525.

100. *AMERON, Inc. v. U.S. Army Corps of Engineers,* 610 F. Supp. 750 (D.N.J. 1985).

101. *Lear, Siegler v. Lehman,* 842 F. 2d 1102 (1988).

102. Cooper, *By Order of the President,* pp. 206–207.

103. Ibid., p. 217; and Kristy Carroll, "Whose Statute Is It Anyway? Why and How Courts Should Use Presidential Signing Statements When Interpreting Federal Statutes," *Catholic University Law Review* 16 (1997): 475.

104. Andrew Sullivan, "We Don't Need a New King George: How Can the President Interpret the Law as If It Didn't Apply to Him?" *Time* magazine, January 24, 2006, pp. 27–28.

105. Antonio Gramsci, *Selections from Prison Notebooks* (New York: International Publishers, 1971).

106. For an excellent discussion, see John Hasnas, "Ethics and the Problem of White Collar Crime," *American University Law Review* 54 (February 2005): 579.

107. The Supreme Court's decision in *Booker v. U.S.,* 125 S. Ct. 738 (2005), declared that judicial use of the sentencing guidelines was discretionary rather than mandatory. The Department of Justice, however, has been pressuring federal judges to continue applying the guidelines. See John S. Baker, "Jurisdictional and Separation of Powers Strategies to Limit the Expansion of Federal Crimes," *American University Law Review* 54 (February 2005): 545.

108. Baker, "Jurisdictional and Separation of Powers Strategies," p. 548.

109. Sara Sun Beale, "From Morals and Mattress Tags to Overfederalization," *American University Law Review* 54 (February 2005): 747.

110. *U.S. v. Hanousek,* 176 F. 3d 116 (9th Cir. 1999). See Hasnas, "Ethics and the Problem of White Collar Crime," p. 609.

111. *Morisette v. U.S.,* 342 U.S. 246 (1952).

112. Hasnas, "Ethics and the Problem of White Collar Crime," p. 606.

113. Memorandum by Larry Thompson, Deputy Attorney General, to Heads of Departments and U.S. Attorneys. Available at www.usdoj.gov/dag/cftf/corporate_guidelines. htm.

114. "The McNulty Memo," *Wall Street Journal,* December 13, 2006, p. A18.

115. Eric Luna, "The Overcriminalization Phenomenon," *American University Law Review* 54 (February 2005): 703.

116. Steven Cohen and William Eimicke, *The New Effective Public Manager: Achieving Success in a Changing Government,* 3rd ed. (San Francisco: Jossey-Bass, 2002), pp. 262–265.

NOTES TO CHAPTER 6

1. Aristide Zolberg, "Moments of Madness," *Politics and Society* 2 (April 1972): 183.

2. V. I. Lenin, *What Is to Be Done? Burning Questions of Our Movement* (New York: International Publishers, 1929), ch. 2.

3. Robert Weissberg, *Polling, Policy and Public Opinion: The Case Against Heeding the "Voice of the People"* (New York: Palgrave Macmillan, 2002).

4. Robert Sobel, *Coolidge: An American Enigma* (Washington, DC: Regnery, 1998), p. 5.

5. David McCullough, *Truman* (New York: Simon and Schuster, 1992), p. 204.

6. Arthur M. Schlesinger Jr., *A Thousand Days: John F. Kennedy in the White House* (New York: Houghton-Mifflin, 1965).

7. Robert Dallek, *Flawed Giant: Lyndon Johnson and His Times* (New York: Oxford University Press, 1999).

8. Alexander Hamilton, *The Federalist*, no. 68, in Clinton Rossiter, ed., *The Federalist Papers* (New York: Mentor, 1961), p. 414.

9. Vamik Volkan, "Narcissistic Personality Disorder and Reparative Leadership," *International Journal of Group Psychotherapy* 30 (1980): 131–152. See also Rufus Browning and Herbert Jacob, "Power Motivation and the Political Personality," *Public Opinion Quarterly* (September 1964): 75–90.

10. Matthew A. Crenson and Benjamin Ginsberg, *Unchecked and Unbalanced* (New York: W. W. Norton, 2006).

11. Stephen E. Ambrose, *Nixon: The Education of a Politician, 1913–1962* (New York: Simon and Schuster, 1987), p. 644.

12. Alonzo L. Hamby, *Man of the People: A Life of Harry S. Truman* (New York: Oxford, 1995), p. 637.

13. Lou Cannon, *President Reagan: The Role of a Lifetime* (New York: Public Affairs, 2000), p. 33.

14. David Frum, *The Right Man: An Inside Account of the Bush White House* (New York: Random House, 2003), p. 57.

15. Stephen Ambrose, *Eisenhower: Soldier and President* (New York: Simon and Schuster, 1990), p. 245.

16. Christopher Matthews, *Kennedy and Nixon: The Rivalry That Shaped Postwar America* (New York: Simon and Schuster, 1996), p. 112.

17. W. Phillips Davison, "Public Opinion Research as Communication," *Public Opinion Quarterly* 36 (Fall 1972): 313.

18. George Creel, *How We Advertised America* (New York: Harper, 1920).

19. Chester Bowles, *Promises to Keep: My Years in Public Life, 1941–1969* (New York: Harper, 1973), p. 93.

20. Quoted in Doris Kearns Goodwin, *Lyndon Johnson and the American Dream* (New York: St. Martin's, 1991), p. i.

21. Quoted in ibid., p. ii.

22. Max Farrand, ed., *The Records of the Federal Convention of 1787*, vol. 1 (New Haven, CT: Yale University Press, 1966), p. 49.

23. Friedrich Nietzsche, *Thus Spake Zarathustra* (Mineola, NY: Dover, 1999), p. 31.

24. Ibid., p. 30.

25. Herbert Marcuse, *One-Dimensional Man: Studies in the Ideology of Advanced Industrial Society* (Boston: Beacon Press, 1964), p. 10.

26. MediaMatters for America, "Where Is Media Outrage over Purported Government Attempts to Restrict Katrina Coverage?" http://mediamatters.org/items/200509080025, September 8, 2005.

27. Matthew A. Crenson, "Guest Editorial," *Baltimore Urbanite*, October 2006, p. 3.

28. Saul D. Alinsky, *Rules for Radicals: A Pragmatic Primer for Realistic Radicals* (New York: Vintage, 1971).

29. Ibid., pp. 141–143.

30. See, for example, Antonio Gramsci, *Selections from Prison Notebooks* (New York: International Publishers, 1971).

31. Alinsky, *Rules for Radicals,* p. 152.

32. William Arkin, "Back to the Bunker: Don't Worry: Washington Has a Plan to Save Itself," *Washington Post,* June 14, 2006, p. B1.

Index

About the Author

Benjamin Ginsberg is the David Bernstein Professor of Political Science and director of the Center for the Study of American Government at the Johns Hopkins University. He is the author or coauthor of many books, including *Presidential Power: Unchecked and Unbalanced; Downsizing Democracy: How America Sidelined Its Citizens and Privatized Its Public; Politics by Other Means; The Fatal Embrace: Jews and the State; The Consequences of Consent; American Government: Freedom and Power; We the People;* and *The Captive Public*. Ginsberg is a frequent radio and television commentator, and his political essays have appeared in such publications as the *Washington Post*. He lives in Potomac, Maryland, just outside the capital beltway, a location he believes gives him both analytic proximity to and critical distance from Washington politics. Ginsberg received his Ph.D. from the University of Chicago in 1973. Before joining the Hopkins faculty in 1992, he was professor of government at Cornell University.